ZIMBABWE

PROFILES · NATIONS OF
CONTEMPORARY AFRICA
Larry W. Bowman, Series Editor

Zimbabwe: The Terrain of Contradictory Development,
Christine Sylvester

*Mauritius: Democracy and Development in
the Indian Ocean*, Larry W. Bowman

Niger: Personal Rule and Survival in the Sahel, Robert B. Charlick

*Equatorial Guinea: Colonialism, State Terror, and the Search
for Stability*, Ibrahim K. Sundiata

Mali: A Search for Direction, Pascal James Imperato

Tanzania: An African Experiment,
Second Edition, Revised and Updated, Rodger Yeager

Cameroon: Dependence and Independence, Mark W. DeLancey

*São Tomé and Príncipe: From Plantation Colony
to Microstate*, Tony Hodges and Malyn Newitt

Zambia: Between Two Worlds, Marcia M. Burdette

Ethiopia: Transition and Development in the Horn of Africa,
Mulatu Wubneh and Yohannis Abate

Somalia: Nation in Search of a State,
David D. Laitin and Said S. Samatar

Ghana: Coping with Uncertainty, Deborah Pellow and Naomi Chazan

*The Central African Republic: The Continent's
Hidden Heart*, Thomas O'Toole

Lesotho: Dilemmas of Dependence in Southern Africa,
John E. Bardill and James H. Cobbe

Kenya: The Quest for Prosperity, Norman N. Miller

*Botswana: Liberal Democracy and the Labor Reserve in
Southern Africa*, Jack Parson

Mozambique: From Colonialism to Revolution, 1900–1982,
Allen Isaacman and Barbara Isaacman

*Senegal: An African Nation Between Islam and
the West*, Sheldon Gellar

ZIMBABWE

The Terrain of Contradictory Development

Christine Sylvester

Westview Press
BOULDER • SAN FRANCISCO • OXFORD

Profiles/Nations of Contemporary Africa

Copyright © 1991 by Westview Press, Inc.

Hardcover edition published in 1991 and paperback edition published in 1992 in the United States of America by Westview Press, Inc., 5500 Central Avenue, Boulder, Colorado 80301

Hardcover edition published in 1991 in Great Britain by Dartmouth Publishing Company Limited, Gower House, Croft Road, Aldershot, Hampshire GU11 3HR

Library of Congress Cataloging-in-Publication Data
Sylvester, Christine McNabb.
  Zimbabwe : the terrain of contradictory development /
Christine Sylvester.
    p. cm. — (Profiles. Nations of contemporary Africa)
  Includes bibliographical references (p.) and index.
  ISBN 0-8133-0690-6 (hc.)   ISBN 0-8133-8248-3 (pbk.)
    1. Zimbabwe—Economic conditions.   2. Zimbabwe—Politics and
government. I. Title. II. Series.
HC910.S95   1991
338.96891—dc20   91-20376
                                                                              CIP
British Library Cataloguing in Publication Data
A CIP catalogue record of this book is available from the British Library.

ISBN 1-85521-256-0 (hc.)

Printed and bound in the United States of America

The paper used in this publication meets the requirements
of the American National Standard for Permanence of Paper
for Printed Library Materials Z39.48-1984.

10   9   8   7   6   5   4   3   2

Contents

Tables

Illustrations

Preface

This book is intended both as an introduction to Zimbabwe and as a guide to the major debates that have shaped academic and political discourse in and on the country. It was a difficult volume to write because at each turn I had to keep this diverse audience in mind and rein in my inclination to wax too theoretical or to give too much detail. In a sense I have produced a book with a content that rides the hyphens of many audience identities and that leaves many questions about Zimbabwe's past, present, and future appropriately ambiguous.

Zimbabwe has beckoned me to return time and again, and for that reason I have accumulated heavy debts to those who made it financially possible to do so and those who always make my travails on the ground easier. Gettysburg College deserves a hearty thanks for its reliably generous funding during the years 1982–1988. To Gettysburg I owe my very first sojourn in Zimbabwe, which occurred under the auspices of an Oxfam America press tour. This introduction afforded opportunities to travel the country widely and facilitated contacts with political, economic, and social figures. Subsequent visits to southern Africa, including a summer stint as a visiting research associate at the Institute for Southern African Studies at the National University of Lesotho (1983), again funded by Gettysburg College, deepened my interest in the region and in Zimbabwe in particular. Between 1987 and 1988 I spent part of my sabbatical year as a visiting research associate in the Department of Economics at the University of Zimbabwe, where I undertook fieldwork for a study on "women," "production," and "progress" in two provinces of Zimbabwe. Some of the research for that project has crept into this book, and I am particularly grateful to Nelson Moyo for expediting the university invitation.

In 1988 I took up a position at Northern Arizona University and found myself again in a delightful funding milieu. In 1990 the university was extraordinarily generous with a paid leave that enabled me to accept an invitation from St. Antony's College, Oxford University, to be a senior associate member for the Hilary and Trinity terms of 1990. Access to the Rhodes House archives and to stimulating discussions with Oxford's many Zimbabweanists led to immeasurable improvements in this book. I am forever grateful to Rhodes Professor Terence Ranger for his invitation and to Deborah Gaitskell for expediting it. This book was completed at Oxford in July 1990 and updated at the point of copyediting in January 1991.

I also wish to thank Kevin Pyle for his unceasing support for my Zimbabwe "fever" and Larry Bowman for suggesting this volume to me and then for forcing me to look closely at the implications of my arguments. Norma Kriger, David Moore, and Jocelyn Alexander read the manuscript in its entirety and, as a result of their insightful comments, may not recognize the final product (although I take all responsibility for its mistakes). I wish to thank Peter Garlake for his hospitality and for his comments on Chapter 1 and David Maxwell for his comments on Chapter 5. Other sources of inspiration and comfort in Zimbabwe include Eunice Kapawu, Emelda Marumure, Vivean Neate, and Elizabeth Peeters.

I dedicate this book to Zimbabwe-watchers everywhere, especially to Zimbabwean academics who, owing to ever-increasing university responsibilities in a new country, must work twice as hard to fit research into their heavy schedules. My hat is off to you and to all Zimbabweans whose double and triple workloads would make me pant with exhaustion.

Christine Sylvester

1

A Historical Kaleidoscope

To begin a portrait of contemporary Zimbabwe it would be useful to sketch the country's history in quick and broad strokes. But Zimbabwe's past and present are fraught with controversies; there is often little consensus on the origins, movements, and general activities of Zimbabweans in early times and considerable debate about trends in political economy today. Many controversies center on issues of historical continuity and discontinuity—such as whether all Zimbabweans, not just former Rhodesians, came from distant lands; whether famous states in Zimbabwe's history collaborated with or were defeated by outside forces; whether the new Zimbabwean state is really new or is an extension of the Rhodesian state; and whether contemporary Zimbabwe follows a development path that diverges from or simply builds on the political economy of Rhodesia.

There is even some controversy about the appropriate questions to ask at this juncture in Zimbabwean history. Which ones are intellectually "fair," and which ones feed what Michael Bourdillon refers to as myths about Africans spun and promulgated under ninety years of white colonial rule?[1] Is it enlightening, for instance, to continue asking about the origins of Zimbabwe's peoples and early states, or does this extend the colonial habit of pronouncing on the "authenticity" of various group claims? Similarly, should we emphasize the powerful—local chiefs and Rhodesian leaders—or does such an approach subvert the narratives of laborers, farmers, women, craftspeople, and spirit mediums (people who communicate the wishes of important ancestors)? Should we ask what happened to the promises of socialism in contemporary Zimbabwe, or by doing so do we take the official rhetoric too strongly to heart, cast our analysis of Zimbabwe in dichotomous terms, and search either for the discontinuity of socialism or for the continuity of Rhodesian capitalism?

We should be aware of the many mine fields dotting the terrain and also recognize that some questions and many "answers" await further

1

excavations. In the case of Zimbabwean prehistory, some basic facts have not yet been established. As for more recent times, even seemingly consensual points about the political economy of Rhodesia and trends in contemporary Zimbabwe will undergo revision as new generations unearth new data and interpretations. Caution in reconstructing Zimbabwe's history must therefore be the watchword. Here the discussion focuses on general trends in the development of the country as well as the areas of dispute.

THE PHYSICAL SETTING

Zimbabwe is a southern African country with a total land area of 390,759 square kilometers. Zambia and the Zambezi River form a border to the north, while Mozambique lies to the east, Botswana is to the west, South Africa along the Limpopo River is to the south, and Namibia (the Caprivi strip) touches the northwest corner. In the east a semi-mountainous region called the Eastern Highlands straddles Zimbabwe and Mozambique, and in the west Zimbabwe and Botswana slip together into the Kalahari Desert.

Much of Zimbabwe is an elevated tropical plateau 650 kilometers in length that is distinct from middle- and lowveld around its edges. The plateau's elevations vary from a low of 152 meters to Mount Inyanga in the Eastern Highlands at 2,594 meters, with an average plateau elevation of 1,500 meters. Generally there is a hot dry season from September to November, followed by a slightly cooler rainy season ending in late March. Zimbabwe is also prone to drought, and there are serious shortages of rain every three to seven years. Zimbabwe does have a winter (although one hardly identifiable as such to most residents of the Northern Hemisphere), when relatively pleasant and dry days quickly take on a cool to cold edge at night, sometimes leaving dustings of frost. Humidity is not a problem on the plateau except during the rains, but steamy daytime temperatures around 36°C are possible off the plateau, especially in the northern resort area of Lake Kariba, near Victoria Falls, and in the lowveld of the Limpopo region.

Most Zimbabweans live in rural agricultural communities and probably have always done so. There are two major cities—Harare and Bulawayo—and several smaller urban centers, including Mutare, Kwekwe, Gweru, Hwange, and Masvingo, which are sites of industrial development or serve as markets for the surrounding areas. Connecting the main centers are good tarmac roads, express buses, and train service. To visit the rural areas is to take a different type of journey on dirt roads, often rutted from rain and use, and then on footpaths that wind unerringly through the bush.

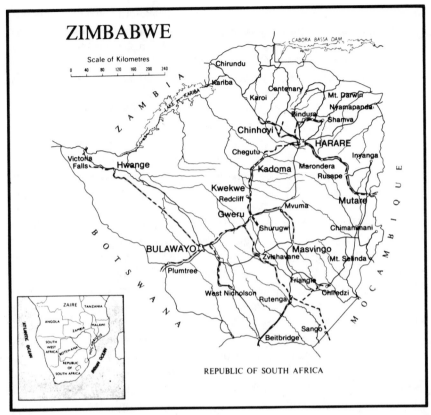

Zimbabwe. *Source: Socio-Economic Review of Zimbabwe 1980–1985.* Harare: Ministry of Finance, Economic Planning and Development, 1986.

A DISPUTED PREHISTORY

It is common to divide Zimbabwe's prehistory into the Stone "Age" of Paleolithic times, which ended approximately one thousand years ago, and the early and late Iron "ages" of this millennium.[2] Nevertheless, the term *ages* is contested in the Zimbabwean context. On the one hand, "ages" suggest characteristic moments in the evolution of technology, economies, and social systems that stand apart from the moments preceding and following them. But on the other hand, the tendency to delineate one age from the next can raise questions about the agents of change—are they local people adapting to new knowledge and conditions or outsiders whose technologies conquer the material culture of their predecessors?[3] There can (but need not) be a political motivation behind questions of origin—namely, to establish the contemporary credentials of various "tribes" and to assign responsibility for achievements and setbacks in Zimbabwe's past.

We do know that between two hundred thousand and one thousand years ago the peoples of present-day Zimbabwe relied on stone tools and weapons and lived by gathering uncultivated vegetables in the wild and by hunting game. Historian David Beach claims Zimbabwe's early inhabitants developed an unusual reliance on hunting and gathering: "Elsewhere in Africa, Stone Age peoples began to plant vegetables or sow crops, and developed special stone tools and even pottery in order to do this, but so far there is no evidence that this ever happened on the Plateau."[4] Archaeologist Peter Garlake disputes Beach's characterization and argues that these people engaged in heterogeneous economic activities that included the domestication of sheep.[5] In either case, these early inhabitants spoke a Khoisan language and developed several living sites in response to local ecological possibilities as well as to movements of groups they met. Their decentralized communities were apparently stable until about A.D. 200, and then one of two things happened.

It is possible that these peoples then began coexisting with more technologically advanced Bantu-speakers who traveled southward from the Sudan belt and eventually absorbed, overwhelmed, or conquered the Stone Age inferiors. If this is the case, these outsiders are the first ancestors of present-day Zimbabweans and are responsible for building several Iron Age plateau states around settled village agriculture, gold mining, and animal husbandry. How many migrations may have taken place, where they originated, and which routes people traveled are still open questions among migration theorists.[6]

Alternatively, the instabilities that migration theorists associate with outside influences could result from local peoples adapting simultaneously or sequentially to conditions of drought, to some newcomers in the region, and to shifting knowledge about technology within their own communities. This interpretation implies that more primitive peoples were not eclipsed by the "true" progenitors of Zimbabwe, who arrived from afar, but rather were themselves "the direct ancestors of the present inhabitants of Zimbabwe."[7] The changes in pottery styles, which archaeologists often read as signs of movement from one age to another, may reflect a local transition from matrilineal to patrilineal power relations: "In a system where wives moved to their husbands' villages on marriage, the continuity of training in pot-making and production would be broken."[8] Trade would also bring technologically different peoples into contact and alter local languages, pottery designs, and tools. The problem in deconstructing the texts on this period is that "there are almost as many interpretations of the ceramic sequence in Zimbabwe

Aerial photograph of Great Zimbabwe. Courtesy Zimbabwe Ministry of Information.

as there are archaeologists of the Iron Age," and there is "a lot of information about pots, but relatively little about people."[9]

One Iron Age controversy, which has to do with the origins of magnificent ruins located near present-day Masvingo, has been laid to rest after tedious debate. According to one school of thinking, the ruins of a two-level walled city known as Great Zimbabwe were surely too impressive to be the work of local Africans:

> When we find an extraordinary phenomenon such as Zimbabwe surrounded by regions hardly yet set upon the road of higher civilisation, it is obvious in what direction we should turn for the explanation. This is not some outburst arising out of native barbarism, like a mutant gene in biology, which from something quite different produces an efflorescence pregnant with a leap forward to higher things. If we find a civilisation such as that of Zimbabwe buried in the jungle of barbarism, we must look for outside influences, just as we have seen was the case in Ethiopia and is here in Nubia.[10]

Thus, in this view Great Zimbabwe was uniquely discontinuous with all surrounding African communities and was said to be built by people with Phoenician, Arabic, Semitic, and/or Hamitic roots. Locals must have supplied [only] the labour, for these stupendous works [had] nothing by which to distinguish them, except that, at a period later than that of the first rock mines, a race of Bushmen left quite a number of their spirited drawings, including one of the Victoria Falls, on the rocks and in the caves of many parts of the country. So much for prehistoric Rhodesia.[11]

Of course, if Europeans could somehow link outsiders like themselves to a glorious civilization in Zimbabwe's past, Rhodesia could be painted as a later moment in a long "distinguished" history of diffused civilization.

Several early archaeologists argued, however, that Great Zimbabwe was a local product, and later excavators used radiocarbon datings to prove this was so.[12] In this effort Peter Garlake's name looms large, and few serious researchers now dispute his claim that the city has indigenous origins.[13] But during the late 1960s Garlake's position ran afoul of the official Rhodesian view that Great Zimbabwe was the work of outsiders, and as a consequence he lost his job as Rhodesian senior inspector of monuments.

There are additional controversies surrounding Great Zimbabwe and the country's complex Iron Age. The next section highlights some of these and explores the historical political economies of four states— Great Zimbabwe, Mutapa, Torwa, and Rozvi—that "were able to exact tribute from other territories over a wide area over a long time and/ or construct large-scale 'prestige' stone buildings."[14] It is useful to bear in mind that although we speak of "great states," everyday life was often conducted in smaller communities ruled by local chiefs.

THE POLITICAL ECONOMY OF PLATEAU STATES

Chiefdoms are known for creating "tension between the forces of centralisation, which allow individuals to build up political and economic power, and competition for authority by rivals."[15] This tension reduces the likelihood that any one chief can accumulate enough power to expand a domain of authority. Accordingly, some believe that the emphasis should be placed not on "the creation of the great states but [on] the consistent replication of these smaller polities,"[16] where subsistence agriculture and pastoralism took place on lands spiritually connected with the dead, particularly with the spirit guardians of the chiefdom.

State building, however, was a feature of the Sudanic period of precolonial African history, which corresponded roughly with Zimbabwe's Iron Age,[17] and that means certain chiefdoms succeeded in preventing divisive power plays within the elite long enough to establish ruling lines. States could then form as resource-extracting "sets of administrative, policing and military organizations headed and more or less coordinated by an executive authority."[18] Zimbabwe's early states, although not the administrative organizations we now know, would have had effective means of coercion, consent, and, sometimes, expansion. None, however, established control over the entire contemporary landmass of the country. Thus, states and chiefdoms coexisted.

Great Zimbabwe

In a country noted for natural attractions—from Victoria Falls to the Eastern Highlands to Hwange Game Reserve—the ruins of Great Zimbabwe do indeed stand out as unparalleled monuments to human enterprise. This one state was the most dominant of what researchers think were seven coterminous states in the region, its name, and now the name of the country, coming from the distinctive stone architecture marking the main capital and smaller regional centers nearby.

Dzimbahwe means "residence of the chief in Shona," and the closely related term *dzimba dza mabwe* means "houses of stone." Zimbabwe had life between the twelfth and fifteenth centuries, however, far before its builders and inhabitants had any contemporary ethnic identity. The name "Shona," Bourdillon notes, "is of recent origin and was applied to all the Shona-speaking peoples only after the British colonization of the country."[19] Thus, it is more accurate to say that Great Zimbabwe was "the residence of the most powerful ruler in the south-eastern interior of Africa, surrounded by the houses of his family, of the families of his tributary rulers and of the officials of his court."[20]

These rulers lived apart from the up to twenty thousand members of the laboring class they controlled from the naturally exfoliated granite hill at the site, later from within a great enclosure built in the valley below. Small openings in the hillside wall suggest lookout points, and tall stone monoliths resemble military projectiles of some type. Walls in the lower valley are approximately 240 meters in length, nearly 10 meters high, and as much as 5 meters in thickness. The image thus presented is of a two-level fortress. Yet it is not clear that this state had enemies let alone opponents capable of launching the horse-and-musket assaults that gave rise to walled cities in Europe. The power and affluence of the ruling classes may explain the edifices, much as aspects of ancient African civilizations in Egypt and Nubia displayed the splendor of divine kingship.

How Zimbabwean elites controlled the masses of the city is a matter of continuing speculation. Most explanations look to religious ideology, control of trade, largesse in the distribution of royal herds of cattle, or a combination of these three realms of power as likely

Hilltop wall of Great Zimbabwe. Courtesy Zimbabwe Ministry of Information.

mechanisms. It is difficult to come to a definitive answer because Cecil Rhodes and other fortune hunters ransacked the site and left behind relatively few cultural artifacts.

That religion may figure into the picture of elite control is suggested by many inexplicable architectural features of the ruins, such as the stone monoliths and a large conical tower in the valley.[21] Several excavated carved stone birds are now used to symbolize the contemporary state of Zimbabwe and are viewed as metaphors for spirits of departed kings.

Trade, however, may have been the central facet of the political economy. Fragments of Islamic and Chinese beads, textiles, ceramics, and glassware bolster this contention. It is also instructive that Great Zimbabwe's "greatest prosperity coincided with the peak in the export trade in gold, as attested on the Indian Ocean coast."[22] But it is unlikely that gold was the engine of elite power because the site is not located at extensive gold reserves. Nevertheless, the shallow goldfields nearby could have figured into trade indirectly through a tributary mode of production whereby peasant villagers paid "taxes" to the nobility in gold and the gold was then used in wider trade networks.[23]

Alternatively, Great Zimbabwe may have been at the center of a complex cattle economy. The evidence for this is its location close to high- and lowveld grazing and the absence of grain-bin foundations,

Zimbabwe bird. Courtesy Zimbabwe Ministry of Information.

storage pits, grindstones, and large concentrations of minerals at the site. A cattle economy, no less than an economy of trade, would require a fairly centralized state and a stratified system of extraction and control of ordinary people that tied use of individual cattle to royal patronage.

Finally, Great Zimbabwe may have had a diversified economy of cattle, gold trade, textile and salt production, and iron making, the integration of which would "demand all the administrative skill, political will and military strength of a state."[24] In that case it is tempting to think of such a state as the center of a golden age.[25] Excavations of areas where ordinary people lived, however, although limited, show urban life at its worst—crowded, muddy, and cramped. Excavations also make clear that high-living kings and courtiers were few in number compared to the many herdsmen–soldiers–mine workers, masons and builders, craftspeople, agricultural producers, and, perhaps, landless peasants in the valley.

Great Zimbabwe's social system broke down during the late fifteenth and early sixteenth centuries, and today there is no consensus on why this happened. It may have become increasingly difficult to maintain herds close by a growing city, gather wood for fuel, and find arable land for food production. Likewise, gold deposits in the area may have been depleted, and trade may have shifted from the plateau-to-sea route near Great Zimbabwe, which had sustained commercial relations with Islamic communities on the Indian Ocean coast, to routes closer to new states emerging in the north and southwest. Each eventuality would provide opportunity for regional centers to assert autonomy from Great Zimbabwe and develop into new states. Mutapa, a dynasty that became identified with a new state, is especially well known.

Mutapa

Portuguese began arriving at the East African Islamic city of Kilwa in 1505, just as Great Zimbabwe was in decline, and heard of a Mutapa dynasty and of a famous ruler by the name of Monomotapa, who governed the northern plateau. Presumably the Mutapa dynasty was a spinoff from the Great Zimbabwe line, but the physical location of the Mutapa capital has never been ascertained, making for considerable speculation about this second state and its rulers.

One tradition has it that Mutapa was a feudal empire dominating the whole northern area of the plateau, the lowlands in the Zambezi valley, and the present-day Tete province of Mozambique. Local communities were vassals of the emperor, notwithstanding their many incidences of rebellion, and the emperor himself was a manipulative ally of the Portuguese—one moment converting to Christianity to seal a trading agreement and the next executing a missionary as a witch-doctor.[26] Other accounts tell of a more restricted domain of political influence and of more insecure relations with tributaries.[27] Details are blurry, nonetheless, and for a state that existed for nearly five hundred years, "there is a surprising lack of scholarly investigation of its history."[28]

There is agreement, however, that in the early seventeenth century Portuguese influence in the area increased, and as it did, resistance grew to the Mutapa custom of paying the emperor a tribute in gold and grain in order to travel freely through his territory. The Mutapa state weakened and several civil wars ensued. Eventually the Portuguese gained the power to depose legitimate Mutapa kings and install others who would give missionaries and merchants total access to the empire's resources, particularly to gold and ivory. Nevertheless, Portuguese power was not constant in the region until the late nineteenth century, and there is little evidence that Mutapa was ever subjected to Portuguese feudal dynasties.

Mutapa's commodity exchanges with the Portuguese favored the Europeans and created enormous gaps between local elites and masses. It has been said that "the king and the chiefs were dressed in cloth of cotton or silk, but the poor nearly went naked."[29] Divisions within classes also occurred: merchants sold prestige cloths directly to ambitious princes, who then developed patronage links to challenge the kings. Meanwhile, some poor people took advantage of the state's preoccupations to engage in illegal ivory trade, and young men often joined the military as *vanyai* (young fighters) or *varanda* (bondsmen or slaves).[30]

For a state that persevered into the second half of the nineteenth century, its cultural life is virtually unknown to us except through Portuguese sources, which are not always considered reliable. In the sixteenth and seventeenth centuries the Portuguese spoke of a high god, named Mulungu or Umbe, whom the people worshipped indirectly through the spirits of dead ancestors. Spirit cults may also have grown up around ancestors of the ruling Mutapa lineage, but Beach argues that this must not be taken as a sign that Mutapa kings were considered divine, as the Portuguese commonly thought. Rather, the king seems to have had access to the most powerful spirits in the land—those of former rulers—which suggests that "religion was based on politics to the extent that it was rooted in the earlier material success of rulers."[31]

Torwa

Torwa, the third great plateau state, was built between the fifteenth and seventeenth centuries, first at Khami and later at Danangombe, both near Bulawayo. Like Great Zimbabwe, Torwa has some impressive stonework, but it is known mostly for the stone platforms that bore huts of the ruling class on hilltop sites, new patterns of decoration and covered passageways, and more elaborate pottery than that found at Great Zimbabwe.[32]

Torwa has attracted neither the archaeological interest that Great Zimbabwe has nor the investigations of trade and commerce that mark the studies of Mutapa. Beach says we do not know whether the rulers of Great Zimbabwe founded this new center, "whether some of the ruling group broke away . . . leaving the old ruler to live in a rapidly diminishing state, or whether a western provincial ruler established his independence and became the focus of new development."[33] To the degree that there are differing interpretations of Torwa, debate centers on the identity of the founding dynasty and the architectural details of the stonework.[34] Portuguese documents suggest the political economy resembled Great Zimbabwe's but also tell of legends depicting a powerful magician at Torwa who could call forth a cloud of bees to dispel invaders. This myth has given rise to the view that Torwa may have been a peaceful state organized around some religious ideology, a story that is countered by evidence that Torwa intervened in Mutapa politics.[35]

Rozvi

By contrast, the Rozvi state has drawn considerable attention, much of it leading to myths as inaccurate as those once associated with Great Zimbabwe.[36] According to legend, Rozvi's origins lie only with one man—Dombo Changamire, a rebellious herdsman of one of the Mutapa leaders who began establishing an independent following around the time of Mutapa's escalating conflicts with the Portuguese. From a base in the northeast, this marauding adventurer migrated with followers to the southwest and led the final attack on Torwa in the 1680s. Changamire also fended off an assault by the Mutapa state in 1684 and attacked and defeated the Portuguese at Maseksea in 1695. By 1700 his successors— themselves always referred to as Changamire—had made Rozvi into a politically influential state different from, yet centered at, Torwa.

Rozvi is known for its powerful armies, which the Portuguese tried to avoid in their quest to monopolize trade with the eastern plateau area of Manyika. How Rozvi could recruit so many military men remains a mystery, for it occupied a prime cattle-keeping location and therefore did not have many young resourceless men seeking patrons through military service. The plight of other classes is also cloaked in obscurity because "there is very little evidence for the economic backing that made the organization of the Rozvi armies, and thus the power of the Rozvi state, possible."[37] That there are no grand cities directly associated with

Rozvi construction could indicate that, despite its military power, Rozvi had less wealth than Torwa, Mutapa, or Zimbabwe.

In any case, the state began to weaken under raids from the south in the 1820s and was dispersed in the 1860s after a new state attained prominence in southwestern Zimbabwe. At that point political power on the northern plateau reverted, as it had often done before, to local chiefs. But Rozvi legends did not die. Beach contends that "even after the fall of the Changamire state the name of 'Rozvi' remained a valued one,"[38] and new inhabitants of the territory remained wary of a Rozvi resurgence into the twentieth century.

THE POLITICAL ECONOMY OF THE NDEBELE STATE

In the early nineteenth century people of the plateau witnessed two waves of migration from south of the Limpopo—raiders in the 1820s and more permanent state builders in the 1850s. The raiders briefly established a state in the Eastern Highlands, caused most local societies minimal damage, and were conquered after 1836 by the state of Gaza, based in Mozambique and for a time on the Mozambican-Zimbabwean border. A more permanent Ndebele state was established by renegade Zulus who converged around the old site of Rozvi. They found little resistance from what were by this time decentralized agriculturally based chiefdoms and built a presence that lasted into the 1890s.

This migratory period is often taken as a point of discontinuity in the history of the Shona-identified plateau states and, especially with the arrival of the "Ndebeles," the Shona-speakers' name for these breakaway Zulus, as the beginning of a clash between "outsiders" and plateau "insiders" that would last well into the 1980s. The Ndebele incursion, in other words, is taken as the start of Zimbabwe's modern ethnic history. But this point of view relies on legends scripted and passed on by the last wave of migrants to enter the area—the Rhodesians—who claimed to have happened on a powerful Ndebele state and its subjugated and demoralized Shona chieftaincies. Just as there are controversies about Zimbabwe's prehistoric ages and their plateau states, so are there controversies about this Rhodesian story line.

Ranger claims, for example, that "if there were indeed people who were conscious of belonging to the Ndebele state they did not and could not think that this was the same thing as belonging to a 'tribe' or an 'ethnicity.' "[39] Thus, the question of insiders and outsiders is murkier than common lore would have us believe. There is also evidence that the Shona were not simply passive victims of outside conquerors but were themselves involved in migrations and state building as active agents of change. Regional overpopulation, it is thought, caused them to enter a general search for fertile land, and their movements in combination with the movements of others helped set off further waves of migration, as people sought to escape new tribute-seekers or find new centers of state power to protect them from other migrants.[40]

We do know the Ndebele state emerged around Bulawayo in the 1850s under a monarchical-civilian structure. The state emulated the Zulu tradition of placing most adult men into regiments (*amabutho*), which were established on a town-by-town basis, and sending these regiments out to incorporate other societies and to restock kraals through regular raiding.[41] Most plateau dwellers were not incorporated forcibly at first, and even as the "Ndebele" king Mzilikazi stole plateau cattle, he consulted "Shona" spirit mediums for guidance, adopted local crops, and used northern trade networks to sell grain and ivory to the eastern coast.[42]

There is some evidence, however, that the new state did behave badly toward peoples who resisted its rule, by kidnapping and mistreating women and press-ganging youth into the army. Moreover, Mzilikazi was apparently wary of a resurgent Rozvi state and prevented Rozvi-identified military recruits from serving in or returning to their home territories. These practices would later create pockets of resistance to the Ndebele state, and when in the 1860s a portion of Mzilikazi's army was defeated by resisters, the Ndebele state moved to dominate militarily all challenging plateau peoples.

Mzilikazi's successor, Lobengula, turned out to be a weaker leader. In 1893 a group of resisters aligned with newly arrived white settlers to end domination by the Ndebele state. Rhodesian lore then built this incident into a story of white pioneers freeing an enslaved nation of Shona from a superior Ndebele nation-state. Ranger argues, however, that the Rhodesians invented the Ndebele as a separate warlike tribe from the Shona and determined that the former had to be carefully reckoned with in early colonial days.[43] This myth ignored the fact that the southwestern plateau state comprised a conglomeration of peoples whose identities and loyalties were fluid: for some the Ndebele state was home, for others it was merely another in a chain of plateau states, and for still others it was a source of oppression.

THE BRITISH SOUTH AFRICA COMPANY STATE

African contacts with Europeans up to the 1890s were limited to trade relations, periodic wars with the Portuguese, a few hostile inter-changes with Afrikaner *voortrekkers* (Dutch settlers from South Africa who traveled north and east to escape British rule in the Cape), and to encounters with individual missionaries. The white settlers were

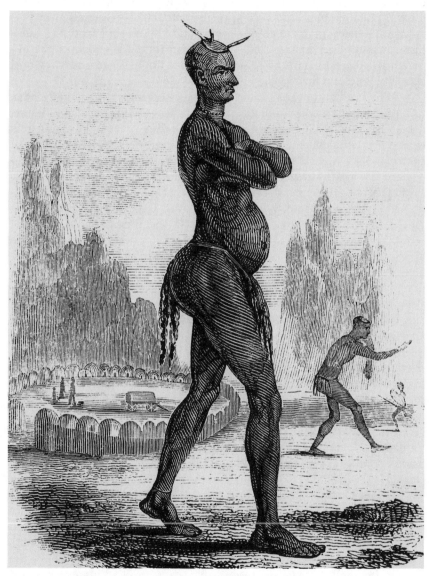

Mzilikazi, circa 1837. *Source:* Captain Sir William Cornwallis Harris, *Wild Sports of Southern Africa.* Courtesy National Archives, Zimbabwe.

different. Although they established what appeared to be just another plateau state, unlike previous states, this one adapted only minimally to local customs and did not incorporate locals except as laborers or inferior collaborators. The timing of the settler entry was also key: the quickening pace of technological innovation in Europe and the move from mercantilism to free-trade imperialism and then to outright imperialism meant Africans faced incorporation, not just into a new regional state but into the formidable capitalist world system as well.

Why the Europeans came, stayed, and behaved differently than had predecessor powers on the plateau is not a subject of continuing debate. In the 1860s explorers and missionaries speculated about gold on the northern plateau, and their tales took on new life when amateur geologist Karl Mauch reported in the South African press that Mashonaland ore existed in great quantities. There was also a German challenge in the region and general British imperialist goals to advance. Nevertheless, it has been said that until 1885 even Cecil Rhodes was unconvinced of the fabled gold and questioned the fitness of the area for settlement. A year later a point near present-day Johannesburg yielded up the first sizable piece of gold in southern Africa, and this unleashed new rumors that a second rand (sizable deposit) existed north of the Limpopo.

The influx of Europeans was then such that Mzilikazi found it necessary to have newcomers arrive only at designated points and then appear for an audience with him. He was not necessarily hostile to them, for he knew from experience with the Portuguese that it made sense to court a few European friends who could act against ruthless traders. Robert Moffat of the London Missionary Society became one such "friend." Moffat tended to treat the king "like a child"[44] and may have joined other missionaries "who constantly advocated 'breaking' the Ndebele military system as the necessary first step in bringing European civilization to the people."[45] In return, Mzilikazi treated Moffat like a madman who could provide guns and contacts to facilitate trade in ivory.

It was far more difficult for Lobengula to hold back the Europeans with these methods. As the leader based closest to South Africa, from whence came increasing numbers of Europeans, it became his burden to deal with each succeeding petition for rights north of the Limpopo, particularly because Europeans assumed he had influence over all the Shona. In 1888 Lobengula placed his mark on the infamous Rudd Concession, thereby granting Rhodes's emissaries rights to "all metals and minerals situated and contained in my kingdom . . . together with full power to do all things necessary to win and procure the same."[46] This treaty became the basis for a royal charter granted a year later to

Rhodes's British South Africa Company (BSAC), empowering it not only to oversee gold mining but to enter treaties, promulgate laws, maintain a police force, and undertake public works in what would become Southern Rhodesia.

For his part in this Lobengula was later depicted as a sellout. But he was not literate in English and was misled by his courted missionary allies into thinking the concession was less extensive than it was. Moreover, we can speculate that Lobengula might have been trying to protect his state from a form of Balkanization through the grant of extensive rights only to Rhodes; and the king may have thought he had the upper hand because the stipulations suggested Europeans could claim for England resources under the soil but not land itself or things on the land.

Treaty in hand, however, Rhodes set about planning an occupation, believing that "although we had a charter we had not got the country, which was occupied by savages."[47] He recruited an armed group of prospector-adventurers and decided to move directly into the legendary goldfields of Mashonaland, thereby circumventing Lobengula's forces in the southwest. In June 1890 Rhodes's "pioneer column" of two hundred young but essentially poor men and five hundred company police left Kimberley, South Africa. Led by Lieutenant Colonel Pennefather, A. R. Colquhoun, and L. S. Jameson, with F. C. Selous as their scout, the men reached the area they would call Salisbury in September and occupied it in the name of Queen Victoria. The pioneers then dispersed into the bush in search of that second rand.

In Rhodes's words the company "began the first groundwork of making a country."[48] Initially, this entailed little in the way of formal government on the northern plateau because Lobengula was thought to retain sovereign rights to the area. In 1891 a British Order in Council declared Mashonaland a British protectorate and laid the basis for a semirepresentative government there consisting of a (white) legislative council of mostly appointed and some elected members, an administrator with ministers, and several departments, including one overseeing "natives," which Rhodes tended to ignore in the belief that "the Shona and Ndebele 'were all pleased and naturally so' by the arrival of the whites."[49]

The company oversaw financial and speculative capital and set terms of entry to the territory. It did not engage in production itself; profits—when they existed—came instead through shareholdings in other companies.[50] One early settler expressed what would become a general sentiment that "instead of having the Imperial Treasury behind her she [the colony] had to depend on a commercial company, and her coat was cut according to their cloth."[51]

Cecil J. Rhodes, 1896. Courtesy National Archives, Zimbabwe.

That cloth, however, could be cut widely. Once it became clear
that the gold of the northern plateau did not exist in the abundance
expected—"less than 800 oz gold were produced in the whole of 1892"[52]—
De Beers and Gold Fields of South Africa saved the company from its
losses and in return received lavish concessions of land—up to 242,915
hectares—in the hope that outside capital would "more rapidly develop
the resources of the territory than the smaller capitals of individual
settlers."[53] By 1896, one-sixth of the country had come under the control
of concessionary companies, their average holdings approximating "the

size of an average English county at the top end of the scale."[54] Individual settlers then began to purchase land from the companies at relatively higher prices than the companies had paid or were given land in exchange for military service in World War I.

It was not agriculture, however, that the BSAC initially had in mind for this land. Historian Stanlake Samkange notes that the first white settlers in the Melsetter region found Africans successfully cultivating "mealie, poko corn, kaffir corn, millet, ground nuts, beans (five sorts), eggs, fruit, cabbages, sweet potatoes, tomatoes, peas, pumpkins, water melons, cucumbers, chillies, tobacco, bananas, lemons—all grown to perfection."[55] Rather than compete with these efficient farmers, the company set its sights firmly on mining and, at every turn until approximately 1907, tried to lure investors by falsely claiming that "everywhere new finds are occurring daily."[56]

Rhodes wanted to open Ndebele territory to investment and settlement but needed a pretext for doing so. In 1893 a "Ndebele" raid on Fort Victoria, which was launched "to punish local Shona who had been responsible for the theft of telegraph wire and for fomenting discord between Lobengula and the Company,"[57] was twisted by Rhodes into a "Ndebele" plan for war against Mashonaland. Claiming the need to protect the "Shona"—even as Lobengula sent a peace delegation to Salisbury—a white commando force moved into Bulawayo and quickly defeated the Ndebele state. Lobengula went into exile, and the company thereby gained legal power over Matabeleland and all territories its state had previously controlled.

What followed was a replay of the earlier settler rush in Mashonaland. Generous grants of land went to commando volunteers and friends, and Lobengula's highly valued cattle became war booty; by 1897 only 13,983 head of cattle remained in African hands throughout the whole of Southern Rhodesia, down from the 200,000 or so the Ndebele state alone had controlled in 1893.[58] The company also installed a system of "native" administration, which in Matabeleland "amounted to frank military despotism by Jameson's [the colony's second administrator] white police."[59]

In 1896 Africans from the northern and southern plateau regions struck back against the settlers with a ferocity that startled even those administrators who knew of company injustices. The timing of the uprising coincided with a plan by Jameson to use police from Bulawayo in an invasion of the Boer Republic of Transvaal, an act intended to "speed the day of a self-governing English-speaking South Africa."[60] The settlers were left unguarded and were subsequently attacked by forces they thought were composed of former "subject peoples" of the Ndebele state. These Shona, it was said, had "beguiled the government

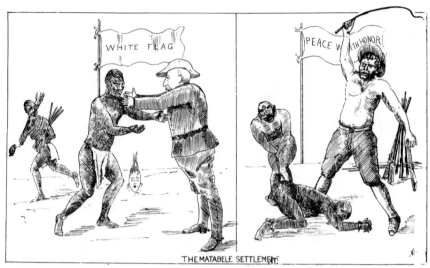

"The Matabele Settlement," cartoon regarding peace negotiations, 1896. Courtesy National Archives, Zimbabwe.

of the country," masterminded and elaborately planned the war in secret—possibly as a means of reviving the Rozvi empire—and struck in a concerted manner on March 24, 1896, the night of long knives.[61] In fact, the first attacks were carried out by remnants of the Ndebele state, and the fighting then spread northward to embrace a number of northern chieftaincies. Rhodes tried to squelch the uprisings through a double strategy of negotiating "Ndebele" land rights on the southern plateau while ferociously working to suppress the attacks in the north, in part by hunting down two spirit mediums who allegedly inspired the warriors, the female medium of the spirit Nehanda and the male medium of the spirit Kaguvi. Fighting lingered, however, until British imperial troops tipped the scales in 1897.

The Rhodesians later credited the "Shona and Ndebele" with a jointly coordinated war effort, and analysts have since debated where the center of the struggle really existed. Ranger argues that certain Shona spirit mediums were indeed central to the combined efforts; Julian Cobbing says prophetic religious leaders were never instrumental in rallying the Ndebele; and Richard Werbner claims religious leaders were involved but did not have the seminationalist political ideology Ranger attributes to them.[62] The latest interpretation stresses the political economy of the situation and suggests that spirit mediums from the northern plateau sought medicine against locusts from certain religious figures in the south and learned from them about the uprisings near Bulawayo. The

Mbuya Nehanda, circa 1896. Courtesy
National Archives, Zimbabwe.

news "triggered a 'ripple effect' in which northern communities resisted or collaborated as the news reached them."[63]

Following the uprisings of 1896–1897 company fortunes waned and then recovered. Millions of pounds had been spent on the war, and Jameson's famous raid into the Transvaal had ruined him and Rhodes, burst the speculative bubble keeping the company semisolvent, and caused Britain to reduce company control of the police. Settlers, particularly those in the north near Salisbury, felt the company had done little to protect them during the uprisings and clamored for greater representation in colony affairs. Rhodes was looking for ways of improving the company's tarnished reputation and in 1897 endeavored to attract investors and reestablish better relations with local settlers by making good on an original charter stipulation that the company construct a railway.

By early 1903 the company's railroad-led development had created a situation in which "demand for labor exceeded supply by some 25 per cent."[64] At the same time, the settlers remained wary of the blacks, and many came to believe, to put it starkly, that "separation, except in so far as labour on a temporary basis was required for the mines, farms and domestic service, was the only safe system if a twentieth century white minority ruling class was to dwell in the same land as a conquered black majority barely emerged from the Iron Age."[65] The Legislative Council created the Rhodesia Native Labour Bureau to recruit workers for the mines, and between 1904 and 1911 the number of black workers (housed separately from whites) rose from about 7,000 to more than 37,000; white workers increased in numbers from 949 to 2,255.[66] The annual value of gold output, supplemented by influxes of capital from South African mining houses, then went as high in 1908 as it had been during all previous years of company oversight.

As the mines boomed, landowners saw possibilities for expanded food production and made it known they resented their African competitors less than they resented special privileges accorded mining, such as its legal rights to wood, water, and grazing lands, and the prospectors who freely operated on farms. Many settlers were poor Afrikaners who had trekked to Southern Rhodesia during the Anglo Boer War, and to them it was important to have titled land, lower rail rates, and company-sponsored agricultural research. The company initially balked at these demands, but between 1907 and 1911 the "number of whites engaged in agricultural pursuits increased by 82 per cent, or roughly 20 per cent per annum,"[67] and the Legislative Council had to be increasingly sensitive to their claims. In 1907 these farmers sponsored a motion to end the rule of a mining-oriented company, and the company thereafter had to labor to change its image, claiming in public relations announcements, for example, that "the prospect of cheap land, easy terms of purchase, and an assured abundant rainfall, is attracting large numbers."[68] By 1914 approximately 2,040 white farmers were cultivating 74,251 hectares of maize and tobacco, and the company continued to hold off the day when its mining focus and new agricultural efforts would definitively clash.

By the second decade of the century the colony had become "hospitable," according to the standards of European men, and Rhodesians became smug, insular, and acquisitive. People from "classes which never had much leisure to dispose of"[69] tried to emulate the British upper classes and succeeded instead in creating a nouveau riche culture. Men found the country particularly congenial, and braggards claimed that "no country in the world [exists] where a man can have a more comfortable bachelor existence, enjoy all the sport he wants and be so much his own master on a comparatively small income."[70] Along with patriarchy there was racism: "His housekeeping is simplified by the essential Kafir, and bachelors all over the territory are always boasting of their boys."[71] Moreover, whites developed "good" excuses for their racial misdeeds: "That either the Company or the individual settlers were guilty of the systematic cruelties attributed to them at one time is highly improbable, for they were living, often as isolated individuals, surrounded by natives who were armed and hostile."[72]

As for the "natives," some were well placed to accumulate by using mine wages to buy farm implements, renting cattle to neighbors, or putting people in their employ. Most, however, defensively struggled to join commodity production as peasants and thereby avoid working for whites. This created social differentiation in the rural areas and broke up the terrain on which the combined forces of state and capital would steadily march.[73]

CONCLUSIONS

The early history of Zimbabwe is noteworthy both for continuities over great expanses of time and for the deep changes associated with discontinuities. That the plateau region saw a series of states, for example, contributes to a sense of its unified history, as do recurring patterns of gold mining, agriculture, pastoralism, trade, and smelting across those states. Historians writing in the 1960s played up a glorious past and often connected the great states to the nationalist struggle looming against Rhodesia.

Yet if one asks questions about struggles within and among the plateau states, one begins to see the outlines of still underresearched differences between privileged precolonial rulers and commoners, chiefs and kings, men and women, youths and elders, and northern plateau dwellers and southerners. Their struggles belie the idea that Zimbabwe's ancestors inhabited a totalizing historical moment from the first days of this millennium until, depending on one's predilections, the 1850s, when the Ndebeles brought rupture, or 1980, when Rhodesian political control ended at the hands of Shona-Ndebele armies.

Notwithstanding both the continuities and discontinuities in pre-colonial times, it does seem the British South Africa Company should be categorized as a different form of plateau political economy whose practices departed sharply from those of Great Zimbabwe, Torwa, Mutapa, Rozvi, the Ndebele state, and the decentralized chieftaincies. The company changed preexisting class structures in response to rules of extractive production no other "outsider" had heretofore imposed, and local practices of community, leadership, and culture—as varied as these were—were twisted ideologically into forms of "depraved savagery" to be ignored, rescued, or tamed by entrepreneurial Europeans riding the crest of Victorian modernization. Although some Africans benefited from the arrival of the Rhodesians, most were set on a path of considerable economic and then political upheaval, as Chapter 2 details.

NOTES

1. Michael Bourdillon discusses *Myths About Africans* in the introduction to his *The Shona People* (Gweru: Mambo Press, 1987), pp. xv–xviii.

2. For two brief but contrasting treatments of African prehistoric ages, see Hosea Jaffe, *A History of Africa* (London: Zed Press, 1985); and Roland Oliver and J. D. Fage, *A Short History of Africa*, 6th ed. (London: Penguin, 1988).

3. Peter Garlake makes his case for continuity in "Prehistory and Ideology in Zimbabwe," *Africa* 52, no. 3 (1982): 1–19; as does Peta Jones in "Farming and Migration in African Prehistory," *Prehistory Society of Zimbabwe Newsletter* 61 (October 1985): 1–6. The more common migration theory of change is associated with T. N. Huffman (e.g.,"African Origins," *South African Journal of Science* 75 [1979]: 233–237); D. W. Phillipson, "The Chronology of the Iron Age in Bantu Africa," *Journal of African History* 16, no. 3 (1975): 321–342; and J.E.G. Sutton, "East Africa Before the Seventh Century," in *General History of Africa*, ed. G. Mokhtar, vol. 2 (London: Heinemann, 1981), pp. 568–592.

4. David Beach, *The Shona and Zimbabwe, 900–1850* (Gwelo: Mambo Press, 1980), p. 5.

5. Garlake, "Prehistory and Ideology."

6. Martin Hall, *The Changing Past: Farmers, Kings and Traders in Southern Africa, 200–1860* (Cape Town: David Phillip, 1987).

7. Peter S. Garlake, *Great Zimbabwe: Described and Explained* (Harare: Zimbabwe Publishing House, 1982), p. 7.

8. Garlake, "Prehistory and Ideology," p. 13.

9. Hall, *The Changing Past*, pp. 15–16.

10. R. Gayre and E. Layland, *The Origins of the Zimbabwe Civilization* (Harare: Galaxy, 1972), pp. 99–100.

11. E. T. Jollie, *The Real Rhodesia* (Bulawayo: Books of Rhodesia, 1971), p. 11. This type of diffusionist analysis appears in James Theodor Bent, *The Ruined Cities of Mashonaland, Being a Record of Excavation and Exploration in 1891* (London: Longmans, 1893); Andries J. Bruwer, *Zimbabwe: Rhodesia's Ancient Greatness* (Johannesburg: Hugh Keartland, 1965); and Richard Hall, *Pre-historic Rhodesia* (Philadelphia: George W. Jacobs, 1909).

12. The indigenists include David R. MacIver, *Medieval Rhodesia* (London: Macmillan, 1906); Gertrude Caton-Thompson, *The Zimbabwe Culture: Ruins and Reactions* (Oxford: Clarendon Press, 1931); and John F. Schofield, "Zimbabwe, A Cultural Examination of the Building Methods Employed," *Southern African Journal of Science* 1, no. 23 (1926): 971–986. For an overview of the diffusionist-indigenist debate see David Chanaiwa, *The Zimbabwe Controversy: A Case of Colonial Historiography* (Syracuse, N.Y.: Maxwell School of Citizenship and Public Affairs, February 1973).

13. Garlake, *Great Zimbabwe: Described;* and Peter S. Garlake, *Life at Great Zimbabwe* (Gweru: Mambo Press, 1982).

14. David Beach, *Zimbabwe Before 1900* (Gweru: Mambo Press, 1984), p. 24.

15. Hall, *The Changing Past*, p. 63.

16. Terence Ranger, *Revolt in Southern Rhodesia, 1896–7* (London: Heinemann, 1979), p. x, noting a critique of his state-centric emphasis in the 1967 edition, offered by David Beach.

17. For a discussion of Sudanic states in Africa, see Oliver and Fage, *A Short History of Africa*, pp. 31–38.

18. Theda Skocpol, *States and Social Revolutions: A Comparative Analysis of France, Russia, and China* (Cambridge: Cambridge University Press, 1979), p. 29.

19. Bourdillon, *The Shona People*, p. 7.

20. Garlake, *Great Zimbabwe: Described*, p. 13. Other important sources on Great Zimbabwe include Peter Garlake, *Great Zimbabwe* (London: Thames and Hudson, 1973); T. N. Huffman, "The Rise and Fall of Zimbabwe," *Journal of African History* 13, no. 3 (1972): 353–366; and R. Summers, *Ancient Mining in Rhodesia and Adjacent Areas* (Salisbury: Trustees of the National Museums of Rhodesia, 1969).

21. Kenneth Mufuka, *Dzimbahwe: Life and Politics in the Golden Age, 1100–1500 A.D.* (Harare: Harare Publishing House, 1983).

22. David W. Phillipson, *African Archaeology* (Cambridge: Cambridge University Press, 1985), p. 206.

23. See debate on this in Hall, *The Changing Past*, pp. 96–97.

24. Garlake, *Great Zimbabwe: Described*, p. 16.

25. This argument is advanced by Mufuka in *Dzimbahwe;* and by Guy Clutton-Brock, "The Zimbabwe Situation," *Southern Africa* (London: Christian Socialist Movement, 1978).

26. W.G.L. Randles, *The Empire of Monomotapa* (Gwelo: Mambo Press, 1979).

27. Beach, *The Shona,* pp. 113–117.

28. S.I.G. Mudenge, *The Political History of Munhumutapa circa 1400–1902* (Harare: Zimbabwe Publishing House, 1988), p. 1. Important sources other than Randles, *The Empire of Monomotapa,* Beach, *The Shona,* and Mudenge, *The Political History,* include D. P. Abraham, "The Monomotapa Dynasty, *Native Affairs Department Annual* 36 (1959): 59–84; D. P. Abraham, "Ethno-history of the Empire of Mutapa: Problems and Methods," in *The Historian in Tropical Africa,* ed. J. Vansina, R. Mauny, and L. V. Thomas (London: Government of Southern Rhodesia, 1964), 104–121; and Allen Isaacman, *Mozambique: The Africanization of a European Institution, the Zambezi Prazos, 1750–1902* (Madison: University of Wisconsin Press, 1972).

29. J. dos Santos, *Ethiopia Oriental,* cited in Randles, *The Empire of Monomotapa,* p. 84.

30. Beach, *The Shona,* pp. 149–151.

31. Ibid., p. 104.

32. Peter S. Garlake, "Rhodesian Ruins: A Preliminary Assessment of their Styles and Chronology," *Journal of African History* 11, no. 4 (1970): 495–513.

33. Beach, *The Shona,* p. 191.

34. For additional information on these debates, see T. N. Huffman, "Great Zimbabwe and the Politics of Space," in *The Indigenous African Town,* ed. M. Posnansky and D. Brokenshaw (London: Heinemann, 1986).

35. Beach, *The Shona,* p. 202.

36. One analyst whose writings perpetrated myths about Rozvi, by erroneously tying the latter to the fall of Great Zimbabwe, was F.W.T. Posselt, the Rhodesian native commissioner for Marandellas. See his *Fact and Fiction* (Bulawayo: Rhodesian Printing and Publishing, 1935); and his *Mambo: A Survey of the Native Tribes of Southern Rhodesia* (Salisbury: Government of Rhodesia, 1927). Corrective accounts have been written by Charles Bullock, *The Mashona,* (Cape Town: Juta, 1928); and Beach, *The Shona.* Other important sources include Ranger, *Revolt in Southern Rhodesia;* N. Sutherland-Harris, "Trade and the Rozwi Mambo," in *Precolonial African Trade,* ed. J. R. Gray and D. Birmingham (London: Oxford University Press, 1970), pp. 243–265; and H.H.K. Bhila, *Trade and Politics in a Shona Kingdom* (London: Longman, 1982).

37. Beach, *The Shona,* p. 245.

38. Ibid., p. 225.

39. Terence Ranger, *The Invention of Tribalism in Zimbabwe* (Gweru: Mambo Press, 1985), p. 4.

40. This discussion relies on analyses in R. K. Rasmussen, *Mzilikazi* (Harare: Zimbabwe Educational Books, 1977); David Beach, *War and Politics in Zimbabwe, 1840–1900* (Gweru: Mambo Press, 1986); and Beach, *Zimbabwe Before 1900.*

41. The literature on the Ndebele state is surprisingly scant. Besides sources noted in note 40, see Julian Cobbing, "The Ndebele Under the Khamalos, 1820–1896" (Ph.D. diss., University of Lancaster, 1976); and Ranger, *Revolt in Southern Rhodesia.*

42. Julian Cobbing, "Review of the Matabele Journals of Robert Moffat, 1829–1860," *Journal of African History* 20 (1979): 313.

43. Ranger, *The Invention of Tribalism.*

44. Cobbing, "Review of the Matabele Journals," p. 313.

45. Rasmussen, *Mzilikazi,* p. 33.

46. Quoted in Ian Phimister, *An Economic and Social History of Zimbabwe 1890–1948* (New York: Longman, 1988), p. 6.

47. Cecil Rhodes, speech at the second annual meeting of the British South Africa Company, November 29, 1892, cited in Jollie, *The Real Rhodesia,* p. 16.

48. Ibid., p. 18. For additional information on the British South Africa Company, see Phimister, *An Economic and Social History,* Chapters 1 and 2.

49. Ranger, *Revolt in Southern Rhodesia,* p. 52.

50. Phimister, *An Economic and Social History,* p. 6.

51. Jollie, *The Real Rhodesia,* p. 18.

52. Phimister, *An Economic and Social History,* p. 9.

53. Ibid., p. 58, quoting P. F. Hone, *Southern Rhodesia.*

54. Paul Mosley, *The Settler Economies: Studies in the Economic History of Kenya and Southern Rhodesia, 1900–1963* (Cambridge: Cambridge University Press, 1983), p. 14.

55. Stanlake Samkange, *Origins of Rhodesia* (London: Heinemann, 1968), pp. 4–5.

56. Phimister, *An Economic and Social History,* p. 9.

57. Ranger, *Revolt in Southern Rhodesia,* p. 92.

58. Ibid., p. 113.

59. Ibid., p. 114.

60. Ibid., p. 80.

61. This rendition is by H. M. Hole, civil commissioner in Salisbury to the secretary of the BSA Company, London, October 29, 1896. It appears in the BSAC Report, *On the Native Disturbances in Rhodesia, 1896–97* (London: 1898).

62. See Ranger's account in *Revolt in Southern Rhodesia.* Also see Julian Cobbing, "The Absent Priesthood: Another Look at the Rhodesian Risings of 1896–97," *Journal of African History* 18, no. 1 (1977): 61–84; and Richard Werbner (ed.), *Regional Cults,* A.S.A. Monograph 16 (London: 1977).

63. Beach, *War and Politics,* p. 147. See Chapter 5 for an interesting rebuttal to Ranger.

64. Phimister, *An Economic and Social History,* p. 26. The following section relies heavily on this work.

65. Robert Blake, *A History of Rhodesia* (New York: Knopf, 1978), p. 157.

66. Charles van Onselen, *Chibaro: African Mine Labour in Southern Rhodesia, 1900–1933* (Johannesburg: Raven Press, 1980), p. 23.

67. Phimister, *An Economic and Social History,* p. 60.

68. Ibid., quoted from BSAC, *Report of the Director of Agriculture for the Year Ended 31 December 1908,* p. 1.

69. Jollie, *The Real Rhodesia,* p. 125.

70. Ibid., p. 197. In *Islands of White: Settler Society and Culture in Kenya and Southern Rhodesia, 1890–1939* (Durham, N.C.: Duke University Press, 1987), Dane Kennedy notes that after the turn of the century, efforts to recruit women

for marriage often took the form of propaganda promising that even a homely girl "looms as a veritable beauty before the excited imagination of the up-country colonist" (p. 36).

71. Jollie, *The Real Rhodesia*, p. 125.

72. Ibid., p. 247.

73. Phimister, *An Economic and Social History*, p. 77. For an excellent discussion of African cultivators in early colonial days, see Terence Ranger, *Peasant Consciousness and Guerilla War in Zimbabwe* (Berkeley and Los Angeles: University of California Press, 1985), Chapter 1.

2

The Contradictions of Rhodesia: State Building, Development, and Struggle (1923–1979)

"To my mind this is a super country, the best on earth, it has everything, sunshine, good soil and the finest people you could find anywhere; in my opinion our black Rhodesians are the finest in Africa, they're fine people and I'm proud of them. If certain people would only get off our backs and let us get on with the job of building up this wonderful country then I believe we could make this thing work."

—white Rhodesian[1]

One of the ironies of Southern Rhodesia (renamed Rhodesia in the mid-1960s) was that there was always something upsetting the whites: at first it was "the natives" and the wilderness itself, then the company and Britain, then a do-good prime minister in the form of Garfield Todd, then Britain again, and finally the "terrs" (black guerrillas). The written, visual, and experiential legacies of the era suggest, however, that Southern Rhodesia was generally better for whites than it was for the country's "fine blacks." This is not to deny that some blacks benefited from collaboration with the settlers or to imply that the experiences of all whites were always devoid of hardship.

To illustrate these themes it is useful to divide Southern Rhodesian history into three overlapping eras. From 1923 until the end of World War II settlers gained "responsible" government from Britain and established racial noncompetition as a principle of political economy. Following the war the colony became involved in the Central African Federation, and until 1965 racial "partnership" was the local development credo, and a moderate nationalism grew in response to discrepancies

29

30

230

THE CONTRADICTIONS OF RHODESIA

between the rhetoric of partnership and the realities of black subordination. From 1965 until 1979 Rhodesia was alone, semiisolated by its refusal to give way to majority rule, and engaged in a fierce armed struggle with guerrillas of two liberation armies.

Like Zimbabwean prehistory, the history of Southern Rhodesia has inspired several controversies. Among these are debates about whether events would have taken a different turn if Britain had exercised more oversight; whether efforts in the 1950s to liberalize the Southern Rhodesian political economy were sincere or were inspired by the desire to strengthen white rule; whether efforts to promote conservation in the African reserves made sense against a backdrop of forced evictions from white-designated lands, which crowded the reserves and helped spawn the nationalist movement; whether unilateral independence from Britain in 1965 could have been averted; and whether Zimbabwean nationalists were too moderate in the 1950s and 1960s and then too divided among themselves in the 1970s to push for a transformed political economy. These questions command debate as new archival and oral sources are discovered and scrutinized, and it is instructive to bear them in mind as we proceed.

RESPONSIBLE SELF-GOVERNMENT AND RACIAL NONCOMPETITION (1923–1945)

On October 27, 1922, voters in Southern Rhodesia went to the polls to determine the political future of the British colony. "Responsible government" was the choice of 59 percent of those who voted. Nevertheless, this was far from an impressive victory: 26 percent of the twenty thousand registered white voters stayed away from the polls, and thirty-seven out of every sixty black voters did likewise (in a total black population of nine hundred thousand).[2] The electorate could have chosen union with South Africa; in fact, white ranchers and tobacco farmers preferred this option for the steady access to South African markets it promised. Continued company rule was another option, which was singularly unpopular because, as one Rhodesian put it, a firm is "bound to be pulled two ways in its governing role."[3] An intermediate position, favored by white maize farmers in Mashonaland, held out against both foreign businesses and union with South Africa, and this translated into votes for a responsible local government, which the nonelite whites hoped to control.

The pitifully low African vote had to do with the franchise requirement: potential black voters had to prove they earned wages of £100 (U.S. $457) per year, at a time when few commanded even £50 (U.S. $228), and had to write fifty words in English. Although this left most Africans out of the balloting, some expressed views on the governance issue in other ways. Lobengula's eldest son, Nyamanda, petitioned for direct British control of African areas and rejected both the union option and the notion that a settler-run government could be responsible. Mwari priests of Matonjeri cave (a cult location) encouraged western Mashonalanders to store grain and prepare for a confrontation with whites. Abraham Twala and Martha Ngano formed the Bantu Voters Association to encourage black votes for responsible government, because in their eyes the new constitution at least entrenched African rights to land and gave Britain extensive powers in the area of "native" affairs.[4]

Responsible government prevailed, and Hardwicke Holderness, a member of the Southern Rhodesian Parliament in the 1950s, later claimed the constitution created something "much more like the government of an independent country than of a dependent Colony," noting with favor that "the machinery operated just as if it were a scale model of the Whitehall prototype."[5] On the face of it this assessment is true. The constitution provided for a single legislative assembly of thirty members empowered to amend, reject, and debate legislation introduced by the government and occasionally by one of its own members. The cabinet, or government, until World War II consisting of only six ministers, was empowered to handle the chief departments of the civil service and the daily challenges of administration. The civil service and judiciary were independent of government and Parliament, and, as in London, a governor represented the British Crown and officially appointed the prime minister as leader of the majority party in Parliament.

The policymaking powers of the colony, however, were meant to be sharply restricted, as the members of the Bantu Voters Association had recognized. Britain said it did not want the Parliament to enact laws for indigenous peoples unless those laws also applied to resident settlers. Britain also prohibited all branches of the state from interfering with the business of the British-based Native Department. In reserving for itself a veto over all matters "native," Britain gave the impression that it would indeed be more liberal in its racial judgments than the white settlers. In fact, however, Britain tacitly agreed with them that Africans needed some protection from rapacious whites but were not ready for European rights. This made it easy for Rhodesian governments to formulate biased policies, submit them quietly for British approval, and then take these policies to the white assembly for a vote. A British blind eye thereby failed to prevent continued literacy and means tests from keeping most blacks disenfranchised and off the common voters' roll (list of registered voters) and generally contributed to the belief in

Salisbury that Southern Rhodesia was more of an independent country than a colony.

In 1924 members of the Bantu Voters Association wanted to know why their rights and interests were being kept down. The settlers did little to respond and focused instead on their own new upsets, which had to do both with Britain's constitutional right to financial control over the colony and the obvious zeal with which that country regulated railroads, mining revenue, currency, and duties. Not unnoticed by all with the interest to see, the new constitution had "produced a thoroughly conservative successor to the Chartered state, so much so that the average session of the twenties resembled more a well-conducted shareholders meeting than a national convention."[6] From 1923 to 1933 the ruling Rhodesia Party tolerated "the deliberate process of penetration instituted by large capital,"[7] thereby mollifying in particular the mining firms in gold, coal, asbestos, and chrome production as a way of building local comparative advantage in a highly competitive mining region. The Rhodesian Chrome Trust and BSAC-dominated asbestos producers co-operated to drive out competitors—by 1929 the colony accounted for more than one-half the world's production of chrome—and the BSAC profited from large-scale prospecting rights granted to its related Wankie Colliery Company in the waning days of company rule.

The Southern Rhodesian government was gradually able to gain some control over colony finances, although not over the quantity of foreign capital in mining. For awhile Africans were able to accomplish an analogous feat by controlling their economic activities and thereby holding off the mine shaft. Most were determined to avoid the Rhodesian Native Labour Board and programs exchanging mine labor for famine relief during lean agricultural years, and they were determined as well to avoid the substandard and well-policed compounds where they could not easily desert their jobs even when wages were reduced.[8] They did so by means of peasantization—making market cultivation work for them. Terence Ranger writes about farmers in Makoni district moving around to maintain access to markets, opening new lands to cultivation, trying new marketable crops, and generally evading white attempts to expropriate African lands. In the mid-1920s these strategies worked fairly well and many black farmers prospered.[9] On the horizon, however, was a government-appointed commission to look into formal land appor-tionment possibilities between the races; in 1926 the Morris Carter Commission ignored the recommendations of blacks and suggested that land be apportioned 37 percent to Africans and 62 percent to whites.

Mine workers already involved in the exhausting business of contract labor found it more difficult to control their economic environment. After 1917 educated workers in the Bulawayo area, and then a cross-section of blacks, joined the religious-political Watch Tower movement, attracted by its prophecy that the Second Coming would coincide with settler political consolidation and later by its denunciation of taxation, mine management, and general white oppression. Between 1925 and 1927 the cost per ounce of gold mined increased as deeper drilling became necessary; the industry responded by cutting black wages. This gave rise to a potentially stronger challenger in the form of the Industrial and Commercial Workers' Union. In practice, however, the union waxed both moderate and militant in its demands for improved wage and working conditions. Only cautiously, for instance, did it first support the wave of mine strikes that broke out between 1925 and 1928. The strike at Shamva was the largest: thirty-five hundred workers walked out, thereby closing the mine for several days, whereupon police and the territorial army finally intimidated the strikers into accepting the management verdict that wages could not rise.

White mine workers were also agitated in the 1920s, both at the thought that black wages might rise relative to theirs and at the possibility that abundant African labor at low wages would threaten their jobs. In 1919 they formed the Rhodesia Mine and General Workers' Association (RMGWA), immediately demanded a 25 percent increase in wages and a forty-eight-hour work week, and struck most large mines until management capitulated. Thereafter mine owners counterattacked through the Rhodesian Mine Owners' Association and forestalled further concessions to strikers through a lockout. What followed next was a move by one class of whites against another:

> Mining capital first destroyed what was left of white unity by systematically favouring members of the much smaller, rival Amalgamated Engineering Union, and then, once the bigger organization was sufficiently demoralized insisted on retrenchments and wage cuts over the protests of both unions. Unable to prevent either the loss of hundreds of jobs or a 12 per cent wage reduction, the RMGWA lost support and by March 1923 was reportedly "defunct." Capital marked its passing by again reducing white wages.[10]

In the 1930s efforts by individuals to control their environment became more difficult for everyone owing to the Great Depression. At the aggregate level, "the national income, never very large, fell from £13.9 million (U.S. $67.5 million) in 1929 to £8.7 million (U.S. $39.5 million) in 1931 as commodity prices plummeted and markets shrivelled. In the first two years of the Depression, railway revenue slumped by almost 50 per cent. Earnings totalled £2.6 million (U.S. $9.1 million) in 1931–32 compared with £5.1 million (U.S. $24.8 million) in 1929–30. Over the same period, base mineral production almost came to a standstill."[11] The only mining industry left unscathed was gold, prices for which increased after Britain went off the gold standard in 1931.

Wages for most mine workers dropped during this period, and between 1930 and 1932 nearly 25 percent of white mine workers lost their jobs to cheaper black labor. This led to new demands by whites for job protection in the economy and to the 1934 Industrial Conciliation Act (amended in 1937), which ended the black-white competition for jobs by barring blacks from the official definition of what, for purposes of official bargaining, constituted an "employee." In return for these new legislative safeguards white workers gave up their right to strike.

Meanwhile, the agricultural sector also became more segregated and class riven. In 1925 approximately twenty-five hundred white farmers were on 12.6 million hectares of land. But only foreign companies could afford imported machinery, chemical fertilizers, and scientific farming through careful seed selection and animal breeding. Many individual landowners were desperately poor because they had little experience with farming and had to rely on tenants and government subsidies to survive. Some tried cattle or took advantage of the high British demand for tobacco in the 1920s; "acreage planted with Virginian leaf approximately doubled every year for four years; from 7,500 in 1925 to 13,000 in 1926 to 30,000 in 1927 to an estimated 50,000–60,000 in 1928."[12] Poor-quality crops in the last years of the 1920s, however, combined with gross arrogance in dealing with British purchasers, meant many planters were out of tobacco production by 1930, and the industry sagged until the 1940s. Overall, "settler experiences in agriculture were unhappy" during this period.[13]

African cultivators more successfully turned their attention to maize, only to meet the prospect of declining prices as the state tried to protect white farmers from the Depression. In response, Africans prepared to grow twice as much and to withhold the grain they had harvested from middlemen traders. But the segregationist thrust in political economy was having a negative effect on African soils; in a move that only complicated the peasant struggle for lucrative agricultural production, the state started a native demonstrator scheme to train reserve area farmers to cultivate on smaller tracts of land or to try new centralizing schemes that operated to separate arable from grazing lands. Rural households that had taken up the plough to cultivate extensively were now accused of destroying the soil and seeking to monopolize large communal plots for individual profit. Although the soils were in need of conservation efforts, farmers found it difficult to understand why methods that in 1919 had contributed disproportionately to the seven hundred thousand bags of maize marketed in the colony[14] were suddenly being discouraged by whites.

TABLE 2.1   Governments of Rhodesia and Zimbabwe

	Terms of Office
Administrators	
L. S. Jameson	1894–1896
Earl Grey	1896–1898
William Milton	1898–1914
Francis Chaplin	1914–1923
Prime ministers	
Sir Charles Coghlan	1923–1927
Howard Moffat	1927–1933
George Mitchell	1933 (July–September)
Godfrey Huggins	1933–1953
Garfield Todd	1953–1958
Sir Edgar Whitehead	1958–1962
Winston Field	1962–1964
Ian Smith	1964–1978
Abel Muzorewa	1978–1979
Robert Mugabe	1979–1987
Presidents	
Robert Mugabe	1987–present

This questioning did not go away when the Reform Party defeated the Rhodesia Party in 1933 (see Table 2.1 for a chronology of governments) and Prime Minister Godfrey Huggins introduced an agricultural rehabilitation scheme and debt moratorium—for white farmers only. The Land Apportionment Act, debated and passed in the 1920s, came into effect in 1931 and granted whites nearly 20 million hectares, as opposed to the 9 million hectares for the black African reserves. This reapportionment entailed massive relocation by peoples with spiritual and economic ties to particular land areas. The act also stipulated that Africans could purchase land only in specially designated native purchase areas, for which approximately 2.8 million hectares were allocated in areas not known for good soils or easy market access.

This era, capped off by the 1936 Native Registration Act compelling black men to have permission to seek urban work or visit urban areas, has come to be known as the period of racial noncompetition. Huggins found the concept useful to hide uneven development behind the myth that there were two separate but equal pyramids of development. The black pyramid allowed a (male) person to become "his own lawyer, doctor, builder, journalist or priest . . . protected from white competition in his own area."[15] Within the white pyramid it was understood that "the black man will be welcomed when, tempted by wages, he offers his services as a labourer, but it will be on the understanding that he

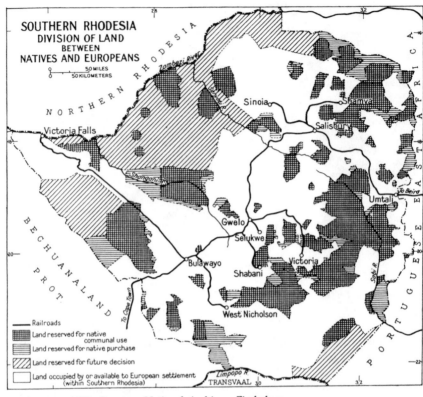

SOUTHERN RHODESIA
DIVISION OF LAND
BETWEEN
NATIVES AND EUROPEANS

50 MILES
50 KILOMETERS

Railroads

Land reserved for native communal use

Land reserved for native purchase

Land reserved for future decision

Land occupied by or available to European settlement (within Southern Rhodesia)

Land tenure, 1932. Courtesy National Archives, Zimbabwe.

shall merely assist, and not compete with, the white man. . . . The interest of each race will be paramount in its own sphere."[16] This doctrine united whites around the Reform Party and set conditions for further exploitation of nonwhite labor and for segregation in housing, services, and farmlands. There were some educated blacks at this time in teaching professions and some relatively prosperous peasants. But there were no official opportunities that in any way matched those for whites.

RACIAL PARTNERSHIP, FEDERATION, AND NATIONALISM (1945–1962)

The big news of the 1940s was that manufacturing was booming, thanks to wartime orders for hard-to-get supplies, incentives provided by worsening South African terms for Southern Rhodesia's primary products, and increasing government support for secondary industry. "Factories increased in number from 294 in 1939 to 473 in 1948, and over the same period their gross output grew from £5.4 million [U.S.

$26 million] to £25.8 million [U.S. $104 million]."[17] This moved manufacturing into second place after agriculture as a source of colony
income and dropped mining to third place. Tobacco was also thriving
again, fully recovered from problems of the late 1920s, and a new wave
of British immigrants contributed to a rate of economic growth in the
late 1940s exceeding 10 percent.

Further industrial stimulation came when Southern Rhodesia joined
Northern Rhodesia (Zambia) and Nyasaland (Malawi) in the Central
African Federation in 1954. This arrangement created a constitutional
division of powers between one federal and three territorial governments.
"Services [with] a specially close relation to the day to day life of the
African people [w]ould remain the responsibility of the Territorial Governments,"[18] while the federal government would have the power to
negotiate trade and treaties with neighbors under the Commonwealth
rather than under the more restrictive Colonial Office.

For white Southern Rhodesians, federation held out the promise
of protected and guaranteed outlets for their products plus access to a
portion of Zambia's substantial copper income. A relatively large settler
population also ensured that Salisbury would be the federation capital
and that favored projects, such as siting a major dam on the southern
bank of the Zambezi rather than deeper within Northern Rhodesia,
would be relatively easy to secure. Moreover, with Southern Rhodesian
industry expanding, the country stood to gain the most from federation
efforts to attract foreign capital and jobs through subsidies, tax rebates,
infrastructural investments, liberal taxation, and generous dividend ex-
patriation.

Yet the good news masked competing interests within Southern
Rhodesia's industrial sector, among its workers, and among Africans in
federation countries. From 1953 to 1957 the Southern Rhodesian manufacturing sector increased from seven hundred to thirteen hundred
firms.[19] Companies producing for the home market sought to stimulate
domestic demand by embracing a more equal wage structure than the
philosophy of racial noncompetition tolerated. Foreign firms, which
accounted for 70 percent of an estimated £233.7 million (U.S. $654.36
million) invested between 1949 and 1953 and often produced for international markets, typically wanted to retain low-cost black labor, as
did profit-conscious commercial farmers and firms in mining.[20] These
differences inspired white labor to worry anew about its fate and led
to white middle-class upsets about black proletarianization at a time
when nationalist fervor was sweeping across British colonies to the
north. Blacks from Northern Rhodesia and Nyasaland also balked at
having Southern Rhodesia as a member on the grounds it would impose
racial noncompetition on them.

Huggins hoped to balance the competing concerns by backing away from racial noncompetition in favor of the catchy new development philosophy of racial partnership. In 1950 he said, "We are anxious to build up this country on the basis of a partnership between the various races, not to use colour as a test of a man's ability and culture. We can only develop and hold this country as partners."[21] The term *partnership* reemerged during the ministerial conference at Victoria Falls in 1951, when details of the federation took shape, and the word was inserted into the preamble of the federation constitution.

This seeming turnabout in development orientation captured government's growing awareness that to accommodate demands of Northern Rhodesia and Nyasaland blacks for a federation free of Southern Rhodesia's racialism, Huggins had to develop "vague principles of government governing policies of all departments in light of which the African's role in state would be progressively redefined."[22] Huggins vaguely suggested that "racial partnership" would place race relations within a businesslike atmosphere, although what he meant by this was never clear. With Roy Welensky, who was the principal architect of the federation and its head from 1956 until its demise in 1963, Huggins coupled "partnership" with "standards," which enabled him to claim that "Africans cannot be admitted to full economic and political rights until they are 'worthy' of them by European standards," a process predicted to take a long time.[23] It was also possible that racial partnership would align a soon-to-be-formed black middle class with whites against Africans ungracious enough to challenge Rhodesian paternalism.[24]

Huggins's promotion of partnership helped secure Southern Rhodesian entry into the federation and brought him its first prime ministership. Back in Salisbury the United Party elected Garfield Todd to take Huggins's place as party head and local prime minister. This New Zealand–born missionary-farmer was deemed a liberal within the context of Southern Rhodesian race relations, and mostly for this reason, his tenure as the head of state was short. But Todd's speeches were peppered with phrases such as "civilized" and "responsible development for Africans," and his actions often suggested considerable continuity with Huggins's.

Todd pursued the partnership agenda at home starting with the agriculture sector. The 1940s had been "a watershed in the agricultural history of Southern Rhodesia,"[25] a time when expanding tobacco cultivation and industrial growth put pressure on the colony's food supply and led to a concern for conservation. How the government handled this pressure, however, is a matter of some dispute. William Beinart argues that efforts initially centered on improving settler agriculture through better farming practices, contour ridging, and state allocation of fertilizers.[26] Ian Phimister counters that there was very little government commitment to conservation until the 1950s and that most efforts to that point centered half-heartedly on the reserves, not on the large-scale commercial sector dominated by whites. After 1947, when for awhile maize and meat were rationed throughout the colony and a considerable amount of maize was imported, the state looked to African agriculture for surplus food production and determined to use authoritarian action, if necessary, "to put right what it considered to be wrong with the ecology and economy of the reserves."[27]

Rural partnership came to be seen, then, not as rectifying land inequities but as remedying the decline in peasant productivity, which Rhodesians had engineered through racial noncompetition, so as to increase food supplies to cities and improve living conditions in the reserves, known then as Tribal Trust Lands (TTLs). This revitalization had to be measured so as to avoid enticing the newly forming proletariat to return to peasant farming and abandon a thriving industrial sector. Moreover, peasant productivity could not rise so high that white commercial farmers would be up in arms about black competition. Despite disagreement about the historical sequencing of conservation efforts—from white farms to black or vice versa—there is some agreement that the reserve focus after 1950 reflected state efforts to blame "African cultivators for problems really created by unjust land division."[28]

A technically oriented conservation ideology was built around the myth that "a" native communal land tenure system stood in the way of sound ecological management, in part because the "native" was superstitious about the causes of good versus poor harvests and because a chief could technically reallocate lands to accommodate new families in his area, thereby undermining cultivator interest in improving holdings or conserving soils. In practice, as Lionel Cliffe points out, this chiefly power was rarely exercised owing to "the necessity of permanent cultivation."[29] Yet to overcome the TTL "bottleneck," the government contrarily endeavored to change customary landholding practice in the reserves while simultaneously squeezing more black families onto spent lands—leaving more good land for whites—and introducing mechanical conservation schemes, such as contour ridging, drain strips, and protected gullies.[30] This was a recipe for serious social upheaval in the TTLs and for acts of resistance to "conservation," as expressed initially through Benjamin Burumbo's wide-ranging African Voice Association and then through more militant nationalist political parties.

The Native Land Husbandry Act (NLHA) was the vehicle of "partnership" in the rural areas, and along with reflecting the conservation ideology, it may have marked "a compromise between the settler farmers and secondary industry."[31] To improve peasant productivity, the NLHA provided for the allocation of individual fields to peasants who had farmed in a particular TTL area in the previous season. This move toward individual land tenure in the reserves was attractive to some Africans; but the act disqualified labor migrants for such land, which meant that workers symbiotically linked to the rural areas by communal land rights could no longer live at the fulcrum of migrant and peasant labor. Women's opportunities through the new scheme were also sharply restricted: widows with children were eligible for only one-third the land men could hold, and all other categories of women were barred from the scheme. All cultivators were now expected to use contour ridging, and pastoralists were often forced to destock rather than increase herds to levels competitive with the commercial market.

The scheme immediately backfired. The TTLs were so crowded that the new plots were often much smaller than the government had promised. A few people could not afford to purchase the right to cultivate a particular plot or run cattle on it, but many more were suspicious of the state and assumed that this land, too, would eventually be taken away from them. Thus, purchased rights came to only .15 percent of all land rights allocated to African peasants and 1.08 percent of all grazing rights.[32] Traditional leaders were bounced between pillar and post as the government first denied them the long-standing power to allocate rural land and then restored that right when it was clear the NLHA was failing. The whole business had the effect, as nationalist Joshua Nkomo noted at the time, of forcing "thousands of Africans off the land—providing a useful float of labour for European enterprises."[33] Although this was part of the plan, the state was soon overwhelmed by the numbers of floaters its scheme had created.

In industry, government reviewed the problem of black exclusion from collective bargaining, established the first Department of Labour— Todd took its ministry himself—and oversaw a debate in 1957 about a new industrial conciliation act. The designation of "employee" was then extended to mining and industrial workers, but the great majority of workers on commercial farms and in domestic labor remained outside that coveted category. Furthermore, no worker could strike unless all grievance mechanisms had been exhausted, a point Todd defended when he authorized the breakup of strikes at the Wankie colliery in 1954 and on the railways in 1956.

A citizen side of partnership aimed at widening the franchise for blacks within Southern Rhodesia while considering "the best means of ensuring that the government of the Territory will remain for all time in the hands of responsible and civilised men."[34] Rejecting universal adult suffrage on the grounds it "would place the European minority entirely in the hands of a black African majority, a majority for the most part uneducated and backward,"[35] the assembly accepted the "temporary expedient" of two special doorways to the common roll for blacks: one required a yearly income of £240 (U.S. $672) and satisfactory performance on a literacy test, and the other required a grammar school education in lieu of an income and literacy test. To appease whites both doors would close when the number of voters registered by either method reached 20 percent of the "ordinary" white voters, who met higher means and/or literacy requirements. This development enabled approximately twelve thousand Africans to vote in the late 1950s—up from one thousand under the old system but still far less than the fifty thousand ordinary voters on the lists—and was liberal only in relation to the two-roll system the federation adopted the same year. To encourage blacks to meet the literacy and education requirements for voting, Todd moved African education out of Native Affairs, where "it was becoming an empire";[36] established the Ministry of Native Education, again reserving the portfolio for himself; and vowed to increase funding for academic as opposed to technical training.

Educated blacks, who would later become prominent in nationalist politics, initially thought well of the partnership initiatives. Nathan Shamuyarira, now minister of foreign affairs, wrote at the time that the Central African Federation would help break down racial barriers and that "Southern Rhodesian whites would even of their own accord, inspired by partnership, pass laws which would let us share political power and economic privileges and enjoy social justice."[37] Joshua Nkomo, head of a series of nationalist parties in the 1950s and 1960s, was initially critical of the federation but stood for its first elections as a black delegate from Southern Rhodesia; he also joined the United Rhodesia Party Huggins had crafted in 1934 and attended its 1956 congress as an experiment in breaking racial barriers at the political level. As for average black Rhodesians, industrial workers were temporarily mollified by partnership wage increases of up to 30 percent, while many peasants evicted from new freeholding areas—and there were 113,000 peasants in this category by 1959—were only seemingly quiescent.

All black classes soon found that their optimism was unwarranted. Despite wage increases in mining and quarrying, the average 1950s wage for workers in Grade A was nine times more than for Grade B workers, and virtually all A's were white and all B's were black.[38] Black unionists had to grapple with hard-line industrial boards and suspicion of normal union activities, such as holding meetings, recruiting members, and supporting black political organizations. People without land or with fewer cattle as a result of the NLHA resisted the state's agrarian policies by refusing to enter labor agreements with purchase area and commercial farmers, often running cattle on their lands instead. Village leaders held angry meetings and protests.

These were the obvious signs of failed partnership. Other indicators were less immediately visible. The 1962 census showed only 60 percent of black children aged seven to sixteen attending school; 46.6 percent of males and 58.7 percent of females born after 1947 had no schooling at a time of increased spending and emphasis on black education.[39] Whereas some categories of black workers showed marginal improvements in wages, commercial farm workers were continually paid such low wages and were provided such substandard compound facilities that their children suffered a nearly 90 percent undernourishment rate. Conservative whites were put off by Todd's "extreme liberalism" and sought to avoid any further upsetting of the balance of privilege—which has since been referred to as "socialism-for-the-whites," owing to the settler tradition of instituting a state that would provide a "near guarantee of an extraordinarily high standard of living."[40] Members of Moral Rearmament, the Capricorn Africa Society, and the Inter-Racial Association held (marginally) interracial teas from the safety of plush suburbs and complained to each other about the conservatives.

Somewhere in between full visibility and quiescence lay Southern Rhodesia's would-be nationalist movement. Prior to the mid-1950s most organizations seeking to improve conditions for Africans took up issues of discrimination and did so on an incremental and individual basis. The Bulawayo African National Congress (BANC), for example, had formed in the 1930s as a welfare organization and by the mid-1950s had made little progress in increasing its membership or broadening its scope of concerns to collective grievance and aspiration. This began to change in 1957 when the BANC merged with a far more militant organization from Salisbury—the City Youth League—which had a reputation for challenging the authority of native commissioners in the rural areas, encouraging peasants to resist the NLHA, and organizing a successful boycott against the increasingly expensive Salisbury bus companies. The merger produced the Southern Rhodesian African National Congress (SRANC), a nationalist organization headed by the moderate Nkomo—whose appointment was intended to attract other educated Africans to the cause—and spirited by a more militant executive committee. The SRANC manifesto shifted attention from individual problems of discrimination to calls for "the fullest freedom for the use of land by competent people regardless of race," full participation of African people in government, "universal suffrage NOW," and "the different races becom[ing] increasingly integrated in social, cultural, economic and political life."[41]

SRANC capped a period of increasing unrest about the cynical half-measures of racial partnership. But a significant proportion of whites was shocked by the organization's demands and blamed Todd for emphasizing racial issues too much. They also disapproved of him for speaking against discriminatory electoral practices in the federation, and when he voted against amendments to the 1903 Immorality and Indecency Suppression Act that would have extended the prohibition of sexual intercourse outside marriage between an African man and a European woman to include such acts between a European male and an African female, many were incensed enough to seek the fall of Todd's government.

Todd's ministers resigned early in 1958. In a special congress of a combined United Rhodesia and United Federal Party, Todd then lost a second ballot attempt to remain as prime minister. His fall, however, did not end the era of ambivalent partnership. Prime Minister Edgar Whitehead proceeded to open the public service to blacks and to repeal Rhodesia's mild pass laws. He also abolished black and white queues at post offices and banks, integrated cinemas and hotels, introduced some interracial sports, and allowed certain blacks to attend white private schools. In 1961 a new constitution under his sponsorship maintained political control in white hands and yet alluded for the first time to a system of one "man," one vote in some very distant future.

This continuity in partnership efforts in part reflected Britain's growing sympathy for African nationalism north of the Zambezi and Southern Rhodesian maneuvering to take advantage of it. Initially some whites thought the federation, which Southern Rhodesia controlled, could be granted independence or at least the status of dominion within the British Commonwealth. But the federation collapsed in 1963, after Northern Rhodesia and Nyasaland were set on the road to majority-rule independence, and Southern Rhodesians shifted their sights to local independence, on white-minority terms. The nationalists were appalled at this possibility and pushed harder to expose cracks in the practices of racial partnership. The state in turn pushed equally hard to silence their voices by banning the SRANC in 1959 and detaining more than three hundred of its members. This merely added fuel to the movement and a new organization, called the National Democratic Party (NDP), quickly arose to replace it. Again Nkomo was at its helm, but the NDP's agenda focused less on exposing unpartnership-like laws in Southern Rhodesia than on encouraging Britain to awaken to its historical prerogatives in Southern Rhodesia and intervene to promote majority rule.

One interim measure that nationalists hoped to secure was better representation in the assembly. The 1961 constitution had offered Africans a mere fifteen seats in a sixty-five-seat lower chamber, and although Nkomo momentarily acquiesced on behalf of the NDP, riots over this quarter-loaf left eighteen protesters dead. The government banned the NDP before it could push harder on this issue and generally strengthened national security measures against nationalists. But the nationalist movement did not go away. The executive of the NDP re-formed the party as the Zimbabwe African People's Union (ZAPU), and when it was about to be banned in 1962, Nkomo moved the executive of this "new" party to Dar es Salaam.

One commentator notes the irony that "a government claiming to be liberal should have enacted legislation so drastic as to need very little amendment by a successor government committed to repression and never even claiming to be liberal."[42] This is all the more ironic given that the goals and methods of early nationalists were very restrained and liberal-minded. They first tried to promote the European agenda of racial partnership themselves, using petitions, protests, and demonstrations to call attention to discrepancies in the logic and performance of racial partnership legislation. By 1961 their agenda was majority rule, but the tactics were still well within the parameters of liberalism because hope reigned supreme that Britain would force Southern Rhodesia to accept the decolonizing "winds of change."

The nationalist emphasis on reform, says Ibbo Mandaza, made it difficult "to recognize the umbilical relationship between imperialism and white settler colonialism."[43] In other words, this emphasis made it difficult to appreciate that Britain was a silent partner with Rhodesia and that the struggle to disentangle the two would require strong measures. Yet nationalism as a phenomenon indicated that the dominant alliance of white agriculture, industry, and workers had created enormous problems for itself in the forms of a self-conscious peasantry and a large industrial work force connected to peasants through migrant labor. Black classes were embittered by the hollow promises and harsh practices of racial partnership, and as a result the Rhodesian state had to conduct a passive revolution—a restructuring of the state and economy—to prolong its reign of privilege.[44]

RHODESIA ALONE AND EMBATTLED (1962–1979)

The Rhodesian Front Party (RF) led by Winston Field prevailed in the colony's 1962 election and set the colony on a solitary course— alone except for foreign firms and fearful or opportunistic allies. The policies of this period were harsh, retrograde, and unabashedly white survivalist; for as nationalism bore down, the British insisted on movement to majority rule as a precondition of independence, thereby inspiring among white Rhodesians the sense that they would have to take matters into their own hands to maintain their way of life.

Ian Douglas Smith. *Source:* Prime Minister's Office. Courtesy National Archives, Zimbabwe.

The most dramatic action of this period was indeed the Unilateral Declaration of Independence (UDI) from Britain, which took effect November 11, 1965. The rationale behind a one-sided break with Britain had existed for some time. The actual timing of the event was determined by the formal collapse of the Central African Federation and the fall of Field to the right wing of his ruling party after he failed in talks with the British to set consensual terms for Rhodesian independence. The timing also had to do with the moxie of Ian Smith, the last of Rhodesia's prime ministers, who took power from Field in 1964.

Smith was the only prime minister of Southern Rhodesia who had been born in the country, and his entire frame of reference was neatly bounded by the Limpopo and the Zambezi. Described by former prime minister Huggins as "devious, parochial and suspicious,"[45] to many white Rhodesians Smith was the standard-bearer of an alliance to restore Rhodesia to Rhodesians by taming the forces of African advancement.

Smith was incorrigible on the issue of minority rule: "I never believed in one man, one vote in any country, including the UK."[46] He hoped to secure Rhodesian independence under the white-rule constitution of 1961 and to that end extracted a pledge from the Harold Wilson government that if freely expressed opinion in Rhodesia accepted the limited terms of franchise in that document, Britain would move ahead with Rhodesian independence. Smith sponsored a meeting (*indaba*) of chiefs and headmen in late 1964 as a mechanism for gathering African sentiments on this issue, and these government-paid elites unanimously backed the idea of independence under the 1961 constitution. Smith then held a referendum for white voters; fifty-eight thousand voted for the proposal, and six thousand voted against it. The Wilson government rejected these travesties out of hand. With stiffening resolve Smith called a general election for May 1965 and asked voters to return a two-thirds majority for the RF, enough to amend the constitution in case unilateral independence became necessary. When his party won all 50 "A" roll seats, in what since 1961 had been a two-roll system of voting, Smith again tried to extract immediate independence under the 1961 constitution. Again the British refused.

UDI was thereupon proclaimed, and for awhile it seemed Rhodesia would get away with its strictly illegal move. Britain ruled out sending troops to counter UDI, and there was some speculation that it had plans to intervene on behalf of the whites in the event of a militant African response.[47] The British did, however, throw Rhodesia out of the sterling area (a special arrangement linking the colony's currency to the British pound), ban its capital exports, seize Rhodesian Reserve Bank assets in London, boycott Rhodesian tobacco imports, and suspend the country from the Commonwealth. In response, the Smith government simply defaulted on British and World Bank loans (guaranteed by Britain), reaping a considerable savings in the process, and balanced the national budget. With every passing day "it seemed more and more absurd for people to think of themselves as having passed through a constitutional revolution and being members of a rebel colony."[48]

In 1966, however, the British encouraged the United Nations to call for a boycott on oil for the renegade colony, and in 1968 the U.N. Security Council imposed comprehensive mandatory sanctions. Despite the well-documented cases of violators (such as South Africa, Portugal, France, Italy, Belgium, Greece, Brazil, the United States, and Japan), Rhodesia then entered a ten-year period of international opprobrium and social isolation. Paradoxically, however, UDI sanctions and isolation fostered a self-reliant prosperity in Rhodesia, with the average annual growth rate by 1968 at 7.6 percent and manufacturing up from 19 percent of gross domestic product (GDP) in 1965 to nearly 24 percent in 1975.[49] Rhodesia's mining industry also flourished when chrome entered the U.S. market openly in 1972, thanks to a Senate amendment to the Strategic Materials Act that enabled the United States to join the Soviet Union in purchasing the mineral from Rhodesia. In 1964, the year before UDI, the value of Rhodesia's mineral production was £26.7 million (U.S. $74.23 million); in 1974, nine years after UDI, it was worth £82.5 million (U.S. $198 million).[50] These successes belied Harold Wilson's prediction in 1966 that the collapse of the Rhodesian economy would come in a matter of weeks, not months.

The post-UDI "miracle" was the result of a state-led effort to survive and flourish under a strict import-substitution regime. Smith forbade foreign firms to remit profits or dividends to parent companies and individual shareholders, and they could not import many essential materials and equipment, divest holdings, or transfer them to other companies without state agreement. Key monetary, fiscal, and infra-structural operations came under state control, and an industrial de-velopment parastatal courted South African capital.

The state also saved money by clipping previous black wage increases and expenditures on black education. To absorb people laid off from sanctions-affected industries, the Smith government increased available acreage in the reserves and restored chiefly authority on the grounds that Rhodesia needed a community development program to restore local decisions to "legitimate" leaders. Land demand in the reserves soon outstripped the available segregated supply, and what followed, as one African community adviser put it, was "despondency, uncoop-eration, illegal land allocations, ignoring [of] the chiefs,"[51] and increasingly organized dissidence headed first by chiefly families, headmen, and male elders and then by younger men, spirit mediums, and guerrillas.

The British tried to recover some initiative by holding talks with Smith in 1966 and 1968 on transition to legitimate independence. In both cases Smith and his ministers found certain British conditions unacceptable, most notably what came to be known as NIBMAR—no independence before majority rule. In 1969, after several complicated enfranchising schemes had been offered and rejected by Smith, the Rhodesian prime minister set forth a new constitution for a Rhodesian republic governed by a lower house (the Assembly) of sixty-six members—with fifty members elected by an A roll of European, Asian, and colored voters and sixteen reserved seats for Africans (eight elected through a B roll and eight chosen by government-selected chiefs, headmen, and councillors)—and a (weak) upper house (the Senate) where Africans would be better represented. Theoretically, the number of blacks in the lower house could rise to 50 percent at the point at which African contributions to income tax equaled those of Europeans; but disparities between white and black incomes promised to hold off that outcome for approximately 980 years. White voters approved the new constitution, and ten days after the March 2, 1970, proclamation of a republic, the RF again won all fifty European seats in the Assembly.

In June the Conservative Party captured the British Parliament and offered to accept Smith's 1969 constitution as a basis for independence if he quickened the pace of African representation and provided the possibility of an African majority in the assembly. Smith agreed, thinking he could finesse the negotiations to go his way, and the British then sent the Pearce Commission to gauge African support for the terms. The commission found that Africans vigorously objected to proposals that did not "accord them dignity, justice or fair opportunities . . . [and] parity of recognition, which was as important to them as parity of representation."[52] Smith simply ignored the report and continued lobbying Britain for minority-led independence.

The Pearce Commission was one of many events that helped steer the nationalist movement down a more militant and violent path. Until 1963 the succession of nationalist parties had been answering calls for racial partnership mostly with their own calls for racial partnership. Nkomo's decision to remove the ZAPU executive to Dar es Salaam was a point of change in the movement. Claiming that an external executive could not properly lead a national struggle and that the ever-moderate Nkomo was more comfortable abroad than in confrontation with the Rhodesians, a small group of ZAPU executives tried to reorient ZAPU and remove Nkomo from office.[53] They were unable to prevail and in 1963 took the drastic and initially unpopular step of forming a separate party called the Zimbabwe African National Union (ZANU), with Ndabaningi Sithole as president and Robert Mugabe as secretary-general. For a year the two nationalist parties fought each other as frequently as they struggled against colonialism, but the government then banned ZANU in 1964, and for the next ten years both ZANU and ZAPU leaders were detained. Party cadres carried on, however, and separately endeavored to recruit youth for military training and to secure external bases and arms necessary for a liberation struggle.

In 1966 the armed struggle began, and it continued, in fits and starts, until 1979. Guerrillas loyal to ZANU engaged Rhodesian troops at Sinoia in April, and a year later a joint force of ZAPU and the South African National Congress (ANC) did likewise in the Wankie area. Both efforts helped to publicize the new phase of nationalist efforts. Militarily, however, they were a disaster. At Sinoia seven ZANU guerrillas died in the barrage of gunfire by Rhodesian Forces helicopters; the joint ZAPU-ANC operations gave South Africa an excuse to send police units into Southern Rhodesia.

Although the nationalists had changed directions, they had yet to devise an appropriate strategy for dealing with an opposing army of superior technological force. David Martin and Phyllis Johnson explain:

> In the Sixties there had been a tendency among liberation movements, and particularly the Zimbabwean movements, to believe that all that was necessary to end white minority domination was to train some guerrillas and send them home with guns: this would not only scare the whites but would ignite a wave of civil disobedience by blacks. It was a belief

psychologically founded on the relative ease other African countries had in achieving independence in the early Sixties. The guerrillas would . . . fire a few shots . . . the people would greet them as liberators, the colonial powers would withdraw and the last white bastions would crumble.[54]

This scenario did not play out in Southern Rhodesia, and from 1968 until 1972 there was little organized guerrilla fighting. Training proceeded as the two parties paused to formulate a more decisive strategy for waging armed struggle.

ZANU forged an alliance with the Front for the Liberation of Mozambique (FRELIMO) and in 1970 started using the Tete province as a gateway to a Maoist-style war in eastern Zimbabwe. Guerrillas trained in Tanzania, the People's Republic of China (PRC), and Mozambique infiltrated and held nightly *pungwes* (meetings) in rural villages to raise consciousness about oppression, particularly about land expropriation under the white government. When possible, the guerrillas also protected villages against Rhodesian Forces incursions, using information provided by a children's intelligence network to plan their actions. Villagers were cross-pressured by the guerrillas and the Rhodesians and were therefore always in danger; but the Zimbabwe African National Liberation Army (ZANLA) methods worked to the degree that guerrillas could confidently hide among rural villagers, gain supplies from them, and recruit new members.

One reason for ZANLA's increasing guerrilla successes after 1970 was the strategic advantage it gained over ZAPU and the Zimbabwe People's Revolutionary Army (ZIPRA) guerrillas when ZANLA took up rear bases in Mozambique. FRELIMO had first offered Nkomo this assistance because it saw ZAPU as the authentic nationalist party and ZANU as a possibly divisive and counterrevolutionary force. The offer, however, lapsed when it became clear that ZAPU was in the throes of an incapacitating leadership struggle between vice president James Chikerema and more militant strategists Jason Moyo, Edward Ndlovu, and George Silundika that was set off by debates about the conduct of the war. Silundika remembers, "Any decision had to be taken by the full executive committee, including Chikerema, and at that time he was not cooperating with J. Z. [Moyo]. The war council, which comprised Moyo and Chikerema and a few commanders, was no longer working. So paralysis was starting within ZAPU at the time when our friends were making these proposals and therefore the question of our responding to them immediately was just not practical."[55]

After that ZAPU underground party branches recruited youths for the war and sent them to ZIPRA rear bases in Zambia. Jeremy Brickhill's recent research on ZAPU-ZIPRA indicates that most of these recruits came out of urban wage employment and had unusually high levels of education, in contrast with ZANLA's peasant-dominated army.[56] ZIPRA moved to a classical guerrilla campaign in the 1970s, working with ZAPU party structures to educate the people for war, and after 1977 it embraced a more conventional war strategy "to resolve a central dilemma of guerrilla war, namely that guerrillas can weaken regimes but not themselves seize power."[57] Part of this strategy entailed training women for a separate military battalion, an approach that differed from ZANU-ZANLA's emphasis on incorporating women into guerrilla companies. In contrast to ZANLA's links with the PRC, ZIPRA relied on ties with the Soviet Union and Eastern bloc countries for arms and military advice.

ZIPRA became associated in the minds of most war analysts (and observers from ZANLA) with its later conventional war strategy and was therefore presented as less radical and less close to the people than the supposedly more politicized ZANLA. Brickhill's research disputes this myth, but once President Kenneth Kaunda closed the Zambian border to Southern Rhodesia in 1973, it was the case that ZIPRA was less fully engaged in a war unfolding mostly in the east near Mozambique. Where ZIPRA did engage the Rhodesians—it operated throughout the south and west of Rhodesia—it was both popular and effective: "Having heard the bangs and seen 'security force trucks burning and soldiers dying and bleeding,' the peasants regarded the guerrillas as possessors of extraordinary power that had never been seen before. Since the performers of this 'mystical power' were sent to 'perform it' by Joshua Nkomo, his name also became associated with some inexplicable legend 'possessing powers to conquer and liberate Zimbabwe.' "[58]

In 1972 ZANLA forces tipped the scales by successfully attacking a white farm in the northeastern Zambezi valley near Centenary. After this it is generally said that they controlled the war. In fact, the former head of Rhodesian intelligence later wrote that "from a winning position between 1964 and 1972, Rhodesian Forces were entering the stage of the 'no-win' war, which lasted from December 1972 to 1976; after that they were fighting a losing war."[59] The turnabout was the result of ZANU's restructured Dare (war council), which now allowed close coordination between the military and political sides of the organization and may also have reflected a revolutionary line brought into the party in the early 1970s in order to link the fighting with a socialist future.[60] It is also the case that the pace of government cutbacks for black education, coupled with reduced jobs in the cities and increased rural contact with guerrillas, led to an enormous number of recruits both for ZANLA and ZIPRA.

We know that most rank-and-file ZANLA guerrillas were neither socialists nor nonsocialists, pure traditionalists nor pure moderns. They carried sophisticated weaponry and also sought out traditional spirit mediums for advice and protection. They welcomed the contribution of women comrades to the effort and even assisted some village women to assert their rights against abusive husbands. The guerrillas, however, also expected women to supply cigarettes, soap, food, and clothes and handed few leadership positions to women during the war. They unquestioningly punished "sellouts" in the villages, even though "the sellout business was a way that some people used during the war to get rid of others they didn't like."[61] They politicized the rural masses around nagging problems with land distribution but threw away these methods of mobilization when necessary, press-ganging some recruits into training in Tanzania, Mozambique, and Eastern Bloc countries. ZANLA guerrillas could also be rebellious: in 1974 a group of them kidnapped several field commanders in order to force them to view deteriorating support conditions at the Mozambican front. The Dare response to this Nhari rebellion was a treason trial at the front and orders for the rebels' execution.[62] Although this was a far-from-ideal fighting force, it was an effective one.

In the early 1970s ZIPRA's shaky comeback combined efficacious action against the Rhodesians in the south and west with problematic action within the organization. In 1971 a group of militants within ZIPRA had attempted to infuse the civilian wing of the party with more socialist content and, for their efforts, suffered the wrath of mainstream field commanders, politicians, and allies in the Zambian government for what became known as the March 11 challenge to the party.[63] In 1972, however, ZAPU also issued a statement giving pride of place to revolutionary consciousness and to revolutionary masses. But when Nkomo was released from prison in 1974, the revolutionary line may have fallen victim to old-guard efforts to end the war through negotiations. If so, he was not the only one to tread this path.

That year the South African prime minister, John Vorster, invited all parties in the Rhodesian conflict to meet and discuss a settlement. Vorster was suddenly interested in a brokering role because Portugal had just withdrawn from southern Africa, leaving Marxist-Leninist forces in power in Mozambique and, as events would prove, in Angola as well. He needed a more moderate outcome in Rhodesia in order to maintain white minority rule in South Africa and thought Smith would hold out on ending the war until the entire population of Rhodesian blacks—and a good many South Africans—became communists. Smith did not believe ZANU and ZAPU could work together toward a common position for independence and therefore agreed to the talks and to a presummit meeting of the still-imprisoned head of ZANU with Nkomo and the other Frontline leaders.[64]

The man who would be Nkomo's main political rival in the future, Robert Mugabe, represented ZANU at these presummit talks. Mugabe told about a prison coup in which Ndabaningi Sithole had been dethroned by other imprisoned ZANU executives for denouncing violence during his trial and for asking other ZANU leaders to do likewise to gain release from detention. The Frontline leaders dismissed this story and reinserted Sithole as ZANU's official head. Mugabe was sent back to prison and to his previous position as party secretary-general. Sithole was summoned from jail by Frontline leaders, and with the other presummit participants he signed the Lusaka agreement creating a united nationalist front for purposes of the upcoming negotiation.

This was not the first time ZANU and ZAPU had tried to work together. In 1971 they created an umbrella organization, the African National Congress (ANC), to lobby the Pearce Commission against Smith's 1969 constitution. This early unity effort was noteworthy for putting Bishop Abel Muzorewa at the head of the delegation and into the political limelight for the first time. Muzorewa was an effective lobbyist, but leaders of ZANU and ZAPU later regretted elevating him because he subsequently lost his militant edge, masterminded the ANC into a third nationalist party (the United African National Council, or UANC), and made himself available for talks with the Smith government throughout the 1970s, claiming sometimes to be the only liberation leader in Zimbabwe. It was his party that became the umbrella organization for the unity effort in 1974; that summit eventually collapsed, owing to mutual claims of bad faith, and so did the ZANU-ZAPU merger with Muzorewa.

In 1975 field commanders from ZIPRA and ZANLA briefly cooperated to form the Zimbabwe People's Army as a way of rising above party competition to conduct the war more effectively. ZIPA was hailed by supporters as a grass-roots triumph over factionalism, but Mugabe and Nkomo came to view it as a counterrevolutionary threat and quickly killed it. In 1976 ZANU and ZAPU then officially merged into the Patriotic Front (PF) in order to prevent the Smith government, and its nationalist turncoat allies such as Muzorewa, from making an independence deal that would exclude them. The PF came alive each time there was a conference on independence and loomed large at the last talks held at Lancaster House in London. Until 1988, however—well past independence—various unities between ZANU and ZAPU were always tenuous.[65]

The turning point in the last phase of the struggle for Zimbabwe was the release of Robert Mugabe from prison in 1974 and his rapid emergence as the only member of the ZANU old guard whom the troops in Mozambique would follow. According to biographers, this intellectual schoolteacher and low-profile nationalist—he was publicity chair for earlier nationalist parties—carefully nurtured his personal standing with ZANLA in the final years of his imprisonment. When released, "he wasn't entirely comfortable with the role of guerrilla leader but no one who heard his impassioned advocacy of the armed struggle in any of his numerous visits to the camps doubted his commitment. And judging by the number coming over the border into Mozambique, he knew he was winning his own battle to create his own power base. Within six months of leaving Rhodesia [in 1975], he had about 10,000 refugees following him, many of them fit for an army."[66] In telling her own story, Sekai Nzenza also tells the story of this man's sudden impact on ordinary Zimbabweans like herself when she says simply, "I knew one man, Robert Mugabe, was going to win. All the comrades I knew talked about comrade Robert Mugabe."[67] And comrade Mugabe did make it known in a 1976 interview that "yes, we are Marxist-Leninists" but ones who consider our "own respective customs and the economic situation which has been established by the settlers."[68]

To this day Nkomo maintains that differences between the parties "were really all about personalities and nothing else."[69] Mandaza says "there is no historical evidence to suggest, as others have been keen to extrapolate from this momentous process of the liberation struggle, that this armed struggle encompassed within it even the idea of a socialist revolution."[70] At the same time, new evidence emerges that some ZIPRA cadres—members of the supposedly less ideological party— were committed to socialism.[71] The text is obviously nuanced and also includes stong elements of ethnic identity—ZANU-ZANLA became Shona identified, and ZAPU-ZIPRA was known as the party of Ndebeles— and considerable interparty rivalry.

The war against the Rhodesians continued despite the sidetracking conferences and abortive unity efforts. By 1976 the Smith government could point to its many "protected villages" and guerrilla casualties as evidence the war was going well, but the Security Force "kill" rate was not keeping pace with the number of "terrorists" infiltrating into Rhodesia, and "there was nothing we could offer the blacks, in the name of government, which was as attractive as the promises now being held out to them by guerrillas."[72] Rhodesia was also increasingly affected by sanctions and by rising Organization of Petroleum Exporting Countries (OPEC) oil prices. As an alarming number of whites left Rhodesia, older white men entered the war.

After several twists and turns involving the handiwork of Henry Kissinger (among others), a rapid escalation of guerrilla pressure in 1977, nationalist insistence on immediate majority rule as a condition for a cease-fire, and Vorster's impatience, Smith was forced into the March 3rd settlement (1978), known more popularly as the "internal settlement." It provided for a one-year transitional government to draft a new constitution for the awkward-sounding state of Zimbabwe-Rhodesia and then for elections to form the first black majority government. This "settlement" was "internal," however, because the blacks whom Smith wooed for the transition government were from a known circle of collaborators—Chief Jeremiah Chirau, Abel Muzorewa, and Ndabaningi Sithole.

Nonetheless, when the results of the constitutional deliberations were presented in April 1979, 1,852,772 out of nearly 3 million war-weary voters turned out for the UANC and Abel Muzorewa. ZANU and ZAPU had not been on the ballot—indeed, they had stepped up the war instead—because they were dissatisfied with clauses of the internal settlement constitution that reserved important cabinet positions for whites; set stringent conditions on black participation in the police, military, judiciary, and civil service; and entrenched certain prowhite provisions for between seven and ten years. Muzorewa felt certain he could persuade the guerrilla rank and file to put down its arms, and white politicians, reluctant to draw back from power, hoped they could control Muzorewa and convince the world to lift sanctions.

In Washington the Carter administration fretted about the guerrilla movements left out in the cold with their weapons; in order for the United States to drop sanctions, the administration wanted an all-parties conference on independence rather than a settlement with Smith's cronies. The British, after sounding out black opinion in Zimbabwe-Rhodesia and among Commonwealth leaders, concurred in this view and started a new diplomatic effort to bring about a more inclusive settlement. In the meantime they also withheld the prized award of renewed trade, travel, and financial arrangements with the isolated country. Then Mozambique sent troops to assist ZANLA, and ZIPRA shot down two Air Rhodesia passenger planes near Kariba. Under Muzorewa's command the national army bombed the Zambian capital of Lusaka, engaged in well-documented massacres in Mozambican camps, and offered gifts to guerrillas who accepted amnesty. Moreover, while proclaiming concern for peasants in protected hamlets, Muzorewa continued the Rhodesian practice of limiting their food supplies to bare subsistence so there would be no surplus to pass on to guerrillas. This "vain man with a passion for flashy clothes, including blue patent leather boots and multicolored tribal robes of his own design,"[73] soon lost his initial popularity, arguably because he did not use his position to distance himself from Smith and the practices of Rhodesia.

Executive council of Zimbabwe-Rhodesia signing internal settlement papers (left to right):
Reverend Ndabaningi Sithole, Bishop Abel Muzorewa, Ian Douglas Smith, Chief Jeremiah
Chirau. Courtesy Zimbabwe Ministry of Information.

In 1979 Prime Minister Margaret Thatcher of Britain sent invitations
to all parties to attend a new conference at Lancaster House for the
purpose of establishing a constitution for genuine independence. There
were many reasons for each side to accept this invitation. Britain wanted
to settle the Rhodesian problem once and for all in order to improve
relations with the Third World. Muzorewa needed a vehicle to show
the still skeptical world of sanctions enforcers that he and his government
were credible and legitimate. Nkomo, Mugabe, and other PF representatives were influenced to attend by the Frontline States (a political
organization of independent states bordering Zimbabwe), many of which
bore the ill effects of continuing warfare in the region; also, they wanted
to head off any turn of events that could strengthen the internal settlement
government in the eyes of the world and at home.

On December 21, 1979, the Lancaster House agreement ended the
war and ushered in the new state of Zimbabwe. The conference had
involved forty-seven difficult and rapid-fire plenary sessions extending
over a period of three months and had confirmed the British as diplomatic
performers of the highest order. But the final agreement, in the words
of two Zimbabwean commentators, offered Africans "the driver's seat
[while] whites would continue to map the route the car must take and
to control the fuel that made it run"[74] and to complain all the way.

CONCLUSIONS

Through eighty years of colonization and resistance to it, the tentacles of the Rhodesian state penetrated farther than the British South Africa Company had managed to do. The state extracted resources and exacerbated social divisions of race, class, ethnicity, spatial location, ideology, goals, and so on. White settlerism even altered preexisting divisions between the sexes by reserving virtually all urban jobs for men and generally relegating all women, white and black, to an artificial, private sphere. At the same time, not every Rhodesian settler was living high and not every African suffered a decline in standards. There were conflicts, tensions, resistance, collaboration, the veneer of success, and an unnamed unease.

The war reversed many Rhodesian myths about backward Africans and African myths about powerful Rhodesians. It provided opportunities for traditional forms of wisdom to reemerge and share space with the techniques and fighting ideologies of modern guerrilla warfare. It brought new leadership to the fore and new political disunities, and as Lancaster proceeded there were odd comminglings of Rhodesian authoritarianism, British liberalism, and some guerrilla Marxism-Leninism. The resultant ensemble of change and continuity is a country that has been termed "a dialectician's dream."[75]

NOTES

1. David Caute, *Under the Skin: The Death of White Rhodesia* (Evanston, Ill.: Northwestern University Press, 1983), p. 27.

2. Calculated from Robert Blake, *A History of Rhodesia* (New York: Knopf, 1978), p. 187. Other sources on Rhodesian history written from a European perspective include D. J. Murray, *The Governmental System in Southern Rhodesia* (Oxford: Clarendon Press, 1970); Colin Leys, *European Politics in Southern Rhodesia* (Oxford: Clarendon Press, 1959); R. Grey, *The Two Nations: Aspects of the Development of Race Relations in the Rhodesias and Nyasaland* (London: Oxford University Press, 1960); L. H. Gann and M. Gelfand, *Huggins of Rhodesia* (London: Allen and Unwin, 1964); L. H. Gann, *A History of Southern Rhodesia: Early Days to 1934* (London: Chatto and Windus, 1965); and Larry Bowman, *Politics in Rhodesia: White Politics in an African State* (Cambridge, Mass.: Harvard University Press, 1973).

3. Blake, *A History of Rhodesia*, p. 174.

4. Terence Ranger, *The African Voice in Southern Rhodesia 1898–1930* (London: Heinemann, 1970), Chapter 5.

5. Hardwicke Holderness, *Lost Chance: Southern Rhodesia, 1945–1958* (Harare: Zimbabwe Publishing House, 1985), p. 33.

6. Ian Phimister, *An Economic and Social History of Zimbabwe, 1890–1948* (London: Longman, 1988), p. 118. I rely on this source for much of my discussion

of Rhodesian political economy. Also see R. H. Palmer, *Land and Racial Domination in Rhodesia* (Berkeley and Los Angeles: University of California Press, 1977); and Giovanni Arrighi, "The Political Economy of Rhodesia," in *Essays on the Political Economy of Africa,* ed. Giovanni Arrighi and John Saul (New York: Monthly Review Press, 1977), pp. 336–377.

7. Phimister, *An Economic and Social History,* pp. 116–117.

8. For a discussion of the conditions of mine compounds and the reasons some workers might be attracted to mine work, see Charles van Onselen, *Chibaro: African Mine Labour in Southern Rhodesia, 1900–1933* (Johannesburg: Raven Press, 1980).

9. Terence Ranger, *Peasant Consciousness and Guerilla War in Zimbabwe* (Berkeley and Los Angeles: University of California Press, 1985), Chapters 1 and 2.

10. Phimister, *An Economic and Social History,* p. 93.

11. Ibid., p. 171.

12. Ibid., p. 136. An outstanding prowhite account of these years appears in Richard Hodder-Williams, *White Farmers in Rhodesia, 1898–1965: A History of the Marandellas District* (London: Macmillan, 1983). Views through pro-African lenses are presented by Ranger, *Peasant Consciousness* and *The African Voice;* A.K.H. Weinrich, *Women and Racial Discrimination in Rhodesia* (Paris: UNESCO, 1979); and A.K.H. Weinrich, *African Farmers in Rhodesia* (London: Oxford University Press, 1975).

13. Phimister, *An Economic and Social History,* p. 125. I am grateful to Jocelyn Alexander for emphasizing this point to me.

14. Ibid., p. 141.

15. *Bulawayo Chronicle,* March 31, 1938.

16. Ibid.

17. Phimister, *An Economic and Social History,* p. 253.

18. This quote is taken from the classic work by Claire Palley, *The Constitutional History and Law of Southern Rhodesia, 1888–1965* (Oxford: Clarendon Press, 1966), p. 345.

19. David Wield, "The Manufacturing Industry," in *Zimbabwe's Inheritance,* ed. Colin Stoneman (London: Macmillan, 1981), p. 154.

20. M. Yudelman, *Africans on the Land* (Cambridge, Mass.: Harvard University Press, 1964), p. 40.

21. Quoted in Leys, *European Politics,* p. 273.

22. Ibid., p. 271.

23. Ibid., p. 275.

24. Palmer, *Land and Racial Domination,* pp. 243–244.

25. Ian Phimister, "Discourse and Disciplines of Historical Context: Conservationism and Ideas About Development in Southern Rhodesia, 1930–1950," *Journal of Southern African Studies* 12, no. 2 (1986): 263.

26. William Beinart, "Soil Erosion, Conservationism and Ideas About Development: A Southern African Exploration, 1900–1960," *Journal of Southern African Studies* 11, no. 1 (1984).

27. Phimister, "Discourse and Disciplines," p. 272.

28. Ranger, *Peasant Consciousness*, p. 312.

29. Lionel Cliffe, "The Conservation Issue in Zimbabwe," *Review of African Political Economy* 42 (1988): 49.

30. Michael J. Drinkwater, "The State and Agrarian Change in Zimbabwe's Communal Areas: An Application of Critical Theory" (Ph.D. diss., University of East Anglia, Norwich, December 1988), Chapter 2. Also see the special issue of the *Journal of Southern African Studies* on the politics of conservation in Southern Africa, 15, no. 2 (1989).

31. William R. Duggan, "The Native Land Husbandry Act of 1951 and the Rural African Middle Class of Southern Rhodesia," *African Affairs*, no. 79 (1980): 230.

32. Weinrich, *African Farmers*, p. 26.

33. Joshua Nkomo, "Statement," *Africa South* (July–September 1959).

34. Holderness, *Lost Chance*, p. 176, quoting from the manifesto of the United Rhodesia Party, 1954.

35. Ibid., p. 179, quoting from the Commission of Inquiry to advise the government on the franchise, 1957.

36. Interview with Garfield Todd, Harare, June 22, 1982.

37. Nathan Shamuyarira, *Crisis in Rhodesia* (London: Deutsch, 1965), p. 16.

38. Ibid., p. 107.

39. David Martin and Phyllis Johnson, *The Struggle for Zimbabwe: The Chimurenga War* (Harare: Zimbabwe Publishing House, 1981), p. 58.

40. Jeffrey Herbst, *State Politics in Zimbabwe* (Berkeley and Los Angeles: University of California Press, 1990), p. 22.

41. Southern Rhodesian National Congress, "Southern Rhodesian National Congress Statement of Principles, Policy and Programme," quoted by Holderness, *Lost Chance*, pp. 200–201.

42. Blake, *A History of Rhodesia*, pp. 330–331.

43. Ibbo Mandaza, "The Post–White Settler Colonial Situation," in *Zimbabwe: The Political Economy of Transition, 1980–86*, ed. Ibbo Mandaza (Dakar: Codesria, 1986), p. 23. That imperial Britain was unwilling to put its power behind its appeals is the subject of several important works, notably, Anthony Verrier, *The Road to Zimbabwe, 1890–1980* (London: Jonathon Cape, 1986); and Elaine Windrich, *Britain and the Politics of Rhodesian Independence* (London: Croom Helm, 1978).

44. This is the thesis of Christine Sylvester, "Simultaneous Revolutions: The Zimbabwean Case," *Journal of Southern African Studies* 16, no. 3 (1990): 452–475.

45. Quoted in Blake, *A History of Rhodesia*, pp. 360–361.

46. Caute, *Under the Skin*, p. 92.

47. For discussions of the British response to UDI, see Verrier, *The Road*; Windrich, *Britain*; and Ken Flower, *Serving Secretly: An Intelligence Chief on Record. Rhodesia into Zimbabwe, 1964–1981* (London: John Murray, 1987), Chapter 3.

48. Blake, *A History of Rhodesia*, p. 388.

49. Government of Zimbabwe, *Transitional National Development Plan, 1982/ 83-1984/85*, vol. 1 (Harare: Department of Finance, Economic Planning and Development, 1982), p. 4.

50. J. Handford, *Portrait of an Economy: Rhodesia Under Sanctions* (Salisbury: Mercury, 1986), p. 122.

51. Quoted in Ranger, *Peasant Consciousness*, p. 162.

52. "Report of the Commission on the Rhodesian Opinion Under the Chairmanship of the Right Hon. the Lord Pearce, May 1972," in *The Rhodesian Problem: A Documentary Record, 1923-1973*, ed. Elaine Windrich (London: Routledge and Kegan Paul, 1975), pp. 228-229.

53. For a further discussion of Nkomo's political career, see Christine Sylvester, "Joshua Nkomo," in *Political Leaders of Contemporary Africa South of the Sahara: A Biographical Dictionary*, ed. Harvey Glickman (forthcoming).

54. Martin and Johnson, *The Struggle for Zimbabwe*, p. 11.

55. George Silundika, quoted in ibid., p. 18.

56. Mentioned in Terence Ranger, "Research Workshop on the Zimbabwean Liberation War" (Harare: September 5, 1990, unpublished report), pp. 1-3.

57. Ibid., p. 3.

58. Lionel Cliffe, Joshua Mpofu, and Barry Munslow, "Nationalist Politics in Zimbabwe: The 1980 Elections and Beyond," *Review of African Political Economy* (May-August 1980): 57.

59. Flower, *Serving Secretly*, p. 119.

60. From ZANU, "The Political Programme: Zimbabwe African National Union Dated 1 August 1972, But With a Note from the Editor Dated November 7, 1973." Quoted and analyzed in David B. Moore, "The Contradictory Construction of Hegemony in Zimbabwe: Politics, Ideology and Class in the Formation of a New African State" (Ph.D. diss., York University, Toronto, 1989), p. 104.

61. Thema Khumalo, "Thema Khumalo," in *Mothers of the Revolution*, ed. Irene Staunton (Harare: Baobob Books, 1990), p. 77. For other discussions of guerrilla violence, see Norma Kriger, "The Zimbabwean War of Liberation: Struggles Within the Struggles," *Journal of Southern African Studies* 14, no. 2 (1988): 304-322; and Norma Kriger, *Peasant Perspectives on Zimbabwe's War of Liberation: Diverse Agendas Under Guerrilla Coercion* (forthcoming). For guerrilla relations with spirit mediums see David Lan, *Guns and Rain: Guerrillas and Spirit Mediums in Zimbabwe* (Berkeley and Los Angeles: University of California Press, 1985).

62. See a discussion of the Nhari rebellion in Masipula Sithole, *Zimbabwe Struggles Within the Struggle* (Salisbury: Rujeko, 1979); Andre Astrow, *Zimbabwe: A Revolution That Lost Its Way?* (London: Zed Press, 1983); David Moore, "What Was Left of Liberation in Zimbabwe? Struggles for Socialism and Democracy Within the Struggle for Independence," in *Liberation Struggles in Africa*, ed. Lionel Cliffe (forthcoming); and, for a different view, Flower, *Serving Secretly*, Chapter 8.

63. Moore, "The Contradictory Construction," Chapter 5; and Owen Tshabangu, *The March 11 Movement in ZAPU—Revolution Within the Revolution for Zimbabwe* (Heslington: Tiger Papers, 1979).

64. For discussions of this and other independence conferences, see Martin and Johnson, *The Struggle for Zimbabwe;* Carol B. Thompson, *Challenge to Imperialism: The Frontline States in the Liberation of Zimbabwe* (Boulder, Colo.: Westview Press, 1985); Windrich, *Britain;* and Stephen John Stedman, *Peacemaking in Civil War: International Mediation in Zimbabwe, 1974–1980* (Boulder, Colo.: Lynne Rienner, 1991).

65. See discussion in Christine Sylvester, "Unities and Disunities in Zimbabwe's 1990 Election," *Journal of Modern African Studies* 28, no. 3 (1990): 375–400.

66. David Smith and Colin Simpson, with Ian Davies, *Mugabe* (Salisbury: Pioneer Head, 1981), pp. 81–82. Relatively little biographical literature has appeared on Mugabe, and to date there is no autobiography. For official pronouncements, see Robert Mugabe, *Our War of Liberation: Speeches, Articles, Interviews, 1976–1979* (Gweru: Mambo Press, 1983).

67. Sekai Nzenza, *Zimbabwean Woman: My Own Story* (London: Karia Press, 1988), p. 71.

68. Smith and Simpson, *Mugabe,* p. 94

69. Interview with Joshua Nkomo, Bulawayo, June 25, 1982.

70. Mandaza, "The Post–White Settler," p. 29. For more supportive statements on ZANU, see Cliffe, Mpofu, and Munslow, "Nationalist Politics," pp. 44–67; and Terence Ranger, "The Changing of the Old Guard: Robert Mugabe and the Revival of ZANU," *Journal of Southern African Studies* 7, no. 1 (1980):71–90.

71. Moore, "The Contradictory Construction."

72. Flower, *Serving Secretly,* pp. 132, 134.

73. Jeffrey Davidow, *A Peace in Southern Africa: The Lancaster House Conference on Rhodesia, 1979* (Boulder, Colo.: Westview Press, 1984), p. 40.

74. Stanlake Samkange and Tommie Marie Samkange, *Hunhuism or Ubuntuism: A Zimbabwe Indigenous Political Philosophy* (Salisbury: Graham, 1980), p. 43.

75. David Gordon, "Development Strategy in Zimbabwe: Assessments and Prospects," in *The Political Economy of Zimbabwe,* ed. Michael Schatzberg (New York: Praeger, 1984), p. 119.

3

State and Politics in Contemporary Zimbabwe

Ibbo Mandaza points out that white settler colonialism in Zimbabwe was a "particular expression of imperialist domination . . . [of] colonialism *par excellence* . . . almost complete in its domination: political, economic, social and cultural."[1] The nationalists could wrestle these forces to the negotiating table but not to their knees.

At Lancaster House the British extracted guerrilla compromises on several constitutional stipulations, and the Zimbabwean government studiously, although not graciously, observed these for seven years. The government then began introducing amendments more in line with its own ideas of a proper constitution for postindependence Zimbabwe. Today, however, it is only slightly less difficult to characterize the ideological and development principles that guide Zimbabwe's public policies than it was when the government was under Lancaster constraints. The terrain of political rhetoric and practice has been crowded with clarion calls to a proworker, propeasant Marxism-Leninism; with authoritarian impulses to define and protect certain "inside" groups; and with a populist liberalism that extols the indispensability of all "the people" and provides for interest-group formation while working to ensure that no portion of the people develops power sufficient to weaken the party-state.

THE CONSTITUTION OF ZIMBABWE

Prime Minister Thatcher's invitation to new independence talks in London contained eleven constitutional proposals. In some respects there was nothing startling in their insistence that an independent Zimbabwe enshrine universal adult suffrage, strengthen the tradition of parliamentary government, and write a bill of rights. Yet intermingled with typical liberal concerns was an interest in privileging certain groups by

61

offering some protection to the white minority in a "country which has been torn by conflict and in which, for the future, all those who have been involved in or affected by that conflict need to feel that their rights will be respected."[2] The British insisted that whites have twenty seats in Zimbabwe's one-hundred-seat Parliament for a period of at least seven years. This would give approximately one hundred thousand remaining settlers twenty representatives, while eight million blacks would be represented by eighty members of Parliament (MPs). The Tories were equally concerned to uphold private property rights, calling for a land program based for at least ten years on the principle of a willing seller (usually a white landowner) and a willing buyer. In Tory eyes, these particular proposals met the requirements of majority rule and at the same time did not pull the rug out from under white capitalist interests.

The PF's proposals also showed some tension between majoritarianism and group protectionism. The front said it sought no special protections for any group: "To incorporate in a purportedly democratic constitution provisions creating a special position for groups or communities or according such groups or communities any preferential treatment on no other basis than those of race and colour is repugnant to the principles of democracy as we understand and cherish them."[3] But the PF also argued for "the right to acquire any land in the public interest [with] compensation being in the discretion of the government,"[4] thereby creating a possible "special position" for itself and for the nonwhite groups or communities it represented. Joshua Nkomo later explained this position in a clever statement that turned antisettler arguments around:

> We knew vast acreages were lying idle, unused and therefore without a market price, in the areas formerly reserved for white ownership. To buy areas adequate for resettling the many land-hungry African farmers who had been confined within the former tribal trust areas would be beyond the financial ability of the new state. What we wanted was an arrangement like that made for Kenya at independence, whereby the British government itself would compensate farmers whose land was taken over in the interest of efficiency and food production. The British argued that the settlers in Rhodesia had been independent for a long time, and Britain could not now take responsibility for them. We replied that we did not regard the white farmers as settlers: as far as we were concerned they were Zimbabweans, and financial arrangements should be made to see that their Zimbabwean land was properly used.[5]

The PF also wanted a strong executive presidency, rather than the weaker Westminster head of state—which country after African country had found ill-suited to their circumstances—and sought to avoid what it saw as intolerable restrictions on the sovereignty of the Parliament of Zimbabwe posed by entrenching certain constitutional clauses for any period of time at all.

By contrast, the Muzorewa-Smith strategy of negotiation was of a cut-our-losses type. It revolved around "sticking fast by the hard-line whites" and reiterated the achievements of the present regime just "like an old-time settler":[6]

> Adult suffrage has been accepted and introduced and this change cannot be reversed. . . . No retrogressive amendments can be made without approval of the black representatives in Parliament. Racial discrimination has been totally abolished. . . . The requirements of previous British Governments have been fully satisfied . . . and nothing should now stand in the way of our Government of Zimbabwe-Rhodesia being granted full recognition.[7]

The only real breach in the Muzorewa-Smith ranks came when Muzorewa voiced optimism that safeguards for whites would eventually prove unnecessary, a comment Smith vehemently decried.

The British agenda ruled the day.[8] Mugabe and Nkomo acceded to Britain's position on reserve seats for whites and to the demand that the twenty seats be entrenched for seven years unless challenged by a consensual amendment by the House of Assembly, something the logic of a racially proportioned legislature made unlikely. The other key compromise was over private property rights. The PF capitulated to the British-cum-Muzorewa stipulation that the government could acquire private property only by purchasing it from a willing seller, if one were available. In other words, there could be no expropriation of unabandoned white land even under the argument, which guerrillas often used in recruitment for the war, that the land had been stolen and should revert to the people at independence.

Observers speculated that the PF caved in on these two key issues of political economy for a variety of reasons. First, leaders of the Frontline States argued repeatedly that it would be worse for the PF to hold out for better terms only to have the British forge a separate agreement with the Muzorewa-Smith forces, a tactic the British repeatedly threatened. Second, the guerrillas knew that "even if the constitution was flawed on points of detail and obnoxious in some of its racial provisions, the fact remained that the main reasons for going to war had been removed"[9]—namely, minority rule under a selective franchise. This argument undercut a view of the guerrillas as social transformers and revealed their limited "political capacity when it came to dealing with the full weight of joint white settler and imperialist intrigue at the

Lancaster House talks, 1979: Bishop Abel Muzorewa and Lord Peter Carrington. *Source:* Central Office of Information, London. Courtesy National Archives, Zimbabwe.

Lancaster House Conference."[10] Third, all parties to the conference believed they would win a fair election and could deal with objectionable aspects of the constitution thereafter. Finally, promises of funding for the new government sweetened the pot: the British hinted at money forthcoming for land purchases, rendering the free-market provision more affordable to those interested in redistributing white assets, and through Kingman Brewster, official U.S. observer to the conference, came a vague pledge of some U.S. financial assistance to the new government should the conference be a success.[11]

The compromise constitution also encapsulated innumerable political possibilities. It was within the grasp of socialist-minded people to build up parallel structures of governance while carefully preserving the old state as a mere shell of power; later, after the mandatory waiting period for consensual amendments elapsed, the Rhodesian state and its white-preserving constitution could be dismantled. Alternatively, a privilege-preserving government could build up the already formidable power of the inherited military and Rhodesia's repressive apparatuses, thereby altering the spirit of the Lancaster agreement while preserving its letter. Or a liberal scenario could play out through judicious use of the state to represent the organized interests of civil society. Thus, the Lancaster

House constitution was unfinished business for virtually anyone with an eye on the state.

THE TRANSITION PERIOD

Once the most difficult constitutional issues were resolved, the British moved to their terms for cease-fire, demobilization, and transition to elections. Muzorewa contended that there was already a popularly elected government in place to oversee the ending of war; in fact, he said, there really was no need for any new elections. The PF wanted an eight-person transitional governing council, on which four of its own would serve, and a U.N. peacekeeping force to monitor new elections. The British were skeptical of both positions—of Muzorewa's because the regime had neither legitimacy nor a sense of fairness, and of the PF's because it would prolong the transition period beyond the three months the British thought optimal. What the British wanted more than anything else was swift and clean movement toward a legitimate black government. If other forces were to supervise the delicate process, chances were that a cease-fire would break down and that the group in charge would try to tamper with the state or constitution. Should that happen, the British would find themselves with yet another failed Rhodesian settlement.

Again the British-led negotiations on transition were often high-handed—as when Foreign Secretary Lord Peter Carrington sent Lord Christopher Soames to Salisbury to serve as the transitional governor before the PF had formally agreed to this. Nevertheless, Mugabe and Nkomo did extract a few concessions along the way. One was that the British governor would rely on a Commonwealth force rather than on the local police to keep everyone honest and peaceful during the potentially explosive demobilizing, campaigning, and voting periods.[12] Another concession concerned the number and location of assembly points for each demobilizing army. Mugabe objected to a plan to corral guerrillas into points near the Zimbabwean borders while Rhodesian Forces personnel gathered at regular company bases near the cities. His fear, of course, was that Rhodesian soldiers would use their strategic locations to gain control over important national infrastructures, while the ex-guerrillas would follow the rules and suffer the consequences in their rural "prisons." The British finally agreed to an additional assembly point for guerrillas in the center of the country, at which point President Samora Machel allegedly sent word from Mozambique that the PF should stop quibbling and get on with the independence. It did.

A cease-fire went into effect on December 29, 1979, and all guerrillas were told to rendezvous by January 4 for transport to assembly points.

British soldiers with their mine-protected Land Rovers, 1979/1980. *Source:* Public Relations Headquarters, U.K. Land Forces, Salisbury Wills. Courtesy National Archives, Zimbabwe.

Despite excruciating tension on all sides, the cease-fire and demobilization plans worked. A particularly amusing account has it that as lightly armed, mostly British, monitoring forces watched with trepidation, the first heavily armed guerrillas emerged from a forest:

> "What do you suppose I do now?" the young officer in charge asked his sergeant major.
> "Sir," came the reply, "this is where you earns your money. You are going out there and meet that bloke in front and you'll say, 'Come on over here and have a cup of tea.'" And that, it seems, is what happened.[13]

The drama of elections then unfolded. A total of nine political parties vied for parliamentary seats in February 1980. Some, such as the all-white RF, led by Ian Smith, and Muzorewa's UANC, were carryovers from previous contests. Others represented pockets of power at the margins of the nationalist movement (National Democratic Union, National Front of Mozambique, United National Federal Party [UNFP], Zimbabwe Democratic Party) or, in the case of ZANU and ZAPU, strongholds of power from the guerrilla war.

Smith's RF ran unopposed in fourteen of the whites-only constituencies and captured all twenty reserved seats on a platform emphasizing

British monitors and PF guerrillas of ZIPRA play volleyball at the PF assembly place code-named "Papa," 1979/1980. *Source:* Public Relations Headquarters, U.K. Land Forces, Salisbury Wills. Courtesy National Archives, Zimbabwe.

the importance of white unity at a time of Marxist threats to free enterprise and to civilized living standards. The UANC, by contrast, barely made a showing, notwithstanding Muzorewa's confident predictions that the first black prime minister of Zimbabwe would be returned to office and notwithstanding the ability of his party to pay for media spots. Running on a platform emphasizing his regime's achievements, Muzorewa simultaneously tried to steal some thunder from the guerrilla leaders by promising land reform, free compulsory primary education, adequate housing, and free health services, and tried to cast his opponents as "Marxist masters" who kept death lists of enemies and who failed to see "whites as the most important part of our economic system."[14] His party ended up with a mere 8 percent of the vote and only three common-roll (black) seats. Parties with shallow roots and indistinguishable acronyms had very short careers; none garnered more than 1 percent of the common-roll vote, not enough to earn any parliamentary seats.

The most interesting electoral developments involved the fates of the PF and a rump of ZANU that Ndabaningi Sithole, the original leader of ZANU, still controlled. On the eve of campaigning, the PF simply collapsed, and the competitive two-party structure of ZANU-Mugabe and ZAPU-Nkomo reemerged. Nkomo claims Mugabe and his team matter-of-factly broke their promise to run with ZAPU as the PF,[15] a development that was foreshadowed at the Lancaster House conference when Robert Mugabe sidestepped a journalist's question about party unity by saying, "We are two parties which are united in a front and, for the moment, we feel that this is adequate so long as we are agreed on a joint programme of action. . . . The question of creating one party will be undertaken as part of an evolutionary process in the course of time. But until we have agreed on every aspect of organization, we cannot say we are exactly the same in every way."[16]

A history of the Zimbabwean struggle graced with an introduction by Mugabe has it that senior ZANU officials wanted to withdraw from the PF on the grounds that the alliance would lose votes in Mashonaland and would not resolve the vexed debate about which of the two leaders and parties had the largest support in the country.[17] In any event, the two movements responsible for the guerrilla war and its conclusion at Lancaster House registered and ran separately—Mugabe's ZANU as ZANU(PF) and Nkomo's ZAPU as PF-ZAPU. Sithole took the unencumbered name of ZANU for his also-ran party on the claim that he was still the proper leader of the original party despite his ouster years earlier.

ZANU(PF), which had been cast as the Marxist scourge of white Rhodesia, did not totally disavow this radical image in its campaign manifesto. Setting forth a revolutionary and action platform premised on socialism, ZANU(PF)'s thirteen fundamental rights and freedoms called for a development fund to acquire land for resettlement; collective villages, agriculture, and state farms; maintenance of the private sector of agriculture only for efficient farmers; government partnership in mining and in decentralized industries; and the right of women to equality with men in all spheres of political, economic, cultural, and family life. The manifesto did say, however, that "private enterprise will have to continue until circumstances are ripe for socialist change."[18] But what the manifesto noticeably did not do was give any credit to its class-similar colleagues in ZAPU: "Through its armed struggle ZANU(PF) alone has been responsible for the constitutional change that removed first, the racist settler regime, and, secondly, the previous regime."[19]

PF-ZAPU distinguished itself programmatically from ZANU(PF) by eschewing all ideologically tinged rhetoric and by wrapping vague policy promises in plain language. PF-ZAPU's manifesto claimed, first and foremost, that land belonged to the people and then went on to proclaim that if elected, the party would eliminate unemployment, ensure everyone a chance to own or rent a home, provide education for every child and more and better hospitals, promote industrial development

TABLE 3.1 National Election Results in Zimbabwe, 1979 and 1980, Common Roll

Party	1979			1980		
	Votes Cast	% of Total	Seats	Votes Cast	% of Total	Seats
UANC	1,212,639	65.4	51	219,307	8.1	3
ZANU(S)[a]	262,928	14.2	12	53,343	2.0	—
UNFP	194,446	10.5	9	5,796	.21	—
ZANU(PF)	—	—	—	1,668,992	61.8	57
PF-ZAPU	—	—	—	638,879	23.6	20
Others	116,440	6.3	—	63,212	2.3	—
Spoiled	66,319	3.6	—	52,746	2.0	—

[a]ZANU(S) is ZANU-Sithole.

Sources: Southern Rhodesia Independence Elections, 1980: Report of the Election Commissioner Sir John Boynton, MC (London: HM Stationery Office, July 1980); Masipula Sithole, "The General Elections, 1979–1985" in The Political Economy of Transition, 1980–1986, ed. Ibbo Mandaza (Dakar: Codesria, 1986), pp. 79 and 83.

and diversification, and establish a nonracial civil service. The party's moderation and loyalties to traditional authority surfaced in promises to codify African customary law and to ensure that "women shall enjoy equal rights with men in all respects, with equal protection by the state of each in *case of abuse of the other*."[20] The manifesto also tipped its hat to the whites by promising them the pensions and benefits which the constitution provided.

Amid charges by some international observers that various parties were intimidating voters—ZANU(PF)'s name was often mentioned in this regard—and that Lord Soames was using the Rhodesian Forces against "unruly" guerrillas, the big electoral contest between ZANU(PF) and the PF-ZAPU began and ended quickly. As Table 3.1 indicates, ZANU(PF) gained nearly 62 percent of the black vote and enough seats (fifty-seven) to form the new government. By contrast, the oldest of the nationalist parties, PF-ZAPU, had become regionally based in Matabeleland and the Midlands and could command only about 24 percent of the votes; this gave it the same number of seats in Parliament as Smith's RF. As for Sithole's ZANU, only 2 percent of voters supported it, not enough to win it any seats.

The ZANU(PF) victory took a good many people by surprise. Right to the last minute, most observers outside the country were predicting either an Nkomo victory—because ZAPU was the oldest and best-known party to Westerners—or a close coalition-necessitating outcome between ZANU(PF) and PF-ZAPU. Voter sophistication, claims ZANU(PF) literature, is what tipped the scales in its favor: "The Zimbabwean masses would not be hoodwinked into even remembering the names of all these numerous parties or their mercenary leaders. They had already gone past the stage of a politically confused people. Well politicized, they talked, sang, dreamt and remembered but one brief slogan, 'PAMBERI NE JONGWE!' (FORWARD WITH THE COCK!) ZANU(PF)'s Party symbol."[21] Less propagandistic writings essentially concur but also draw attention to the popular belief that only Mugabe and his party could stop the war, control the guerrillas, and provide honest and articulate leadership.[22] The other parties might have sounded more moderate—at least one writer finds, however, that peasants in Mashonaland, the base of "radical" ZANU(PF)'s power, knew little about socialism[23]—but they were too tied in voter's minds to a Rhodesian politics of manipulation, privilege, and accommodationism. After all, there was already one party that could be counted on to continue, or attempt to continue, the old ways without embarrassment—the RF.

Robert Mugabe astutely took to the air on the night his party prevailed and soothed the feathers of a ruffled nation-in-the-making. He talked, as one source recalls, "of turning swords into ploughshares to rebuild the war-torn nation, of the need for reconciliation and not recrimination, and he assured whites that they had a place in the country as Zimbabweans."[24] He quickly followed these words with the appointment of General Peter Walls, former head of the Rhodesian Forces, to oversee the integration of three armies into one loyal to Zimbabwe. Former RF deputy leader David Smith became minister of commerce and industry, and Dennis Norman of the Commercial Farmers Bureau was made minister of agriculture. Mugabe promised to bridge the ZANU-ZAPU divide through coalition politics within and outside Parliament and proceeded to offer four ZAPU members cabinet positions and three junior minister posts. For Nkomo, Mugabe had in mind the ceremonial position of president of Zimbabwe, but Father Zimbabwe held out for the more powerful Ministry of Home Affairs.

On April 18, 1980, Zimbabwe threw an independence celebration of grand and funky proportions. There was solemn pomp and circumstance by day, as the British flag was lowered and the newly designed Zimbabwean flag—featuring one of the Great Zimbabwe birds—was hoisted. Nighttime brought the reggae sounds of Jamaica's Bob Marley and the Wailers.

STATE AND POLITICS IN THE FIRST FIVE YEARS

When we came into power, most of our energy was directed at changing the colonial situation. More recently we have been able to concentrate on transforming the political and economic institutions of Zimbabwean society and transforming the thinking and the minds of the people. It is around these three issues that our basic program for the new Zimbabwe revolves.[25]

The emphasis in this vague statement, by the now minister of foreign affairs, on "transforming" suggests a comprehensive effort to reorient the structures, priorities, and policies of Rhodesia. This would be in keeping with ZANU(PF)'s campaign pledges. But a more reformist future loomed in *The Transitional National Development Plan* (*TNDP*) of 1982 and brought to the forefront the more parenthetical comments Mugabe had made in the past about the need to avoid pushing socialism too hard before conditions were ripe:

> While the inherited economy, with its institutions and infrastructure, has in the past served a minority, it would be simplistic and, indeed, naive to suggest that it should, therefore, be destroyed in order to make a fresh start. The challenge lies in building upon and developing on what was inherited, modifying, expanding and, where necessary, radically changing structures and institutions in order to maximize benefits from economic growth and development to Zimbabwe as a whole.[26]

Readers of these early statements could form one of three conclusions about the ruling party and the future. Possibly ZANU(PF) was Marxist-Leninist and had every intention of sweeping away the capitalist-bourgeois traditions it had just agreed to at Lancaster House. Possibly ZANU(PF) was a Marxist-Leninist party that knew better than to alert the bourgeoisie that its days were numbered and sought instead to strengthen the political economy before making that leap into scientific socialism. Or, perhaps, there was a big difference between a liberation force outside and opposed to the system and the duly elected government of a state, and ZANU(PF), to its credit, knew when the Marxist jig was up. By 1983 a fourth interpretation had emerged—ZANU(PF) was all for reconciliation between blacks and whites but not between blacks in ZANU(PF) and blacks in PF-ZAPU.

These positions capture the main questions about politics and state building during Zimbabwe's first five years of existence—namely, was Zimbabwe becoming socialist, and was the government justified in leading an antidissidence campaign targeted at ZAPU and its sympathizers in Matabeleland? The public record of those first years contains a few clues to the answers but generally sketches the outlines of a government cross-pressured by Marxist, authoritarian, and liberal goals.

Whither Socialism?

From the first day of Zimbabwean independence, Robert Mugabe publicly held to the line that ZANU(PF) was a Marxist-Leninist party committed to leading the people into a scientific socialist future. He also said that to fulfill this goal Zimbabwe had to institute a single-party system to represent worker and peasant interests and build grass-roots organizations to aggregate and articulate those interests. Thus, "the People as a Nation cannot necessarily be homogeneous in respect of their cultural or racial backgrounds, but this diversity should become more a source of our cultural wealth than a cause of division and mistaken notions of groupist superiority philosophy."[27] If this meant there would be "class struggle in all arenas: the party, the state, the work-place,"[28] the socialist outcome was not in doubt, at least according to Mugabe.

But at the same time, the ZANU(PF) government also backpedaled from its ideological hard line. ZANU(PF) policies came to resemble a democratic socialist potpourri composed of a little nationalization of industries—mainly of the Rhodesian banking system and the South African–controlled media; a little influx of new foreign capital; careful safeguarding of the commercial farming sector; an increase in public spending on education, health, and housing; the establishment of local government committees, youth and women's groups, and workers' committees; a little land resettlement; and an age of majority bill giving women the same status as adults that men enjoyed under the law. Many of these specific policies are discussed in Chapters 4 and 5. The point to make here is that the potpourri approach showed an activist government moving to correct some imbalances from the past, but the pot did not contain the ingredients Mugabe placed on the label. A few briefly sketched cases illustrate the gaps.

After independence, 35,763 out of approximately 60,000 ZANLA and ZIPRA ex-combatants were given what is referred to as the "coal dust handshake"—a Z $2,420 demobilization pay (worth half that amount today in U.S. dollars) spread over a two-year period. "Some of the former guerrillas failed to claim that allowance because they had been charged with dissident activities . . . and some missed the June 30, 1983 deadline for registration and were simply left out."[29] Many who did receive the money pooled it to form cooperatives—which subsequently were left to struggle almost totally on their own. Others looked for jobs or the vocational and academic education they had sacrificed to fight the war. By 1990 as many as twenty-five thousand ex-combatants were still unemployed, and "some who acquired 'O'-level [secondary education] [we]re denied vocational training" on the grounds that the O level was the upper limit of rehabilitation.[30] In postindependence Zimbabwe the market was flooded with job candidates presenting similar qualifications, and to compensate ZANU(PF) did little to bring young ex-combatants into government and bureaucracy. Also, former Rhodesian Forces members, including Africans recruited for "dirty tricks" operations against the guerrillas, could claim two allowances—a medical compensation and a retirement pension—if they had been injured and retired on medical grounds. Ex-combatants did not receive this twin benefit because they were never members of the national army. In 1990 Chris Pasipamire, the secretary-general of a new war veterans association, lamented that he and a few others had to "worm into" the ZANU(PF) central committee because it was clear that "certain politicians showed no interest in us during the past 10 years."[31] Was the government forgetting the warriors while committing the war itself to historical memory? Was it failing to compensate people in disadvantaged classes for their contributions to "socialist" Zimbabwe relative to those who fought socialism?

A related issue of compensation emerged around the government's approach to acquiring land for peasant cultivation. In 1982 the government pledged to resettle 162,000 families on white-owned lands by 1986. By 1990 it had succeeded in resettling only about 52,000 families on 3.3 million hectares—only 2,000 families in Matabeleland—and by way of explanation said the Lancaster House constitution required that landowners receive "adequate compensation," which a financially pressed system could not offer. It did not escape notice, however, that "the Government s[aw] itself as being required by the constitution to pay the market price of any land . . . as a lower price would not in its view be 'adequate.'"[32] In Zimbabwe rural property values increased dramatically within two years of independence because of speculation. Luke Mhlaba, a lecturer at the University of Zimbabwe, notes that the government could therefore have legally defined "adequate compensation" to mean "the original purchase price plus the cost of capital improvements, with a certain allowance for general inflation."[33] The term *adequate compensation* could also have been interpreted in light of clauses in the constitution that stipulated that the interests of the "public generally" or "a section" of the public had to be promoted. Perhaps the infrastructures of rural development were not yet fully hammered out between conservationists and technicians interested in increasing rural crop outputs, and the result was go-slow development. Or was it that the "Marxist" state feared driving away "indispensable" white farmers in the process of making room for peasants whom it also described as indispensable?

The government also sidestepped its calls for a one-party system by promising to honor the constitution and avoided proclaiming itself the de facto single party of Zimbabwe, as had been done elsewhere in Africa. With a bill of rights guaranteeing assembly and multiparty organization, ZANU(PF) spokespersons took care to point out that single-party rule would come with time and only after a popular referendum. In the interim ZANU(PF) would earn the trust and respect of all Zimbabwean citizens necessary for one-party rule. Was this an admission that many party officials were opposed to the single-party system, or was it commonsense caution?

These inconsistencies intrigued western and local analysts, a few of whom, such as John Saul, wondered whether ZANU(PF) was even waging a cautious rearguard war of position (an indirect, rather than a shooting, war) against the bourgeoisie.[34] Marxist-Leninists within the party were hoping that by making representative institutions of the colonial era more genuinely representative and accountable, the ruling party was simply doing its homework and building the political base of a national democratic stage.[35] Trotskyites threw up their hands at the latest drift in policy, having already labeled the nationalist struggle as a socialist sellout,[36] and businesses in Zimbabwe breathed sighs of relief as they watched Mugabe implement not only the freedom of assembly stipulation but the willing buyer/willing seller clause of the constitution.

In hindsight these varied interpretations of government actions in the first five years of independence suggest considerable slippage of theory on the ground. Rob Davies has pointed out that

> in historical practice, few, if any examples can be found of socialist parties which have followed fully Lenin's dictum, and smashed the old state structures. Rather there is a continuous range from more to less substantial changes to inherited structures; where on this continuum the transition is made between revolutionary and reformist practices is debatable and requires a "theory of transition." We would argue that some of the weaknesses of the Zimbabwean transition can be attributed to an unwillingness to face up to the implications of developing such a theory clearly.[37]

Put differently, in the first five years of independence, ZANU(PF) did not flesh out the contents of its radical rhetoric or make clear precisely how a future single party would fit into the larger scientific socialist picture.[38] The party's many policy initiatives therefore constituted a blurred picture of Zimbabwe's future.

As the gaps emerged between declarations and policies, many government and party officials started to follow the petit bourgeois path to advancement. Members of Parliament exhorted the people to work hard for socialist development as these same MPs moved into the suburban houses whites were vacating and drove expensive cars purchased in South Africa. The ruling party seemed at sea on the issue of public servant comportment and continued to hold tedious weekend rallies to preach about good government to the people who were theoretically supposed to be helping shape socialism in Zimbabwe.

In 1984 the prime minister tried to take the petit bourgeois problem in hand by pushing a weak version of Tanzania's leadership code through the second ZANU(PF) party congress. High-ranking party loyalists committed themselves to restrictions on the number of properties they could own and to other tenets stipulating proper comportment. But party leaders could get around the code by putting their assets in other people's names. Moreover, "the adoption of a leadership code seems to defeat the whole concept of equality in a society, because what it basically means is 'socialism' for the leadership and capitalism for those with the potential to lead society but [who] would rather accumulate capital without the strictures of the leadership code."[39]

As for the "preachy" top-down government style, this created both resentments among traditional authorities and new sources of legitimacy for them. David Maxwell's postwar interviews with spirit mediums in the northern Nyanga district indicate a local feeling that the government lacked gratitude for traditional forms of knowledge respected by guerrillas during the war: "The government does not respect the ancestor spirits. They have taken part of their power for their own."[40] Jocelyn Alexander reports a different type of response among some chiefs and headmen in Chimanimani district who claimed to continue as the living repre-sentatives of the ancestors but who bolstered this authority by becoming chairs of new village development committees (these were established by a directive from the prime minister in 1984 to increase popular participation in local development) and members of ZANU(PF). Although the state "had a tremendous impact on local institutions by way of legislating the division of power between them, creating new institutions, controlling resources available to them and privileging a certain kind of knowledge,"[41] the complex authority of rural leaders was something no one at the top truly controlled.

By 1985 a second wave of analytic writings had recognized, as Colin Stoneman points out, that "the complexity of the Zimbabwean reality . . . cannot be categorized simplistically as being in the process of either building socialism or consolidating capitalism . . . [because] whatever government or party leaders may say or desire, powerful internal and external forces are at work over which individual politicians have relatively little control, although they may have some leverage."[42] The Marxist-Leninist story, which Mugabe may have hoped to coalesce into a hegemonic ideology and development path, was fragmenting.

The Antidissidence Campaign

That fractured story was then pushed out of view by fragments of organized dissidence against the ZANU(PF) government that began in 1982. In that year Mugabe dismissed Joshua Nkomo from his position as minister of home affairs and seized most of his properties without compensation. The precipitating incident was a cache of arms found on two farms linked to Nkomo through ZAPU; these arms were sufficient in quantity to equip at least one battalion of soldiers with everything from AK-47s to some surface-to-air missiles (SAM-7s). The government brought no formal charges against Nkomo himself but did detain two ex-ZIPRA commanders, Dumiso Dabengwa and Lookout Masuku, on the grounds that they were conspiring to use the weapons to overthrow the government.

Nkomo called the dismissal that he claimed to have heard on the radio "silly" and later explained that the cache must have been made during the demobilization period, when ZIPRA soldiers received confusing orders about where to assemble and disarm. He understood that the guerrillas were to take their weapons and leave the Bulawayo area for assembly points in the countryside, and he ordered them to do so. Authorities in charge of the transition told the soldiers to return to assembly points near Bulawayo to be disarmed. Nkomo suggested that most of his soldiers did return, but some may have dropped their weapons at ZAPU farms because they feared a trap.[43]

Actions against Nkomo and his chief wartime strategists undoubtedly accounted for a sharp increase in army desertions by former ZIPRA soldiers between mid-1982 and 1983 and may have resulted in a sudden upsurge of robberies in Matabeleland and grisly events involving abduction and murder of foreign tourists and the death of a white man on his farm near Bulawayo. But Nkomo steadfastly disavowed any connection with these events and maintained that it did not take ZAPU to tell people "things are going wrong in Zimbabwe."[44] To the government Nkomo was simply a bad loser in the 1980 elections and was now stoking Shona-Ndebele animosities in order to get revenge. Accusations and counteraccusations flew until the government gained the upper hand in 1983 by unleashing a counterinsurgency unit of North Korean–trained troops—the infamous Fifth Brigade—on Matabeleland. The mostly ex-ZANLA guerrillas in the brigade operated under the terms of the Emergency Powers Act, which began during UDI and which Parliament continued to ratify until mid-1990, and were widely accused of indiscriminate beatings, property burnings, extrajudicial executions of children, and bayoneting of pregnant women under the charge that "a dissident made you pregnant." Aside from these direct assaults, there were nightly curfews and a government installation in Bulawayo where suspected dissidents were tortured.[45]

The government said its critics misunderstood relations between dissidents and the local peasants who harbored them—the very argument

Smith had used against the guerrillas during the war. Nkomo also behaved as he had in earlier times and in 1983 fled in disguise to London for five months. The Mugabe government, by contrast, departed from its earlier posture of humble reconciliation to promote a cult of personality around the man who supposedly had been reluctant to be a guerrilla leader. Banners at the ZANU party congress in 1984 proclaimed Mugabe the "Authentic and Consistent Leader of the Zimbabwean People." The crowd regularly chanted, "Viva Mugabe! Viva the One-Party State! Pasi ne (down with) Nkomo!" At one point approximately five hundred young males swarmed into an already tightly packed stadium from three directions, loudly—frighteningly so—proclaiming loyalty and obedience to ZANU and commitment to smashing the state's ZAPU enemies, thus blurring lines between ZAPU and South Africa as the people's enemies.

The cumulative attacks on ZAPU drove Nkomo into a series of on-again, off-again negotiations with ZANU officials for an eventual merger of the parties. Leaders of other parties were not included in these talks: Muzorewa was "preventively detained" for one year on charges of collaborating with South Africa to destabilize Zimbabwe, and Ian Smith was prevented from traveling abroad on more than one occasion because of the security threat many thought he posed.

One could argue endlessly about the dangers to the new government that dissidence, banditry, and leaders of opposition parties presented, but it was perplexing to see the new government wield the old military apparatuses of the state, much as Smith might have done in a similar situation. It was around the issue of dissidence that the "Marxist" government of Zimbabwe earned a reputation for mixing democratic socialist policies with considerable authoritarianism.

Living with South Africa

South Africa posed a demonstrable threat to Zimbabwe in the early days of independence and not just through its support of dissidents. Soon after Mugabe took office, South Africa began to impose sanctions against its neighbor, abrogating a long-standing bilateral trade agreement by which Rhodesia sold it radios, clothing, and steel products; disallowing Zimbabwean migrant labor and deporting forty thousand mine workers; and withdrawing South African technicians and locomotives from the Zimbabwean rail lines. "The crisis reached a peak in August 1981 . . . [when] transport disruptions were so serious that there were fuel shortages in Zimbabwe, while the country was losing $5 million per week due to lost exports."[46]

South African businesses thereafter put pressure on Pretoria to cease injuring their prospects in the new country, but this did not stop

South Africa from backing acts of sabotage against Zimbabwean army vehicles and ammunition storage areas or from bombing ZANU(PF) headquarters. Pretoria apparently believed Mugabe was even more dangerous to South Africa than his more consistently Marxist colleague, Samora Machel, in Mozambique, because in the first two years of Zimbabwean independence it seemed that

> while Machel embraced Marxism-Leninism, Mugabe practised social democracy. While Machel harboured ANC guerrilla cadres, Mugabe rejected them. While Machel accepted Soviet military aid, Mugabe preferred British military assistance in the merger of Zanla, Zipra and the Rhodesian army. Internationally Mugabe's political prestige soared and it was postulated . . . that Mugabe was a potential "African Bismarck." Little of this was welcome to Pretoria in 1981. Mugabe was doing the unthinkable: making African revolution respectable, even moderate.[47]

The ZANU(PF) government handled the threats posed by an insecure southern neighbor largely by combining a pragmatic approach to coexistence with a strong antiapartheid posture. Mugabe invited the head of the South African National Intelligence Service and a former head of its Military Intelligence Department to Harare in 1982. Until 1990 he maintained the "gentlemen's" agreement not to harbor ANC guerrillas and in return understood that South Africa would not conduct serious military actions against Zimbabwe. The Zimbabwean government also behaved judiciously with respect to South Africa's considerable capital investments in the country and was tolerant of a business situation in which neither Harare nor Pretoria could "take action against the other without inflicting equivalent damage on itself."[48] All these actions gave the new government breathing space, but, at the same time, South Africa weighed heavily in the Mugabe regime's calculations of military policy. In January 1981 Mugabe stated that "Zimbabwe would have to create a large army at the expense of economic growth because Pretoria 'poses a threat to our democracy.'"[49] Ronald Weitzer claims the force buildup was then rather cynically used against ZAPU dissidents.[50]

STATE AND POLITICS AFTER 1985

Zimbabwe's second national elections were held in 1985, five years after the first round, as stipulated in the constitution. Despite ZANU(PF)'s contradictions, no one seriously thought the Mugabe government would be turned out of office. Perhaps, however, the occasion of elections would prompt ZANU(PF) to clarify its program, particularly if the opposition parties put forth clear visions of the future.

During the first three months of 1985, the country was still reeling from political turmoil, and one election observer suggested that had the election been held in March instead of early July, as originally planned, "it could not have been free and fair."[51] Indeed, opposition party spokespersons argued precisely this case and sought to embarrass the government, delay the elections, and sway voters. Problems in establishing a new constituency system, rather than the cries of opposition parties, finally led to a postponement until June–July, and during the nineteen-day campaign period the government placed no legal restrictions on party participation. Six parties ran candidates for the eighty common-roll seats, while one party, one so-called election group, and several independent candidates contested the white seats.

The Election Campaigns of 1985

ZANU(PF) candidates and supporters ran an inconsistent campaign that alternately touted and downplayed socialism, boasted that the elections would be a preliminary referendum on the single-party issue, and avoided the single-party theme altogether. ZANU(PF) declared itself the only party capable of achieving national unity, rooting out colonialism, and providing nonpersonalist leadership[52] and had harsh words for its opponents. The ZANU(PF) candidates, however, had virtually nothing to say about the party's economic policy.

PF-ZAPU and UANC ran defensive campaigns in which they depicted ZANU(PF) as the source of dissidence in Zimbabwe. PF-ZAPU's election slogan was "Think Positive, Vote Positive: Power to the People," and its most noteworthy strategy entailed denouncing Marxism and extolling the virtues of multiparty pluralism while offering few concrete policy departures from ZANU(PF). The UANC adopted the slogan "The Winners" and shared the same problem PF-ZAPU had in distinguishing the only nominally Marxist program of ZANU(PF) from its own more liberal preferences. Both parties drilled away at the evils of a future one-party system and cast ZANU(PF) as a threat to free enterprise and expression. An additional three common-roll parties ran low-visibility campaigns bordering on nonexistence.

The race for the twenty relatively inconsequential white seats was more dramatic. The old RF of Ian Smith registered as the Conservative Alliance of Zimbabwe (CAZ) and did nothing to disguise its profound belief that "standards" had declined under majority rule. This time, however, Smith was challenged by disgruntled RF members who formed the Independent Zimbabwe Group (IZG) and espoused a conciliatory style of politics with blacks under the assumption that the future lay with a single black party and not with separatist white politics. (Privately, however, some IZG spokespersons regretted that services had been allowed to deteriorate from the days of Ian Smith.) In addition, a few candidates ran as independents, arguing that even the IZG was an anachronistic whites-only party.

The white elections were held in the waning days of June, and the results seemed to stun everyone. Against some hopes that Ian Smith and the old RF were has-beens, the CAZ won fifteen of the twenty seats reserved for whites against the new-style IZG's mere four-seat showing. Of the seven independent candidates who refused to associate either with the CAZ or the IZG, only one prevailed. Mugabe denounced the pro-CAZ outcome as proof most whites had not changed, had not accepted the government's generous offer of reconciliation, and did not deserve special considerations in the future.

ZANU(PF)'s rebuff by the whites did not recur in the common-roll elections. This time around, ZANU(PF) improved its 1980 showing by 15 percent and won sixty-three seats in Parliament (and a sixty-fourth seat in one delayed contest). As indicated in Table 3.2, PF-ZAPU won only fifteen seats instead of its previous twenty and saw its electoral margin slide from 24 percent of the vote in 1980 to approximately 19 percent, almost all of it confined to Matabeleland. The UANC dropped even further. During the 1979 internal settlement, it had 65 percent of the vote, and in 1980 this dropped to 8 percent; in 1985 "The Winners" received less than 3 percent of the vote, and not even Abel Muzorewa was able to win a seat.

Although ZANU(PF) had prevailed again, what the victory meant in ideological terms was not clear. The campaigns had shown that Zimbabwean politics was becoming a shadowy netherworld of persuasive pretense, with almost all parties taking stands in theory to which they were actually opposed in fact: thus, reactionary CAZ candidates came forward as champions of multiparty democracy, which they had seemingly feared when they ran Rhodesia; and ZANU(PF) candidates ran under a Marxist banner that fluttered alongside the party's liberal-authoritarian policies. The stage was thereby set for continuing contradictory trends in state building and politics.

The New Issues

Since the 1985 elections there have been two major issues in Zimbabwean politics—the nature of national unity under ZANU(PF) leadership and corruption among high government officials. There has also been concern about ZANU(PF)'s role in shaping state and society, especially now that ZANU and ZAPU have merged, and about the future of the party system. All reflect "a vigorous debate on the forms and content of 'democracy' in contemporary Zimbabwe."[53]

TABLE 3.2 National Election Results in Zimbabwe, 1985 and 1990

Party	1985			1990[a]		
	Votes Cast	% of Total	Seats	Votes Cast	% of Total	Seats
ZANU(PF)	2,233,320	75.1	64	1,654,864[b]	75.4	116
PF-ZAPU	558,771	18.8	15	—	—	—
UANC	64,764	2.2	—	9,551	.44	—
ZANU-Ndonga	36,054	1.2	—	18,631	.85	1
ZUM	—	—	—	364,544	16.6	2
CAZ	18,731	52.4[c]	15	—	—	—
IZG	13,513	37.8[c]	4	—	—	—
Independents	1,486	4.2[c]	1	7,541	.34	—
Other parties						
Common roll	376	.01	—	494	.02	—
White roll	311	.86	—	—	—	—
Spoiled ballots						
Common roll	78,861	2.6	—	139,375[d]	6.3	—
White roll	1,721	4.8	—	—	—	—
Presidential Election						
ZANU PF (Mugabe)				2,026,976	78.3	
ZUM (Tekere)				413,840	16.0	
Spoiled ballots				146,388	5.7	

[a]Unofficial.

[b]Includes total votes for four constituencies in Masvingo where two ZANU-PF candidates competed for one seat.

[c]These figures are for white-roll votes. All other figures are for common-roll votes.

[d]Does not include Kambuzuma constituency where spoiled ballots were unconfirmed as of April 3, 1990, when this table was prepared.

Sources: Chronicle, Sunday Mail, Herald, April 1, 2, and 3, 1990; Registrar-General, 1985 General Election Report (Harare: Government Printer, September 1985).

Unity. The unity issue came to life immediately following the 1985 elections and soon became entwined with the question of ZANU(PF)'s role within society. In what has been referred to as Days of Madness, supporters of the victorious party went on a postelections rampage in some communal areas and several high-density (black) towns and burned, looted, and destroyed property owned by known supporters of opposition common-roll parties. That members of ZANU's Women's League and Youth League figured prominently in these activities created the impression that revenge was sanctioned by the ruling party hierarchy and foreshadowed the banning of PF-ZAPU. No vengeful actions surfaced against so-called antireconciliation whites, and there was little talk about an imminent banning of white electoral organizations.

In the wake of the Madness a new round of dissident activity, centered mostly in Midlands province, left several ZANU(PF) officials dead, and there was considerable speculation that South Africa had resumed aid to the dissidents after a hiatus of two years. The press and independent magazines carried pleas for a return to the early postindependence climate of tolerance for political diversity and reconciliation and warned that problems in Zimbabwe could be further exploited by South Africa.

ZANU(PF) answered these calls mainly by stepping up its merger negotiations with PF-ZAPU as of November 1985 and by alternately halting its public harangue against opposition parties and stepping up efforts to undermine PF-ZAPU. On the one hand, Mugabe emphasized that the people had spoken through their support of ZANU(PF) in the recent election and that there was no option other than reconciliation. But he chose his words carefully and was more gentle than in the past:

> We would hope that the majority of the small segment which is ZAPU will respond to the call to join hands with us. . . . A situation of conflict can never, ever, bring about a ZAPU victory, never, ever, bring about the power that Nkomo is thirsting for. That can never come. The only way in which honour can come to Nkomo and ZAPU is to accept the reality of the political decision made by the people. . . . I invite them, and I want to lend weight to that reality and extend my invitation, my hand of friendship to them to join us.[54]

On the other hand, the talks limped on, despite periodic rumors that closure was near and despite a few gestures of friendliness, such as the release of several ZAPU detainees in 1986; indeed the Mugabe government had detained and tortured ZAPU and ZIPRA members after the elections and had attempted to destroy ZAPU branch-level organizations. Against this backdrop, it would be an understatement to say that ZAPU members were suspicious of "unity."

Starting in 1987, the government made several course adjustments. First came a bill to remove reserved parliamentary seats for whites. This landmark turn from racial privilege—a move in the direction of political discontinuity with Rhodesia—was made possible by the sheer passage of time, for the clause had been entrenched for only seven years, and by ZANU's success in prying ZAPU from a possible alliance with the whites against the amendment. On passage of the measure white incumbents resigned, and the remaining parties in Parliament submitted lists of interim legislators to the government, which an electoral college of assembly and senate members then reviewed. This came just weeks after Ian Smith was expelled from the House of Assembly on the grounds that in direct violation of an official policy of no support of apartheid, he had encouraged the South African government to stand up to the sanctions imposed on it by Western nations. His ouster helped make the abolition of white seats more palatable to those who worried about the future of multiparty politics.

The second government initiative called for movement from a parliamentary executive system to what the justice minister referred to as an African type of presidential system, which the PF had advocated at the Lancaster House conference. Under the proposed system, power and "executive Authority [are] vested in a President who is not a member of the legislature. He is assisted by a cabinet of Ministers, all of whom are members of the legislature. The Ministers, however, merely assist the President; he is not bound to take their advice and may decide matters in his own deliberate judgement."[55]

The system made sense to ZANU(PF) on several levels. First, real and titular power would conjoin in one office. Second, the model would minimize conflict between executive and legislative branches because ministers would be "members of the legislature and owe their tenure of office partly to Parliament, partly to the President."[56] Third, the system would reduce intragovernmental competition by making the president head of state, the executive of government, and commander in chief for a term of six years, which would be repeatable without limit (although the House of Assembly could put through a vote of no confidence).

Parliamentary debate on the executive presidency was generally subdued and centered on the unlimited terms of office and presidential powers to declare war and to dissolve Parliament. Apropos of considerations of continuity and discontinuity, an interesting moment came when the minister of justice rebutted a critique of the presidential system sent by David Beach, the distinguished historian of precolonial Zimbabwe. Beach argued against the executive presidency on the grounds that it reminded him of Zimbabwe's past monarchies and conjured up images of the succession battles, civil wars, suspicion of rivals, and personalism that had plagued precolonial states. In his words, "If they [Zimbabweans] adopt the full executive Presidency proposals in the belief that this is a desirable and natural re-creation of the glories of the pre-colonial Shona and Ndebele monarchies, then they will have only themselves to blame."[57] The minister called the warning "worthless" and suggested that the executive presidency merely culminated a period of growing discontinuity between past and present that had to do with the nationalist movement and changes associated with modernity; this presidency was not a search for past glories.

The third initiative saw Joshua Nkomo accept Mugabe's aggressive handclasp and join ZAPU to ZANU(PF). This man of frustrated ambition, who could not deflect ZANU(PF)'s relentless efforts to stigmatize and marginalize ZAPU, was then reabsorbed into government as a special minister in the president's office in charge of welfare matters. Other ministerial changes further accommodated the new party partners. Heretofore there had been five ministers of state in the prime minister's office and nineteen regular ministries. Now there were three senior ministers including Nkomo in the president's office, seven ministers of state, and twenty-one regular ministries. A few portfolios changed hands, at least one long-standing ministry was divided into two (the Ministry of Education became the Ministry of Higher Education and the Ministry of Primary and Secondary Education), and one new ministry merged with another (Co-operatives joined Community Development and Women's Affairs). Although this made for a puzzling bureaucracy, the sight of key ZAPU people working alongside ZANU ministers softened the encumbrances. On December 30, 1987, one week after the historical merger of ZANU and ZAPU into ZANU, Robert Gabriel Mugabe was selected by the electoral college as the first president of Zimbabwe. He was inaugurated the following day for a foreshortened term of three years, after which a general election would be held. The festivities of the day rivaled the first inauguration, with air force displays, assorted marching bands, interminable speeches, and dancing into the night.

With the merger accomplished—except for ratifications at upcoming ZANU and ZAPU party congresses and a lengthy process of amalgamation that lasted until early 1990—and a new presidential system in place, it was time to review the steady grant of emergency powers to the executive. Early in January 1988 the government asked for a six-month extension, citing internal problems of banditry and external problems posed by the rebel Mozambique National Resistance (MNR) force in Mozambique and South Africa's campaign of regional destabilization. The measure was debated in the assembly and then passed without opposition. A few months later the president offered amnesty to ZAPU dissidents. This seemed to seal a new covenant with the people that henceforth the state's enormous emergency powers would be directed only at outside enemies.

A consensual renewal of emergency powers was repeated in June 1988. By then one could detect a slight shift in the political winds as the healing of overt political divisions among blacks put white politics under close scrutiny again. Letters to the press asked why whites were not attending unity rallies and joining ZANU PF. Why were they remaining aloof from mainstream trends? Were they saboteurs at heart? In the debate to renew the state of emergency, the minister of home affairs defused the "white problem" with these words: "Not every white man is a bad man, nor is every black man a good man—we realize that. However, the facts are what they are: the majority of saboteurs happen to be whites and people tend to wonder whether the whole white community is now inclined with the South African interests of destabilizing Zimbabwe. . . . I think we are now grown up as a nation and we can desist from such temptations."[58]

This response highlights the populist qualities in Zimbabwean politics after 1985—that is, the appeal to a more united people not riven by class or race. At its center was the ZANU-ZAPU merger metaphor; implicitly, if ZANU and ZAPU could surmount their differences, all Zimbabweans could do likewise. That the party merger has not been an entirely peaceful and voluntary affair has gotten a bit lost in the rhetoric of unity and in some of the state's actions.

The Rural District Council Act of 1988 illustrates some of the ambivalences in the merger metaphor. Under its terms, two colonial institutions of rural government are to merge into one—the rural councils, which used to comprise mostly commercial farm interests, and the historically less powerful district councils established to administer TTLs, now communal areas. (As of early 1991 the act had yet to be implemented.) The government said the merger would reduce bureaucratic redundancy and promote common interests across agricultural sectors. Yet to vote for a district councillor, the act stipulated that a person must be a resident of a communal land or resettlement area or must own immovable property or pay rent for accommodations. Persons housed by their employers cannot expect the same rights as contributing citizens, argued one MP, because "one must feel he owns something, has something to protect."[59] (This principle is also embedded in the Urban Councils Act of 1987, which disenfranchises domestic workers living rent free on the premises of their employers.) The property clause would have the effect of prohibiting most commercial farm workers—a large and especially poor group of workers in Zimbabwe—from participating in council elections. Moreover, in cases of multiple-spouse marriages, only the longest married wife would have the privilege of voting. Thus, in the new merger-oriented Zimbabwe some are still excluded, and this has contributed to a decline in party influence in some rural areas.[60]

There have been other contradictions around the themes of merger and unity. One has to do with the behavior of privileged officials relative to the less privileged majority. The other has to do with how the government has handled a direct challenge to unity in the form of a new opposition party.

Corruption. In August 1988 a popular columnist for the *Sunday Mail* commented that a "new Zimbabwean 'glasnost'" was reigning among free-speaking MPs.[61] Indeed, with the dissidence problem "solved" by party merger, the climate for national debate about the country's problems brightened considerably. In Parliament discussions about the attractions and liabilities of a one-party system, at least one MP warned his colleagues that such a party would surely "constitute a few, to oppress the workers and the peasants."[62] Longtime party official Edgar Tekere made even more pointed comments on a problem that had simmered on the back burner for years—corruption within the governing hierarchy—by insinuating that Mugabe was protecting "insider" offenders. The names of possible criminals then appeared in a series of *Chronicle* articles charging that high government officials were engaged in illegal car deals.

The ZANU(PF) government went on the defensive. Tekere was removed from his post as provincial head of ZANU(PF) in Manicaland, and protests by university students against this action were denounced. *Chronicle* editor Geoffrey Nyarota was rewarded for the investigative reporting of his newspaper by a promotion upstairs to steady his pen. These efforts to intimidate critics into silence merely stirred more discontent, and by early 1989 it appeared that Mugabe was facing a serious crisis in public confidence around the issue of corruption and what was happening to those who exposed it.

The government then astutely appointed a special commission to look into the car scandal. On what became known as the Willowgate scandal, named for the state factory in Harare where cars were illegally procured for profitable resale above the legal price, the Sandura Commission held public hearings in early 1989. These attracted large crowds eager to express their lack of sympathy for the accused—such as Maurice Nyagumbo, who had been with ZANU from its earliest days—by groaning and whistling. The commission found that indeed a number of officials had padded their pockets. As a result, Mugabe took resignations from five key ZANU(PF) officials. For a moment public opinion was assuaged, as judged by an informal opinion survey conducted by the *Sunday Mail* for April 16, 1989, that indicated great satisfaction with how government had handled the matter.

But the jubilation of people who could not afford the government's fixed price of Z $27,000 (U.S. $12,420) for a Toyota Cressida, let alone the black market price of Z $110,000 (U.S. $50,600), soon sobered as news hit the press that one of the guilty, Nyagumbo, had committed suicide, apparently out of humiliation. Mugabe reacted to this news by pardoning all convicted Willowgate ministers from their prison sentences, insisting only that they pay fines and resign from Parliament. This move seemed tremendously unpopular, and rumors flew that Mugabe was trying to prevent the convicted from revealing more extensive networks of corruption in places high enough to include his wife, Sally. The depth of the crisis became clear when Tekere founded a new political party— the Zimbabwe Unity Movement (ZUM)—to contest Nyagumbo's vacated seat. Although the government tried to prevent ZUM from holding campaign rallies, it garnered one-third of the by-election votes in a solidly ZANU(PF) constituency.

In July 1989 Tekere took to the podium at the University of Zimbabwe and urged students to "get out there and bury the corpse of this rotten government." He said, "ZANU tells us we are unified and integrated now, but we are not or there wouldn't be ZUM." The meeting was halted after an hour, and departing students engaged the riot police in a round of rocks versus tear gas. By October 1989 the entire university was reputed to be behind ZUM, and that month the University Council closed the institution for an indefinite period (it did not reopen until April 1990 and then a new wave of student protests started in October over a new bill to reduce the university's independence). Student leaders were detained for destroying a Mercedes Benz owned by the vice chancellor, Walter Kamba, and for wrecking several offices after Kamba refused to condemn the police actions on the campus as violations of academic freedom.

The 1990 Elections

Against this backdrop of crisis, resolution, and renewed crisis, the state prepared for the 1990 elections. Parliament supported a government suggestion to do away with the ceremonial senate in favor of a single legislative chamber of 150 seats; of this total, 120 seats would be elected on a constituency basis, 8 would be held by the country's provincial governors (nominated by the president), 10 seats would go to traditional chiefs, and the remaining 12 would be appointed by the president. Mugabe also reshuffled several ministries, notably merging Industry into Trade and Commerce and Women's Affairs into Political Affairs, and establishing a new ministry, Education and Culture. Parliament also renewed the ongoing state of emergency—for the twenty-fifth straight year—in January 1990 by a vote of sixty-nine to three in order to stand prepared for possible difficulties posed by the MNR in Mozambique and/or by Zimbabwe's own opposition parties.

As state matters settled, ZANU PF became absorbed by preelection party business, which seesawed dizzily between the poles of popular democracy and top-down control. ZANU PF announced a major party congress for December 1989 and quickly held provincial elections to elect new party officials and congress delegates; in one interesting outcome Dumiso Dabengwa, the former ZIPRA commander detained in 1982 because of the arms cache, was elected united ZANU chair of Matabeleland North. The party also held the congress of its Women's League and stipulated that the top positions in the league were noncontestable; the presidency went to Sally Mugabe. Then party primary elections selected candidates for the 1990 general election. For the first time, Zimbabweans could "elect their true candidate to represent them in the single-chamber Parliament . . . [and] remove those in their midst whose leadership record (at least among them) had not been exemplary."[63] The party, however, did not tolerate too much democracy if it meant senior party members could be rejected by their constituents: in Bindura district the minister of community and cooperative development, Joyce Mujuru, suffered resounding defeat in the primary by a junior ZANU PF candidate, whereupon the party nullified the election and banned the winner from recontesting it; in the second round, Mujuru won a "landslide victory."

At the congress of the newly united ZANU, Joshua Nkomo and Robert Mugabe dissolved the central committees of their respective parties and the delegates voted for 160 members of a new central committee and for 22 Politburo members. Mugabe became the party president, and a new joint vice presidency went to Nkomo and to prominent ZANU leader, Simon Muzenda; a white was also elected to the central committee of ZANU PF—Professor Reg Austin of the University of Zimbabwe law faculty. The addition to ZANU of new personnel, however, did not alter the radical style of Mugabe's rhetoric. Amid considerable debate and criticism, Mugabe insisted that Marxism-Leninism be inscribed as the leading ideology of the new party and that the one-party notion be carried forward. These directional affirmations came at the moment of mass anticommunist activity in Eastern Europe and were barely interrupted by news that the ostensibly Marxist-Leninist Ceauşescus, heretofore on friendly terms with Mugabe, had been executed in Romania. Mugabe rushed to say, however, that a socialist society would not be imposed in Zimbabwe and when adopted would not fall prey to the errors of Eastern European–style regimentation.

For a brief moment another party formed to challenge ZANU PF. Called the Zimbabwe Active People's Unity Movement (ZAPU), it hoped to represent people in Matabeleland skeptical of the unity process. When the parties and candidates registered for the 1990 elections in late February, however, the reconstituted ZAPU was already defunct and the final entrants were ZANU PF; ZUM; Muzorewa's old UANC (minus a retired Muzorewa); Sithole's old rump of ZANU, called ZANU-Ndonga (Sithole himself was in the United States); and a mysterious NDP. ZAPU, which one Matabeleland MP had dismissed as reflecting "another ambitious nonentity,"[64] threw what little weight it had to ZUM. Only ZUM and ZANU PF contested all available seats in the new unicameral Assembly.

ZANU PF's election manifesto [which changed the acronym from ZANU(PF) to ZANU PF] proclaimed unity, peace, and development and lauded ten years of achievements in health, education, rural development, and transport. The party promised that the tenth anniversary of independence would see the willing buyer/willing seller clause finally amended so government could acquire private land for resettlement on its own terms with or without the cooperation of commercial farmers. Addressing more than four rallies a day in the short three-week campaign, Mugabe denounced ZUM vociferously and defensively made promises— of one thousand new buses to alleviate transport problems for urban commuters, pay increases for nurses, more paved roads in rural areas, and greater trade union power in the future to negotiate wages without government involvement. ZANU PF candidates avoided discussing the party pledge to form "a socialist society or system in the country . . . [which] must derive from Marxism-Leninism as an ideology"[65] and said little about future single-party rule. They took every opportunity, however, to warn Zimbabweans that

> the forces of reaction, racism, division and retrogression which were soundly defeated retreated into the background, but they continue to regroup with new tactics, and new faces. They seize on disgruntled elements of the ruling party who have lost positions in which they totally failed to perform, or unemployed youths, or diehard racists, and try to recover lost ground. These reactionary and inimical forces keep changing tactics but never the objectives of oppressing, exploiting, and dominating our people.[66]

Indeed, ZUM did have drawbacks. It was led by Tekere, a "disgruntled element" of the ruling party known for a temper so hot that it had led him to kill an older white farmer in 1981, a crime for which Tekere was acquitted on a legal technicality. Tekere was also known as a hard-drinking malcontent who may have been free from the stain of corruption but did not seem cut from presidential cloth. ZUM itself made the tactical mistake of forming a united front with the remnants of the "forces of reaction, racism and division" of Ian Smith. Smith was ostensibly retired from politics by 1990, but in discussions with the ZUM-CAZ hierarchy a day before the elections, I was struck by the reverence younger colleagues of both races showed him and the power he therefore continued to wield. ZUM paid this no mind and said the front was a sign of the true racial reconciliation that had eluded ZANU PF. Tekere then announced that within twelve months of a ZANU PF "victory"—he thought the elections would be rigged—the country was destined for political turmoil, thereby suggesting a coup or war that no one wanted. Finally, ZUM, ignoring its thoughtful party manifesto in the last days before balloting—a text that raised the question of whether it was best to have a powerful presidency or a more limited prime minister (which ZUM preferred) and rang the alarm on government ministries doing ZANU PF support work (for example, Political Affairs and Youth, Sport, and Culture)—joined ZANU PF in a match of leader bashing, Tekere's unconvincing salvo being that Zimbabwe was led by an unintelligent man.

In three days of polling in late March, ZANU PF won all but 4 of the 120 constituency-based seats in Parliament. (Five ZUM candidates defected to ZANU PF immediately prior to the balloting, thereby giving the ruling party 14 uncontested victories, and one election in Chimanimani was postponed owing to misprinted ballots.) ZUM gained 2 seats in Manicaland, and ZANU-Ndonga held down 1 seat in Chipinge district. Unlike the 1985 elections, however, when more than 80 percent of the electorate voted, in 1990 less than 60 percent of eligible voters cast ballots, and 6 percent of the votes were spoiled, sometimes by voters writing across presidential ballots words to the effect that they supported Mugabe but not a one-party state.[67] The Electoral Supervisory Commission pronounced the elections, which gave ZUM less than 20 percent of all ballots cast compared to ZANU PF's 75 percent, free and fair, but there was considerable grumbling in the streets and in the alternative media about ZANU PF's subtle intimidation tactics and less subtle use of the media.[68]

Mugabe proclaimed the election a landslide victory for ZANU PF and a mandate for a one-party state. But it was noteworthy that there were no celebrations in the streets after this ZANU PF victory. On April 1 the government-controlled *Sunday Mail* seemed to crystallize the fears of ZANU PF opponents by saying in an editorial that "the election is over and with that, one aspect of the democratic process in our country has had its day."[69] And yet a scant four months later the government allowed the Emergency Powers Act to lapse without requesting an extension, presumably because the state of emergency had been lifted in South Africa. Before doing so, however, the government turned its emergency powers against teachers and nurses who were illegally striking for higher wages.

At the September 1990 meeting of the new ZANU PF Central Committee, the party officially abandoned Mugabe's dream to transform Zimbabwe into a legal one-party system. *Parade Magazine* reported at the time that "the President seemed determined that [Committee] members speak their minds without inhibitions, and . . . invited those who are normally reticent, the party hacks, to contribute. . . . The consensus . . . was so overwhelming there was no need for a vote. When the debate ended, President Mugabe revealed the Politburo [of ZANU PF] had come to a similar conclusion."[70]

With an eye on the changes shaking single-party rule in Eastern Europe, the rejection of such rule by the South African Communist Party, and the existence of ZUM in Zimbabwe, Mugabe could persuade only a few close associates—including loyalists in the ZANU PF Women's League—to hold the course on an eventual single-party system in Zimbabwe. *Parade* heralded the victory for "democrats," while *Moto Magazine* expressed the hope, often dashed in the past, that there would now be a "tolerance that excludes threats and harassments of the people."[71]

CONCLUSIONS

As Zimbabwe moves into the 1990s, ZANU PF becomes increasingly populist-liberal in orientation, albeit with lingering tinges of authoritarianism at the edges and concern in some quarters that the Marxist-Leninist line should not be cast off altogether. ZANU PF has helped shape a hybrid political system deft at managing some of the more extreme challenges from the "old Rhodie" right and from radical left flanks, and the party may now be moving away from a notion of national unity that was always too simple and hidebound to be convincing. As entreaties and heroic displays of magnanimity overtake threats, denunciations, and detentions, it is nonetheless unclear whether ZANU PF has abandoned its simultaneous tendency to be patient with "the people" and to rush to accusations when certain groups show too much independent thought and "dissident" action. Suffice it to say that ZANU PF mirrors and reinforces all the inconsistencies of the country's many inheritances. Its policies also illustrate some of the strengths—and unpredictabilities—of a party government that asserts but still lacks hegemony.

NOTES

1. Ibbo Mandaza, "The State in Post–White Settler Colonial Situation," in *Zimbabwe: The Political Economy of Transition, 1980–86,* ed. Ibbo Mandaza (Dakar: Codesria, 1986), pp. 21, 22.

2. "Lord Carrington's Statement in Reply to the Patriotic Front's Papers," October 9, 1979, in Goswin Baumhogger, with Telse Diederichsen and Ulf Engel, eds., *The Struggle for Independence: Documents on the Recent Development of Zimbabwe (1975–1980),* vol. 6 (Hamburg: Institut fur Afrikakunde, Dokumentations—Leitstelle Afrika, 1984), pp. 1102–1103.

3. "The Basic Political Position of the Patriotic Front," Press statement in Dar es Salaam on August 18, 1979, in Robert Mugabe, *Our War of Liberation: Speeches, Articles, Interviews, 1976–1979* (Gweru: Mambo Press, 1983), p. 117.

4. "The Patriotic Front's Response to British Constitutional Proposals," October 8, 1979, in Baumhogger et al., eds., *The Struggle for Independence,* vol. 6, p. 1101.

5. Joshua Nkomo, *Nkomo: The Story of My Life* (London: Methuen, 1984), p. 196.

6. Ibid., p. 195.

7. "Responses to British Constitutional Proposals," in Baumhogger et al., eds., *The Struggle for Independence*, vol. 6, p. 1101.

8. "Lord Carrington's Statement," p. 1103.

9. David Martin and Phyllis Johnson, *The Struggle for Zimbabwe: The Chimurenga War* (Harare: Zimbabwe Publishing House, 1981), p. 319.

10. Mandaza, "The State," p. 30.

11. For a detailed analysis of the Lancaster House conference, see Jeffrey Davidow, *A Peace in Southern Africa: The Lancaster House Conference on Rhodesia, 1979* (Boulder, Colo.: Westview Press, 1984).

12. See Ph.D. dissertation in progress by Susan Rice, "The Commonwealth Initiative in Zimbabwe, 1979–1980: Implications for International Peacekeeping," New College, Oxford University. The issue of monitoring forces is also discussed in ibid.

13. J. Newhouse, "Profiles: A Sense of Duty," *New Yorker*, February 14, 1983, pp. 77–78.

14. "A. Muzorewa's Speech Launching the Election Campaign of the UANC," January 6, 1980, in Baumhogger et al., eds., *The Struggle for Independence*, vol. 6, p. 1266.

15. Interview with Joshua Nkomo, Bulawayo, June 25, 1982.

16. Robert Mugabe, September 25, 1979, in Baumhogger et al., eds., *The Struggle for Independence*, vol. 6, p. 1066.

17. Martin and Johnson, *The Struggle for Zimbabwe*, p. 328.

18. "Election Manifesto of ZANU/Patriotic Front," January 25, 1980, in Baumhogger et al., eds., *The Struggle for Independence*, vol. 7, p. 1309.

19. Ibid., p. 1308.

20. "Election Manifesto of the Patriotic Front," January 16, 1980, in ibid., pp. 1282–1283 (emphasis added).

21. "The Party: ZANU(PF) Wins—The People Win," *Zimbabwe News: Official Organ of the Zimbabwe African National Union (Patriotic Front)* 12, no. 1 (March–July 1981): 2.

22. Masipula Sithole, "The General Elections, 1979–1985," in Mandaza, ed., *Zimbabwe*, p. 84.

23. Terence Ranger, *Peasant Consciousness and Guerilla War in Zimbabwe* (Berkeley and Los Angeles: University of California Press, 1985), Chapter 6.

24. Martin and Johnson, *The Struggle for Zimbabwe*, p. 330.

25. Nathan Shamuyarira, from Christine Sylvester, "An Interview with Nathan Shamuyarira and Comment on the Zimbabwean Situation," *Alternatives* 8, no. 3 (Winter 1982–1983): 485–486.

26. Government of Zimbabwe, *Transitional National Development Plan: 1982/ 83–1984/85*, vol. 1 (Harare: Department of Finance, Economic Planning and Development, 1982), p. 1.

27. "Election Manifesto of ZANU/Patriotic Front," p. 1309.

28. Rob Davies, "The Transition to Socialism in Zimbabwe: Some Areas for Debate," in *Zimbabwe's Prospects: Issues of Race, Class, State and Capital in Southern Africa*, ed. Colin Stoneman (London: Macmillan, 1988), pp. 20–21.

29. "A Luta Continua," *Parade and Foto-Action* (April 1990): 7.

30. Captain Ngiyi, Letter, *Parade and Foto-Action* (April 1990): 67.

31. "A Luta Continua," p. 7. Norma Kriger also discusses this point in "In Search of a National Identity: The Politics of War Heroes" (1990, unpublished paper).

32. Luke Mhlaba, "Burying the Lancaster House Constitution," *Parade and Foto-Action* (April 1990): 12.

33. Ibid., p. 13.

34. John Saul, "Zimbabwe: The Next Round," *Monthly Review* 32, no. 4 (1980): 1–42. See discussion of this position in Christine Sylvester, "Continuity and Discontinuity in Zimbabwe's Development History," *African Studies Review* 28, no. 1 (1985): 33–34.

35. The hard-line Marxist position was often articulated in the official circular of ZANU(PF), *Zimbabwe News*, and reappeared in the Zimbabwe African National Union Central Committee Report, *Second Congress of the Party, 1984* (Harare: ZANU, 1984).

36. This is the general tone of Andre Astrow, *Zimbabwe: A Revolution That Lost Its Way?* (London: Zed Press, 1983).

37. Davies, "The Transition to Socialism," p. 20.

38. On whether single-party rule is essential to socialism, see W. Shaw, "Towards the One-Party State in Zimbabwe: A Study in African Political Thought," *Journal of Modern African Studies* 24, no. 3 (1986): 373–394.

39. E. Mukonoweshuro, quoted in "Leadership Code Undemocratic," *Moto Magazine*, no. 54 (July 1987): 7.

40. David Maxwell, "Religion and the War in Northern Nyanga District Zimbabwe" (Paper presented at St. Antony's College, Oxford, March 1990).

41. Jocelyn Alexander, "Land Resettlement and Agrarian Reform: The Chimanimani Case" (Paper presented at St. Antony's College, Oxford, March 6, 1990).

42. Colin Stoneman, "A Zimbabwean Model?" in Stoneman, ed., *Zimbabwe's Prospects*, p. 4. Other writings in this second wave include Mandaza, "The State"; Davies, "The Transition to Socialism"; Colin Stoneman and Lionel Cliffe, *Zimbabwe: Politics, Economics and Society* (London: Pinter, 1989); Christine Sylvester, "Zimbabwe's 1985 Elections: A Search for National Mythology," *Journal of Modern African Studies* 24, no. 2 (1986): 229–255; and Christine Sylvester, "Simultaneous Revolutions: The Zimbabwean Case," *Journal of Southern African Studies* 16, no. 3 (1990): 452–475.

43. Author interview with Nkomo discussed in Christine Sylvester, "An African Dilemma," *The Progressive* (January 1983): 40–43. Joseph Hanlon hints that the head of the Central Intelligence Organization in Hwange, Matt Calloway, ordered an ex-ZIPRA officer to cache the arms. See Joseph Hanlon, "Destabilisation and the Battle to Reduce Dependence," in Stoneman, ed., *Zimbabwe's Prospects*, pp. 32–42.

44. Ibid.

45. See Lawyers' Committee for Human Rights, *Zimbabwe: Wages of War, a Report on Human Rights* (New York: Lawyers' Committee for Human Rights, 1986); and Andrew Nyathi with John Hoffman, *Tomorrow Is Built Today: Experiences of War, Colonialism and the Struggle for Collective Cooperatives in Zimbabwe* (Harare: Anvil Press, 1990).

46. Joseph Hanlon, "Destabilisation and the Battle to Reduce Dependence," in Stoneman, ed., *Zimbabwe's Prospects*, p. 34.

47. Michael Evans, "The Security Threat from South Africa," in Stoneman, ed., *Zimbabwe's Prospects*, p. 221, drawing on L. H. Gann and P. Duignan, *Africa South of the Sahara: The Challenge to Western Security.*

48. Roger Martin, *Southern Africa: The Price of Apartheid—A Political Risk Analysis*, Special Report no. 1130 (London: Economist Intelligence Unit, July 1988), p. 21.

49. Ibid., p. 225, quoting Robert Mugabe in *Herald*, January 29, 1981.

50. Ronald Weitzer, "In Search of Regime Security: Zimbabwe Since Independence," *Journal of Modern African Studies* 22, no. 4 (1984): 529–557. For a discussion of Zimbabwe's security system, see Ronald Weitzer, *Transforming Settler States: Communal Conflict and Internal Security in Northern Ireland and Zimbabwe* (Berkeley and Los Angeles: University of California Press, 1990).

51. Brian Wrobel, "Intimidation, Political Freedom, and the Common Roll," in *Zimbabwe: Report on the 1985 General Elections*, ed. Millard Arnold, L. Garber, and B. Wrobel (Washington, D.C.: International Human Rights Law Group, 1986), p. 4.

52. This discussion of the 1985 election is taken mostly from Sylvester, "Zimbabwe's 1985 Elections." Also see Masipula Sithole, "The General Elections: 1979–1985," in Mandaza, ed., *Zimbabwe*, pp. 75–98.

53. L. M. Sachikonye, "The Debate on Democracy in Contemporary Zimbabwe," *Review of African Political Economy*, nos. 45–46 (1989): 117.

54. Robert Mugabe, *Hansard*, August 7, 1985, p. 301.

55. E. Zvogbo, Address to House of Assembly, *Hansard*, October 27, 1987, p. 1556.

56. Ibid., p. 1557.

57. D. Beach, cited in ibid., p. 1579.

58. M. Mahachi, *Hansard*, July 12, 1988, p. 120.

59. E. Chikowore, *Hansard*, March 8, 1988, p. 2891.

60. From interviews in Mazowe area in 1988 and Alexander's presentation on Chimanimani district, "Land Resettlement."

61. A. Saxon, "Hansard Gems Well Worth Digging," *Sunday Mail*, August 7, 1988, p. 7.

62. L. Nzarayebani, *Hansard*, July 19, 1988, p. 301.

63. "Guided Democracy . . ." *Parade and Foto-Action* (April 1990): 19.

64. Sidney Malunga, from a discussion at St. Antony's College, Oxford, March 9, 1990.

65. ZANU PF, *ZANU PF Election Manifesto 1990* (Harare: Jongwe, 1990), pp. 3–4.

66. Ibid., p. 1.

67. Interview with ballot-counting observer, Harare, April 1, 1990.

68. "The Dirty Campaign," *Parade and Foto-Action* (May 1990): 13–21. For further discussion of the 1990 election see Christine Sylvester, "Unities and Disunities in Zimbabwe's 1990 Election," *Journal of Modern African Studies* 28, no. 3 (1990): 375–400.

69. "New Chapter," *Sunday Mail*, April 1, 1990, p. 6.

70. "Democrats Triumph as Central Committee Rejects One-Party State," *Parade Magazine* (November 1990): 7.

71. Ibid.; and "Comment: We Commend," *Moto Magazine*, no. 94 (November 1990): 1.

4

The Political Economy
of "Growth with Equity"

The economy Zimbabweans inherited languished during the war but still emerged as one of the strongest in Africa. Its potential lay in considerable arable land, a history of food self-sufficiency in most years, adequate water supplies, diversified minerals, and a growing industrial sector in which manufacturing accounted for more than 25 percent of GDP. It was also an unequivocally capitalist economy—that is, dominated by private capital and driven by a logic of capital productivity for profit. Owing to the strong interventionist role the UDI state played, however, this was not a free-market system.

Today the Zimbabwean government approaches this economic inheritance in ways that seemingly contradict its stated socialist aspirations and sometimes may be at cross-purposes with simpler needs. "The economic philosophy proposes planning and socialism, whilst the practice inhibits or humanizes capitalism, adds a little state enterprise, and provides social services, adding up to a national capitalism much like European welfare-state capitalism, but without the scale of productive capacity needed to sustain it."[1] This chapter explores the contradictions in Zimbabwe's approach to economic development and the debates that follow in their wake, bearing in mind the question of how specific economic policies affect ordinary Zimbabweans.

THE ECONOMY AT INDEPENDENCE

The Rhodesian economy weathered international sanctions until 1974, when it entered a period of sharp decline owing as much to situation-specific constraints as to trade cutoffs; indeed, there is evidence that, thanks to South Africa and other sanctions-busters, UDI Rhodesia was never fully alone, except with its fears. UDI did cause Rhodesia's export earnings to drop and import costs to increase, primarily because the government had to work through expensive intermediaries. The country was also isolated from international financial markets at a time when petrodollars were being liberally recycled as loans to Third World countries. Nevertheless, government control of profit repatriation by foreign firms ensured the economy of investible financial surpluses, while exchange controls imposed by the Treasury and Reserve Bank enabled the state to direct available resources to industrial diversification. Under the weight of sanctions and new internal policies, the economy shifted away from a reliance on standing commodity exports, such as tobacco, and toward the import-substitution industries of metal working, mining, and agro-industry and to the export-capable sector of manufacturing. The relative shares of GDP accounted for by agriculture and manufacturing reflected the changes: during this time, manufacturing's share of GDP increased to 26 percent, while agriculture's dropped to 18 percent. With an overall growth rate of 6 to 7 percent, the Rhodesian government accomplished between 1967 and 1975 what the International Monetary Fund (IMF) often mandates now for countries seeking its assistance, namely, economic stabilization.[2]

The post-UDI boom, however, could not be sustained, primarily because the apartheid-like economy had built-in limits on local demand but also because sanctions made engaging in normal trade more difficult and costly. The OPEC jolts, along with generating loanable funds, caused a major recession in industrial countries in the West that had been involved in limited or extensive sanctions-busting, and this, too, cut into the Rhodesian boom. The armed struggle then took its toll: Zambia closed its border with Rhodesia in 1973, and the new government of Mozambique followed suit, which led to higher transport costs, foreign exchange losses, and increased reliance on South Africa. In addition, the Rhodesian government funneled one-fourth of the total budget into defense in 1976 and imposed new restrictions on the use of dwindling foreign exchange. Between 1976 and 1979 imports dropped by about 40 percent, business expectations sank along with profits, and there was little in the way of new fixed investment. Income per capita also declined by almost 12 percent (see Table 4.1) as the employment growth of the boom years turned negative, and capacity utilization fell from 98 percent in 1974 to 70 percent in 1978. On top of all this, the region suffered two droughts.

After 1978 the economy was buoyed by the independence talks and began to recover from the depths of recession. In 1980 GNP grew at a spectacular rate of more than 11 percent, the first increase since 1974, as sanctions were lifted and relatively high mineral prices prevailed on the international markets. Moreover, as an independent state Zimbabwe could now join international financial institutions and seek legitimate

TABLE 4.1   Economic Indicators for Rhodesia, 1969–1979 (Z $ million)[a]

Indicators	1969	1971	1973	1976	1979
GDP	1,001	1,244	1,553	2,179	2,780
GNP	983	1,101	1,262	1,353	1,312
GNP per capita (dollars)	193	200	214	208	184
GDP at factor cost by industrial sector					
Mining and quarrying	—	121	138	147	133
Manufacturing	—	117	150	150	152
Agriculture, livestock, forestry	—	117	107	132	115
Balance of payments on current account					
Merchandise	32	3	89	154	139
Services	−5	−25	−58	−71	−134
Balance of payments on capital account	10	31	52	11	182
Gross fixed capital formation[b]	145	221	330	402	380
Total external debt	145	130	113	78	353

[a]At constant 1969 prices, R $1 = U.S. $2.80.
[b]At 1987 prices, Z $1 = U.S. $.59.

Source: Government of Zimbabwe, Transitional National Development Plan: 1982/83–1984/ 85, vol. 1 (Harare: Government Printers, November 1982), pp. 108, 109, 113, 125, 129.

foreign aid. The government signed the Second Lome Convention and thereby received Europe's guarantee to purchase twenty-five thousand metric tons of Zimbabwean sugar, provide funds to support refugee repatriation and resettlement, and institute a foot-and-mouth disease control project. The World Bank lent Z $38 million (approximately U.S. $60 million at that time) to help finance a coal mining project at Hwange, for which the Export-Import Bank of the United States authorized funds for equipment. In December 1980 Zimbabwe also secured two international commercial loans to improve the rail and air systems. With Zimbabwean export earnings up 27 percent, the U.S. Department of Commerce optimistically described Zimbabwe as "a unique opportunity for American investment in a nation eager for new capital and new technology, with material and human resources to put them to work profitably."[3]

Despite the sense that Zimbabwe was emerging as the economic pride of Africa, it soon became clear that the country also "inherited a physical infrastructure with a huge backlog of repairs and maintenance and a stock of capital which was overaged, largely worn-out and in bad need of replacement."[4] Real output was increasing (nearly 12 percent in 1980), but overall employment was increasing only 2.6 percent. Shifts to capital-intensive methods and crops meant that a 1980 increase in agricultural output was accompanied by a drop of 2.4 percent in formal agricultural employment. Moreover, there was such unevenness in the wage structure that the 1981 average income of urban workers was fourteen times that of peasant farmers, and commercial farm workers made even less than peasant farmers. Manufacturing was up in volume of output over 1979, but so also was its use of foreign exchange, which prompted Ministry of Economic Planning and Development officials to suggest "a greater need for export expansion to finance an increasing volume of industrial imports."[5] Rustling in rural areas during the war and disease after dipping and inoculation programs were curtailed led to a drop in cattle from 3 million to only 2.3 million by independence. In 1980, then, Zimbabwe's economy was full of promise, as Table 4.2 indicates, but also scarred by wartime damages, by dependence on external markets, and by decades of state-sponsored inequities in jobs, wages, housing, land, and education.

ECONOMIC DEVELOPMENT
POLICIES IN THE FIRST FIVE YEARS

The government was quick to pronounce "Growth with Equity" the twin concerns of development. As in the realm of its self-proclaimed socialist politics, however, the government was slow to give the slogan content and is still disinclined to plan the details of a growth-with-equity system or indicate how such a system could advance socialist aspirations.

A year after independence the first broad outlines of economic policy were drawn, followed eighteen months later by a transitional development plan. The first document, *Growth with Equity*, stated at the outset that "government is determined to forge ahead with the task of building a progressive, non-racial and egalitarian society which draws on the energies and abilities of all its peoples."[6] But exactly what the government has meant by "progressive" and "egalitarian" has been unclear. Whereas *Growth with Equity* spoke of establishing "progressively a society founded on socialist, democratic, and egalitarian principles,"[7] the *Transitional National Development Plan, 1982/83–1984/85*, the more complete and detailed of the two early documents, lauded the "opportunity to create a new order, to rid Zimbabwean society of vestiges of exploitation, unemployment, poverty" and so on but reiterated that "the challenge lies in building upon and developing on what was inherited."[8]

TABLE 4.2 Economic Indicators for Zimbabwe, 1980–1989 (Z $ million)[a]

Indicators	1980	1983	1986	1988	1989
GDP	3,441	6,306	7,902	8,295 [b]	—
GNP	3,394	6,058	7,518	—	—
Real GDP growth rate (%)	11.3	−3.4	2.0	5.3	4.0[c]
GNP per capita (dollars)[d]	472	730	784 [e]	—	—
Price inflation (%)	7.3	13.8	19.7	14.6	11.5[c]
GDP at factor cost by industry					
Mining, quarrying	285	393	372	529	—
Manufacturing	802	1,441	1,726	2,197	—
Agriculture, forestry	451	544	1,121	1,203	—
Balance of payments					
Current account	−439 [f]	−454	15	81.5[g]	—
Capital account	310 [f]	299	60	152 [g]	—
Gross fixed capital formation	528	1,238	1,320	1,333 [g]	—
Total external borrowings	415	987	2,223	3,099	—
External debt/service ratio (%)	—	—	33	32.4	—
Reserves minus gold	427	151	213	357	—

[a]At 1989 prices, Z $1 = U.S. $.46.
[b]At factor cost.
[c]Estimate.
[d]At 1987 prices, Z $1 = U.S. $.59.
[e]1984 figure.
[f]1981 figure.
[g]1987 figure.

Sources: Government of Zimbabwe, Quarterly Digest of Statistics (Harare: Central Statistical Office, March 1989), pp. 13, 19, 63, and June 1989, pp. 13–14; Economist Intelligence Unit, Country Report on Zimbabwe and Malawi, no. 1 (London: EIU, 1990), p. 2.

Taken together, it seemed the state was pursuing a nationalist development style in which the state would work on behalf of lower classes to improve social services and consumption levels, and mollify the monied classes by encouraging the profitability of capital and opportunities for external investment and trade.[9] The strategy relied on the largesse of all key economic groups in the country, even though there may have been some concern to check the ambitions of bourgeoisies. Thus, pragmatism emerged as the watchword, and "transformation" came to mean "balance."

It is worth noting that if balance between capital and labor, between external market pressures and internal priorities, could be accomplished in Zimbabwe under this development style, it would mark a departure from Rhodesia's various schemes of racial privilege. But the agenda of exquisite balance has not always been played out in the policy realm.

Privately owned manufacturing has been targeted for expansion under an export-led model, while cooperatives, which can be more democratically organized and run and in which local initiative can be high,[10] have languished. Although the working classes are touted for their contributions to the economy, the government has seemed ill-disposed to improve the appalling problem of unemployment through creative and workable rural development strategies. To appreciate these and other ambivalences in the Zimbabwean approach, let us consider macroeconomic and sectoral tendencies in the postindependence economy.

Macroeconomic Targets

Twenty-two months after independence Zimbabwe was in the throes of a drought described as one of the worst of the twentieth century. The world capitalist economy was in recession, and the Zimbabwean economy was growing at only 2 to 3 percent, down from the spectacular growth rate of the first fiscal year. At that difficult moment, the *TNDP* called for a real growth rate of 8 percent each year until 1984. It set new job creation at a target rate of 3.2 percent per year, virtually ignoring the trend toward job retrenchment that was accompanying the global economic slowdown. The *TNDP* offered 4.8 percent as the rate of growth in labor productivity over the plan period, despite evidence that productivity was actually down; looked forward to new investments of approximately Z $6 billion; and projected 23 percent of Zimbabwe's GDP going to gross fixed investment. None of this was reasonable in a time of recession. Moreover, with manufacturing output declining by nearly 3 percent in the first ten months of 1982, the *TNDP* breezily asserted that exports, led by manufacturing, would rise about 35 percent. Finally, perhaps the most unsettling assertion was that government would seek a deliberately negative balance on current account in order to ensure economic growth. Zimbabwe was underindebted at independence, but a planned negative balance could become large very quickly.

Rumors flew that the *TNDP* was tailored more for home consumption than for the technical planning community. Yet the exaggerated targets also showed investors and donors that Zimbabwe was serious, both about expanding its productive capacity and about courting capitalist approval and assistance. Sectoral specifics varied in degree of feasibility and specificity. Agriculture received the most, but not necessarily the most careful consideration, while manufacturing and mining were painted with broader strokes.

The Agricultural Sector. Agriculture has been called the most important sector in Zimbabwe. Although it is second to mining in earnings of foreign exchange and contributes less to GDP than manufacturing does, it is the sector most people rely on for their livelihoods. It is also an important focal point of culture and was the rallying point for mobilization in the armed struggle. Government targets agriculture, therefore, as a major locus of equity while striving to enhance its considerable growth potential.

At UDI the government wanted to stimulate growth in agricultural output, attain self-sufficiency in food production and raw materials, diversify the structure and output of the sector, and maximize its foreign exchange earnings.[11] To these ends government introduced preplanting producer prices for certain controlled crops such as maize and cotton, economic incentives for crop diversification, and an agricultural finance corporation to provide credit to farm owners. Accordingly, between 1965 and 1974 the real value of agricultural output grew at nearly 8 percent, subsequently dropping below 1965 rates during the slump. Most of the boom was accounted for by six thousand commercial farms: "They produced 90 percent of the marketed maize (the main staple) and cotton (the main industrial crop) and virtually all the tobacco and other exports, including almost all the other food crops—wheat, coffee, tea, sugar, etc."[12] Moreover, the commercial sector accomplished this without cultivating extensively; estimates put total cultivation at less than one-third of arable land.

The 47 percent of the land (approximately eighteen million hectares) located in less fertile areas of the country was cultivated by nearly seven hundred thousand household-based farmers. During UDI years "land degradation sometimes reached such an advanced stage that it was said regeneration processes w[ould] require several decades before the vegetation and soil cover [could be] returned to a productive state, even assuming that population pressures c[ould] be relieved and appropriate reclamation begun immediately."[13] Government pricing policies did little to help small farmers in subsistence and cash cropping because prices were based on expected market realities from good soil conditions, not on the vagaries of production in poor agro-ecological regions far from centers of marketing.

Growth with Equity and the *TNDP* listed ten objectives for an agricultural sector marked by this inheritance. Five would benefit commercial farmers by encouraging growth in aggregate output, food self-sufficiency and security for the entire southern African region, and food exports as sources of foreign exchange. These objectives were "identical with those for the UDI period" and were to be pursued "through the same policy instruments as before."[14] The other five objectives focused specifically on rural victims of past land appropriation policies and were more potentially transformative: government vowed to conduct a land resettlement program to ensure fair distribution of landownership and use, provide accelerated improvement in living standards in rural areas, integrate the commercial and "communal" sectors into one agricultural sector, and encourage greater productivity of land and labor and infra-structural and social service improvements. Importantly, the plans called for diversifying the forms of agricultural production such that commercial and peasant farming would continue as the backbones of the sector, supplemented by more socialist production through cooperatives and state farms.

To help fund some of these projects, the government held a donor's conference in March 1981 called the Zimbabwe Conference on Recon-struction and Development (ZIMCORD). Reminding foreign governments of promises made to the PF during the Lancaster House talks, the government appealed to forty-five countries and organizations for funds to help complete the refugee and reconstruction programs, for land resettlement and agricultural development, and for training and technical assistance. The conference netted pledges of nearly Z $1.3 billion (ap-proximately U.S. $1.9 billion), mostly in loans with riders stipulating that Zimbabwe had to use between 10 and 30 percent of the assistance to purchase goods and services from the donor country. The largest donor was the World Bank, with Z $287.5 million (U.S. $417.3 million) in new soft-term loans, followed by the United States pledging Z $140.6 million (U.S. $204 million), and the European Economic Community (EEC) with Z $107.8 million (U.S. $156.3 million).[15] Not all pledges were honored and some were slow in arriving. For this and reasons noted in Chapter 3, as well as drought, the government could not reach the *TNDP* goal of resettling 162,000 families between 1982 and 1985.

Those who were resettled could opt to establish a household in villages designed for family cultivation on five-hectare plots with some communal grazing (Model A). Alternatively, there was the option of coop-erative production, with fifty to two hundred individuals jointly owning all assets (Model B). A third option combined household retention of land or tenant farming with employment on large capital-intensive state farms (Model C). For pastoralists, the government later devised a grazing scheme for villages established along the lines of Model A (Model D).

The great majority of resettled people (thirty-five thousand by mid-1987) chose the least collective and most individualistic of the options, Model A. Successful candidates had to satisfy the government that they were landless, unemployed, and males or widows; in a country where a large proportion of farming is done by women, "women other than widows were not eligible in their own right" for land in resettlement villages.[16] Some early Model A schemes struggled—one study showed only two with an overall net farm profit in 1982–1983.[17] Those located in fertile areas, however, and lucky enough to be supplied with adequate physical infrastructure by the government, began to flourish during the first five years of independence. Both the form of Model A resettlements and the stipulations government imposed concerning "appropriate" participants and land use resonated strongly with NLHA-era thinking. Moreover, Model A schemes were subject to an old conservation ideology barely dressed up for the independence era: "If soil erosion rates are allowed to continue at existing levels the soil over large areas of Zimbabwe will be destroyed."[18] Michael Drinkwater argues, as part of an ongoing debate about government resettlement policies, that predictions of this sort have been vigorously advanced since the 1920s and have been based more on physical observation than on careful study. He notes that "even since independence, an acceptance that land apportionment has caused the fundamental inequalities in the communal areas, has had little impact on the physicalist and technocratic approach to production constraints."[19] Hence the government replicated and reinforced a set of colonial policies that "the people" fought to escape.

Ex-combatants gravitated to the cooperative model, using demobilization allowances or funding by donors to cover start-up costs. Model B schemes came to be viewed as the hard-core socialist subsector of agriculture, even though "production cooperatives are not necessarily socialist units, since they must function in a capitalist system as collectively organized profit-making entities."[20] By 1984 there were only forty-one such farms in existence, and many of these were undersubscribed and struggling to generate surpluses. Several had not received government establishment grants by their second season of operation, and many complained that it was nearly impossible to get loans from commercial banks. Under severe drought conditions in 1983, some collective farms found it impossible to function in anything but name only. In part this had to do with the very limited resources Model B participants brought to their enterprises relative to some Model A people: Model B settlers were usually young men with little farming experience, ex-commercial farm workers with no tools of their own, and older foreign workers from Malawi and Mozambique.[21]

State farms, the Model C option, had a prior history in Zimbabwe, and at independence eighteen such estates were brought under the wing of the Agricultural and Rural Development Authority (ARDA) parastatal. The new government subsequently acquired several more estates and looked to turn the subsector into a successful example of large-scale socialist production along three lines: pure state farms producing strategic commodities such as cattle, seeds, and selected food crops; nucleus estates encouraging individual tenant farmers to use the latest techniques of farming; and agro-industrial estates integrating commodity production with processing.[22]

Collective farmers. *Source:* Ministry of Education; photographer, J. Musekiwa. Courtesy Zimbabwe Ministry of Information.

The assembly line at an ARDA farm. Photographer, B. Kanyama. Courtesy Zimbabwe Ministry of Information.

Many former estate workers stayed on, and others were attracted by prospects of better conditions under majority rule management than were usually found on commercial farms; in the 1984–1985 fiscal year there were more than eighteen thousand state farm workers, up one thousand from the 1981–1982 fiscal year. But contrary to worker expectations, the subsector continued to mimic the capital-productive approach of the private sector. Worker housing remained of a poor standard, hours and conditions were harsh, and it was usually the case that the estates hired more seasonal than permanent workers in order to avoid paying benefits. Most seasonal workers were women, and on one farm I visited in 1988 single women who "fell pregnant" were forced to vacate farm hostels. The practical result of this policy was that pregnancy ended a woman's already tenuous farm employment because there was no place for her to stay; it also allowed state enterprises to circumvent Labour Relations Act stipulations that employers must present a formal case for any dismissal. As for permanent workers, government increases in minimum wages did not translate into better living standards because companies successfully made the case whenever the minimum wage was raised that they simply could not meet these costs and should be given a waiver.

Along with new schemes for land use and resettlement, the Zimbabwean government endeavored to increase the productive capabilities of farmers living in former TTLs. It distributed seeds and fertilizers, reactivated Agritex (an agricultural technical and extension service), stipulated that women producers could now have their own grain marketing board cards, and empowered the Agricultural Finance Corporation (AFC) to make more loans to communal farmers. Voluntary organizations also provided some credit and finances for marketing depots and technical services. These inputs, taken together, contributed to the well-publicized boom in the communal areas (CAs) indicated in Table 4.3.

Sales from CA crops and livestock, however, were still lower by at least one-third than those for the smaller commercial sector, with its better access to marketing facilities, longer history of AFC credit, irrigation, and locations in higher rainfall zones. Moreover, the postindependence peasant "miracle" did not affect all peasant cultivators evenly. The majority of good harvests occurred in only three areas of the country—central Mashonaland, Midlands, and Manicaland—where soil quality was good to begin with. Credit for peasant farming continued to be in short supply, and more than 70 percent of AFC loans still went to commercial farmers. Access to draft power also became problematic: between "19.5 per cent and 33.3 per cent of the households surveyed had no draught animals, while 4.8 per cent had over 10."[23] In the past,

TABLE 4.3 Summary of Sales of Principal Crops and Livestock, 1970–1986[a]

Production Location	1970	1973	1976	1979	1980	1983	1986
Crops							
Communal areas	2.7	8.2	18.2	12.2	22.0	65.0	221.9
Commercial areas	80.9	124.9	225.4	249.2	350.1	451.0	960.5
Crops and livestock							
Communal areas	7.2	14.1	26.7	15.4	27.2	54.3	246.1
Commercial areas	118.8	201.2	310.3	361.0	465.6	660.6	1,184.8

[a]At 1989 prices, Z $1 million = U.S. $460,000.

Source: Government of Zimbabwe, Quarterly Digest of Statistics (Harare: Central Statistical Office, March 1989), p. 37.

peasant cultivators could augment their investible resources from farming by engaging in migrant labor. Although this practice still continued, as many as 40 percent of communal farmers and most women-headed households had few reliable sources of off-farm income, and it was predicted that "with reduced formal employment and concerns over the creditworthiness of the bulk of small farmers, capital for inputs will increasingly have to come from on-farm production."[24] All this meant that "at the most, 20% of the peasantry [were] gaining from the reforms."[25]

To some, even Zimbabwe's most impressive farming accomplishments have had ominous undertones. Zimbabwe is nearly self-sufficient in the basic food crops poor people can afford; also, new local and export crops of soy beans and sunflower seeds have been introduced, and some communal farmers now cultivate exportable cotton and burly tobacco. Yet these unexpected and unprecedented gains caused University of Zimbabwe professor A. M. Hawkins to issue a warning in 1985 that communal and commercial agriculture was producing too much maize for the needs of the country: "The wider economic concerns range from the impact that such a situation is bound to have on the trading account of the GMB [Grain Marketing Board] on the one hand to the inflationary implications of stock-building of that magnitude."[26] In years since 1985, Agritex has pointedly encouraged farmers in all categories to deemphasize maize relative to other grains, groundnuts, and soybeans. Michael Drinkwater, however, raises the possibility that peasants were really marginalized within ZANU(PF) ideology (despite TNDP promises) and that the technocratic "miracle" papered over the tension:

> ZANU(PF) won the 1980 elections because it gathered the support of most of the Shona peasantry during the Liberation War . . . and the peasantry supported ZANU because they wanted to recover the land taken from them and to eject administrative coercion. The dilemma the government

faces is that on the one hand it needs to appease the peasantry in order to retain their support, but on the other hand it fears a peasantry, led by old lineage leaders, being permitted access to most of the agricultural land. If the latter scenario took place the state's power would be severely weakened. . . . [Thus] 'Thesis Six' of the resolutions passed at ZANU(PF)'s second party congress in August 1984 [says] an ideal socialist agricultural system in Zimbabwe would have two "arms": large-scale state farming and the cooperative farming movement. Where does this leave the peasantry, [except] as a "residual sector"?[27]

As for the "privileged" commercial farming sector, the nearly four thousand white farmers who remained in Zimbabwe were slowly joined by approximately three hundred black farmers with titled land; in the Nsiza Rural Council area alone, which is in the north of Insiza district in Matabeleland, "57 of 114 commercial farms are now owned by blacks."[28] This sector then continued to produce about 75 percent of the total agricultural output and contributed 41 percent of foreign exchange earned in 1984. Yet it was clear that large farms often maintained sizable tracts of uncropped lands where they could allocate three to five hectares for one cow, "double what the average peasant household has."[29] Even though the government criticized land underutilization, farmers could disguise such lands by integrating them with productive fields or by shifting use patterns. Government was also critical of farm labor losses, which occurred at the rate of 35 percent between 1979 and 1984, mostly because farmers preferred to capitalize their production rather than conform to minimum wage legislation. Daniel Weiner thinks it is "indicative of continued imbalance in the agricultural sector that it is the farm labourers, not the farmers, that are being displaced."[30] This subsector is so reliable, however, that government has been reluctant to destabilize it.

Growth with equity policies in the agricultural sector, therefore, have emphasized land productivity over land use transformation and the commercial somewhat over the peasant and greatly over the cooperative farming sector. These priorities certainly reflect shortages of funds: in 1985 a new agricultural cooperative needed an establishment grant of Z $109,554 (U.S. $67,961)—"Z $63,000 (U.S. $39,060) for a tractor, Z $4,000 (U.S. $2,480) for oxen and implements, Z $20,000 (U.S. $12,400) for buildings, and so on"—but total government allocations to all agricultural cooperatives in that year were only Z $984,000 (U.S. $610,080),[31] in part because the economic slowdown in 1982–1983 led to a 52 percent budget cut for the Ministry of Lands. Under a nationalist development approach it is also important to maintain and expand the productive capacity of a sector while accommodating popular pressures for a more equitable distribution of assets. Model A farming goes far toward accomplishing the second goal, and the government advances the first by promoting commercial farming and taking a private managerial and profit approach to state farms. As a result, farm workers and landless peasants are left alone until they organize and articulate demands, and government has avoided "squandering" resources on a small cooperative subsector. The simultaneity of the approaches, however, promotes class formation in the rural areas, raises questions about the ambitions of a rising petit and bona fide agrarian bourgeoisie, and can maintain the myth of sharp lines between various subsectors of agriculture when in fact all are involved in the capitalist cash economy.[32] This simultaneity also obscures a more basic problem: the majority of Zimbabwe's rural population does not have access to a reasonably productive material base. Postindependence subsidies have continued to benefit mostly the large-scale farming sector, and that sector has continued to use prime land in capital-intensive, rather than labor-intensive, ways.

While the Zimbabwean government circumvented the agricultural crisis affecting most of Africa, successfully took on the regional role of food security, and produced a more reliable harvest of grains than South Africa, the country also suffered regular food shortages at the regional level that miscoordination among government agencies, mainly the GMB and the Department of Social Services, periodically exacerbated. Therefore, along with appeals for simple fine-tuning of an already robust agricultural sector, one heard the muted cries of food-short peasants during Zimbabwe's first five years of independence.

Manufacturing and Mining. Mining and manufacturing were singled out in government plans as pump-priming sectors of the economy—mining because it was the leading earner of foreign exchange, although contributing only 8 percent of GDP, and manufacturing because of its contribution to GDP (see Table 4.2). These sectors also generated considerable tax revenues for the state through direct taxes on companies and indirect sales and excise duties. The bottlenecks here, however, included high levels of inherited foreign investment in industry (much of it South African and British), less now in mining, and the fact that neither subsector absorbed the volume of workers it should: total industrial employment accommodated only about 4 percent of the country's working population, with mining taking 6 percent (about sixty-seven thousand workers) and manufacturing about 16 percent (about one hundred seventy-nine thousand workers).

Both *Growth with Equity* and the *TNDP* emphasized that the state would increase local participation, ownership, planning, and control of the mining sector and continue producing the forty minerals historically mined, the most important of which are listed in Table 4.4. Subsequently,

TABLE 4.4   Mineral Production in Zimbabwe, 1978–1988 (000 tons)

Minerals	1978	1980	1982	1984	1986	1988
Asbestos	248.9	250.9	197.7	165.3	163.6	186.6
Gold (fine oz)	399	367	426	478	478	481
Chrome (fine oz)	477.8	553.5	431.6	476.4	553.1	561.6
Coal[a]	3,065	3,134	2,769	3,109	4,047	5,065
Copper[b]	33.8	27.0	24.8	22.6	20.6	16.1
Nickel[b]	15,701	15,074	13,309	10,251	9,732	11,489
Iron ore	1,123	1,622	837	925	1,115	1,020
Silver (fine oz)	1,109	949	918	895	840	704
Cobalt	17	115	98	77	76	122
Tin metal	945	934	1,197	1,209	1,079	855
Other[c]						

[a]Coal sold but not produced.
[b]Quantity relates to metal content.
[c]Includes precious stones, phosphate, tantalite, magnesite, limestone, and lithium. No figures on tonnage, but total Z $ value for each year is comparable to the value for gold (average = Z $200,000) between 1978 and 1982 and then exceeds gold earnings by Z $100,000 to 600,000 between 1983 and 1988.

Source: Government of Zimbabwe, Quarterly Digest of Statistics (Harare: Central Statistical Office, March 1989), pp. 43–44.

the state established ownership of the iron and steel industry through the parastatal Zimbabwe Steel and Coal Authority and put tin mining under the parastatal Kamativi. The state is now the largest shareholder in the coal mining industry, with Anglo-American retaining management, and in 1984 it formed the Zimbabwe Mining Development Corporation, which bought out most South African interests in copper. Government participation in mining has also been evident through a mineral marketing corporation that oversees all international mineral and metal trade except gold, which the Reserve Bank of Zimbabwe buys. In this subsector, then, the state has intervened forcefully in ownership, but mineral processing is still in the hands of multinational corporations.

In keeping with its mixed-economy objectives, the government also looked with favor on the formation of mining cooperatives. By 1985 eleven chrome mining cooperatives were in existence but with members barely eking out an income; mining cooperatives distributed as little as Z $51 (U.S. $32) to members in 1985 (although one was able to pay Z $173 [U.S. $107]) because the government had not made sufficient money or training available and members often had little experience in business or even the skills needed for production. Moreover, there was some concern that "chrome cooperatives [we]re being established precisely to allow the big mining companies to lay off staff, and thus to effectively

Meat factory. Courtesy Zimbabwe Ministry of Information.

pay the same miners less money,"[33] based on individual production rather than equal pay standards.

Compared to plans for agriculture and mining, the government's intentions for private and cooperative manufacturing have lacked clarity and detail. The future of capital goods, which "provides a base for self-sustaining industrialisation and opportunities for training and development of skill,"[34] was not addressed in the first two development statements. The role of Zimbabwe's small chemical industry was understated in the early plans, despite the fact that Zimbabwe spends Z $5 to $6 million per year just importing resin for its plastic industry. Problems have also arisen in the textiles industry, which produces nearly 15 percent of the gross output of manufacturing, because cotton ginning capacity is not keeping pace with expanded outputs of Zimbabwe's cotton crop, even though the country may have a comparative advantage in this area. Zimbabwe could also stand to shift its manufacturing sector from a heavy reliance on metals, metal products, foodstuffs, drink, and tobacco to the production of more machinery.

Manufacturing cooperatives are twice as numerous as agricultural cooperatives but have been undersupported by the Ministry of Industry and Technology, which sees them as poor investment risks. The Small Enterprises Development Corporation has been equally profit oriented and concerned with providing seed money for conventional rural and urban businesses. Foreign exchange restrictions affect the operations of all manufacturing cooperatives, as do difficulties in procuring export licenses and even "stands," or spaces for work, from city and rural councils.

In order to bring more financial support to the mining and manufacturing sectors—particularly mining, which was hard hit by the global recession of the early 1980s—the government devalued its currency by 25 percent between December 1982 and January 1983. This move increased import costs for manufacturing, exacerbated already existing balance-of-payments problems, and led to a larger program of economic austerity and increased short-term borrowing. Zimbabwe had already "exercised the usual virtually automatic right to a drawdown in the low conditionality first credit tranche"[35] from the IMF in the first year of independence. In 1983 the country returned to the trough and found the IMF wanted it to correct a "debt service ratio [which] stood at an estimated 30% . . . a 300% increase in 3 years from the 1980 levels"[36] by reducing its spending, devaluing the dollar further, and compressing domestic demand. Under these terms the IMF granted Zimbabwe a U.S. $375 million loan of which $316 million was on standby until Zimbabwe adhered to the stipulated conditions.

In 1984 the IMF suspended the standby arrangements because Zimbabwe failed to meet IMF performance targets. The government had acted to curb the outflow of foreign exchange, freeze local prices, and reduce public investment on infrastructure. It was not, however, about to cut military spending, wages, or education expenses, and these amounted to 8.5 percent of GNP relative to 6.3 percent spent on productive sectors and 3.4 percent on production services. Although Zimbabwe was thus initiating its own rules of structural adjustment, its continued spending priorities played some havoc with an inherited problem of unemployment and still left it with a total government and government-guaranteed debt that had increased from U.S. $520 million in 1979 to almost U.S. $1,450 million in 1984.[37]

Increased foreign investment was one way out from under this burden. In 1982 the government issued guidelines according to which foreign capital would be welcome if it could make a "contribution to the economy, including the training of Zimbabweans"; enter joint ventures with domestic and state concerns; avoid diluting existing domestic participation in enterprises; undertake "intensive use of local raw materials and processed inputs . . . [and enter] areas in which labour-intensive technology and technology appropriate and easily adaptable is promoted"; and generate "exports within a reasonable period."[38] Government steadfastly refused to sign an agreement with New York's Overseas Private Investors Corporation—which insures private firms against financial losses that result from property expropriation, suspension of income and dividend remittances, and war/riot damages—arguing that the constitution of the country specifically prohibited the transfer of private property through any mechanism other than a willing buyer/willing seller mode. At the same time, the investment guidelines and the constitution alluded to "reasonable notice" of government intention to acquire property and authorized nationalizations in the interests of defense, public safety, or public order. This two-sided pledge—to uphold the willing buyer/willing seller clause and to provide compensation if it was not abided by— unsettled the nerves of would-be investors in the early years of Zimbabwean independence. Zimbabwe's strict foreign exchange controls also dampened their enthusiasm because it put a brake on imports.

The few firms drawn to Zimbabwe under these terms were not always then forced to conform to the rules. Government courted the food-producing and -processing company of Heinz for nearly nine months and in the final agreement allowed it to take over the ailing local firm of Olivine through a 51 percent controlling interest arrangement with the government. This ran counter to the guideline that existing domestic control should not be allowed to pass to foreign investors. But because the local firm was probably thereby saved from bankruptcy, Mugabe proclaimed, "Heinz and we are newly wed, and we are more than that. I think we have had our first child and there is great happiness in the family, indeed."[39] Dandy Chewing Gum was approved on the basis of its export potential, willingness to locate outside a major city, and plans to employ one hundred people; as for the company's product, chewing gum was certainly superfluous to Zimbabwe's development needs.

In addition to low levels of foreign investment the government had a difficult time attracting manufacturing and other nonfarm production and services to rural areas. It had anticipated that a growth-point strategy would eventuate in "Rural Service Centres which . . . provide all basic infrastructure, ha[ve] a strong residential component and offer a wide range of services. [These] will automatically attract rural non-farm activities . . . the whole range of activities connected with trading, manufacturing, construction, transport, and government and other services."[40] There are 450 such points now, and the program has brought modern bus stands, drains, market stalls, and new commercial ventures to areas of the country that had been barren, shabby, and eroded.[41] Eighty percent of the produce sold in such centers, however, comes from commercial farms, and virtually no major industry has relocated outside the preexisting town structure.[42] Some firms, in fact, have moved from smaller towns to large urban areas, prompting jokes about Zimbabwe's "death points."

Zimbabwe's overall scorecard for industrial development, therefore, was mixed during the first five years after independence. It seemed "government controls ha[d] reduced the freedom of isolated capitalist firms . . . [but without] creat[ing] an alternative dynamic, whether socialist or of a state-capitalist type."[43] One implication of government controls is that the interests of historically dominant and new entrepreneurs were reinforced during this time, while those seeking to enter the promised land of growth with equity struggled. Another is that Zimbabwe was indeed attempting to finance welfare-state capitalism "without the scale of productive capacity needed to sustain it."

Labor. Labor problems plagued government from the earliest days of independence. In 1977 more than 90 percent of black wage workers in Salisbury were living below the official poverty line, and 34 percent were unemployed or working in the nonwage informal sector.[44] The 1980 independence ceremonies had not even been held when a series of strikes broke out around the country, unleashing "a Pandora's box of militant labour protest and industrial action . . . a smouldering cauldron of labour restiveness,"[45] a crisis of expectations. By June more than sixty-five thousand industrial workers had been involved in strikes, mostly for higher wages but also in protest against a history of racist supervisors and arbitrary dismissals. The strikes spread to the nursing and teaching professions in 1981, and in 1982 bus drivers and railway firefighters struck.

The Mugabe government first admonished the workers to channel their complaints through the very arbitration procedures that had historically held them back. It then blamed the labor actions on "subversives" and called some strikes "nothing short of criminal."[46] When these tactics did not bring results, the new minister of labour said of workers, "I will crack my whip if they do not go back to work" and empowered the Swift Transport Company, controlled by British capital, to fire one thousand strikers and rehire people on a selective basis.[47]

These coercive moves reduced some militance, and the remainder of it was seemingly assuaged by minimum wage legislation introduced in 1980. As Table 4.5 shows, wages for industrial workers were set at Z $70 (U.S. $101.60 before devaluation) per month. Miners received a minimum of Z $43 (U.S. $62.41), plus other provisions, and agricultural and domestic workers were awarded Z $30 (U.S. $43.50) per month, plus housing and food subsidies. These minimums were increased dramatically in 1982 and thereafter went up yearly at a declining rate (except for 1987, when government instituted a wage and price freeze to bring down an inflation rate of nearly 20 percent [see Table 4.2]). The minimums, however, were never sufficient to hoist most workers above the poverty line of approximately Z $120 (U.S. $80) per month,

TABLE 4.5   Average and Minimum Monthly Wages by Sector, 1976–1984[a] (Z $)

Sectors	1976	1978	1980	1981	1982	1983	1984
Agriculture							
Average	19	23	32	53	71	80	—
Minimum	—	—	30	30	50	55	65
Mining, quarrying							
Average	73	94	131	177	214	236	270
Minimum	—	—	43	58	105	110	120
Manufacturing							
Average	129	150	196	242	280	313	329
Minimum	—	—	70	85	105	115	125
Private domestic							
Average	19	22	29	35	54	57	70
Minimum	—	—	30	30	50	55	65

[a]Average combines wages of professional skilled and semiskilled workers, with the minimum wage geared to the lowest skill and experience level.

Source: Government of Zimbabwe, Statistical Yearbook, 1987 (Harare: Central Statistical Office, 1987), p. 54; and Government of Zimbabwe, Socio-Economic Review of Zimbabwe, 1980–85 (Harare: Ministry of Finance, Economic Planning and Development, 1986), p. 91.

and by 1985 inflation had taken such a chunk out of wage increases that real wages were actually below what they had been in 1980.

To make wage policy stick in the face of industry concerns about lowered profits, government made it difficult for employers to fire workers and in 1985 followed up with the comprehensive Labour Relations Bill, which set forth a code of regulations on employment, wages, collective bargaining, settlement of disputes, registration of labor unions and organizations of employers, and duties and rights of workers' committees, employment councils, and boards. Hailed by the government as a bill of rights for all workers, including agricultural and domestic laborers, whose terms of employment were not covered by the predecessor Industrial Conciliation Act, the Labour Relations Act was also a vehicle for controlling the outbreak of future strikes. Workers in "essential services"—electricity, water, mining, communications, transport, fire service, sewage, sanitation, health, food and production, delivery, supply, and so on—which are most of the industries in Zimbabwe, were prohibited from striking. Others could strike only if redress of grievances had been attempted, unless issues of occupational safety were involved or the existence of a workers' committee or trade union was in question. The minister of labour was given extensive powers under this act to intervene in trade union administration and to annul collective bargaining agreements if they were injurious to consumers or to the economy.

Another wave of strikes, however, broke out that year, this time by workers in agro-industry who charged that their employers refused to follow wage increase guidelines. The outcome, alluded to earlier in this chapter, was that government modified wage stipulations for the 355 commercial farming, parastatal, and multinational corporations that argued they could not afford a large increase in wage bills during a recession. Agricultural workers thereby received a reduced increase of Z $85 (U.S. $52.50) per month, and workers classified as agro-industrial (the categories are a source of some confusion) were paid Z $35 (U.S. $21.70) a month less than the stipulated minimum. In 1984 the unemployment rate, inclusive of people engaged in the nonwage informal sector, was estimated at 14 percent, and a large number of seasonal workers were simply unprotected by most labor legislation.[48]

After the first wave of strikes, the government formalized the worker organizations involved in the unrest into workers' committees and works councils. The committees were to represent worker interests to firm managers and the government, while works councils, composed of workers and management, would serve as vehicles for communication within firms. Since then, these worker organizations have become liaison committees among workers, management, and state and operate mostly to "create 'harmonious' relations for the employer's benefit rather than extend workers' power over job control issues."[49]

The government also began regulating trade unions, most of which had been plagued by splinter elements. To discourage the latter, the government formed an umbrella organization, the Zimbabwe Congress of Trade Unions (ZCTU), whose aim was to register only one union from each industry. The new ZCTU, however, was soon accused of fomenting, rather than resolving, union splintering and of engaging in corrupt and inefficient practices. Certain of its leaders were accused of everything from nepotism to mismanaging funds, from failing to pay staff minimum wages to bullying affiliated unions and capitulating too readily to government agendas. At the second congress of the ZCTU in July 1985, people deemed more reflective of and sensitive to the rank and file of Zimbabwean workers were elected to head the organization. Charges of corruption and so forth kept recurring, however, and women union members added the complaint that they were given only token roles in the ZCTU and other unions.[50]

The First Five Years Revisited

In the first five years of independence references to a future economy catering to peasants and proletarians abounded. The signals to the left were "balanced," however, by moves to the center-right and by policies that encouraged peasant production as long as large-scale farming was not discouraged. The outcome—perhaps intended, perhaps not—was a mixed economy. Those years saw the repression of worker militance, caution toward foreign investors, and an emphasis on outward-oriented trade. There was some nationalization of key industries and modest support for cooperatives. Government's wage policy stayed within the structural boundaries of inherited inequity, yet expenditures on education and the military soared. Even though it seemed Zimbabwe was becoming a "socialist country without the prospect of socialism,"[51] it was at the same time not becoming an unregulated capitalist free-for-all.

THE ECONOMY SINCE 1985

In 1986 the *First Five Year National Development Plan, 1986–1990* was issued. This plan, the government claimed, was different from previous development statements because it recognized setbacks suffered in the early years of independence, including sustained unemployment, a growing budget deficit, a 33 percent debt/service ratio, a 20 percent inflation rate, and a manufacturing sector dependent on imports for intermediate and capital goods. The plan noted that trends in 1985, the last year of the *TNDP*, were improving slightly and repeated the pledge to transform the economy, improve employment opportunities, and so on. But this time the targets were more modest.

The Big Picture

The plan projected an annual growth in GDP of about 5 percent, subject to normal rainfall and a steadily improving international economy; increased investment in Zimbabwe's three productive sectors of agriculture, mining, and manufacturing; and improvements in the country's transportation system. Instead of holding to the earlier (and failed) commitment to resettle 162,000 families, the government pledged to settle only 15,000 families per year and to reorganize land use patterns in the communal areas in order to ensure self-sufficiency in food and cut the high costs of repeated drought relief in some areas. In a pilot villagization scheme begun in 1986, Agritex worked with communal area district councils to "consolidate" at least one village per council jurisdiction by demarcating arable from grazing lands, instituting irrigation schemes, and improving access to water for people and livestock. Reform of land use in the CAs represented a shift in emphasis from the first five years, when the focus was on resettlement, and inspired an ongoing debate about the points of strength and weakness in Zimbabwe's approaches to rural development.[52]

The five-year plan offered few departures from the *TNDP* for the mining sector, but the government claimed it would "increase its participation in the manufacturing industry because it is both the key sector in overall economic development, as well as the decisive sector in the physical restructuring of the economy."[53] It targeted subsectors of manufacturing for greater linkage with mining and committed itself to enter countertrade and other "offsetting programs" in order to reduce the import bill for capital goods. Cooperatives emerged once again as important vehicles for production, and government also spoke of encouraging small-scale industries as subcontractors and producers of basic consumer goods. As for unemployment, there was intent to create twenty-eight thousand jobs annually, still too few to absorb the 214,177 school leavers that the Ministry of Education projected for 1990,[54] with new investments coming from domestic and foreign sources at the ratio of sixty to forty.

Leftists, fearful that this plan represented a drift toward structural adjustment, began piling up arguments against it. One commentator said quite pointedly that the plan "doesn't seem to aim at a genuine socialist development—despite all the expressed intentions . . . [because it] favours exports over local markets; foreign needs over local ones; capital intensive over labour intensive industries; urban over rural development; and foreign capital over local capital."[55] The plan's target figures for resettlement, such critics claimed, were not based on precise estimates of how many people needed land and wanted to be resettled. And in accommodating only a fraction of job seekers, the plan was seen to "take not a 'people-oriented' approach to planning, but a 'production-oriented' approach to it. In other words, instead of asking how the 8,5 million people of Zimbabwe can best employ themselves in creative and productive work, the Plan sets out 'production targets' and on that basis it has determined how many people can fit into those targets."[56]

It was more common, however, for the socialist idealism of the first five years to drop away or simply lose its bite and be replaced by more technical considerations about the performance of the telephone system and commuter buses, about cement shortages and a rising crime rate, about spare parts for cars and more foreign investment. This shift in emphasis was well under way when the minister of finance, economic planning, and development, Bernard Chidzero, opened his 1987 budget statement to Parliament by saying that "the economic picture in 1986/87 turns out to be worse than I projected this time last year."[57] GDP had grown only about 0.2 percent, primarily because agricultural value added had fallen by an estimated 12 percent under conditions of erratic rains, and efforts to keep imports low had had an adverse effect on industrial production. These performances threw the economy off the more modest targets of the five-year plan: "The three major productive sectors—agriculture, mining and manufacturing—taken together actually declined by 3.5 per cent . . . [and] if we are to meet our Plan target of overall average annual growth of about 5 per cent over the five-year Plan period, growth for the remaining four years will have to average at least 6 per cent annually."[58]

In 1988 the economy improved marginally under a 5 percent growth rate, which reflected a good rainy season and some improvement in manufacturing. But it was still necessary to wrestle with shortages of foreign exchange, import levels under the economy's requirements, and unemployment reaching nine hundred thousand. Expenditures were running 9 percent over revenues (down from 22 percent the previous year), and the foreign debt, a mere 21.9 percent of total central government debt in 1980, was 40 percent by the middle of 1988. The debt/service ratio, however, had dropped a bit from the previous year and stood at a little more than 32 percent; Chidzero estimated that "per every dollar we spend, twenty cents is borrowed, of which five cents go to finance recurrent expenditure."[59] The leading indicators for 1989 showed a growth rate slowed to between 3 and 4 percent, although mining was doing particularly well and agriculture was again strong. By now concern had shifted again from monitoring economic performance to devising a program of sustained recovery.

Export-oriented trade figured prominently in the recovery effort as a source of much-needed foreign exchange. From 1984 on, as Table 4.6 indicates, the government recorded a favorable overall trade balance for Zimbabwe. Table 4.7 shows, for instance, that the United Kingdom, the Federal Republic of Germany (FRG), Netherlands, Italy, France, and Switzerland accounted for 33 percent of Zimbabwe's exports in 1987 and 32 percent of its imports. The United States was the sixth largest market for Zimbabwean goods in 1986 and moved into fourth place in 1987. Only with South Africa did Zimbabwe chronically run a trade deficit, while at the other end of the spectrum the socialist bloc countries together and singly did not make the top ten of trading partners with Zimbabwe; in 1987 the PRC contributed less than 2 percent of Zimbabwe's external markets and less than 1 percent of its imports. Zimbabwe's history of slight trade surpluses with most partners, however, could not keep pace with mounting levels of foreign and domestic debt, and in 1987 the government instituted an export-promotion loan program for agriculture and mining; manufacturing was already covered by a similar program to orient it away from import substitution and toward overseas markets in textiles, clothing, processed foods, leather, furniture, and horticulture.[60] Although it was uncertain whether the world economic situation could sustain the export strategy, the government tried to

TABLE 4.6　Principal Commodity Exports and Imports, 1979–1985
(as % of external trade)

Commodities	1979	1980	1983	1985
Exports				
Food products	17	13	15	16
Beverages, tobacco	13	16	23	24
Crude materials except fuels	23	22	18	19
Manufactured goods	34	36	33	32
Machinery, transport, radio,				
TV, electrical equipment	5	2	2	2
Imports				
Machinery, transport, radio,				
TV, electrical equipment	23	26	34	29
Mineral fuels, electricity, etc.	30	24	21	24
Manufactured goods	17	19	15	16
Chemical and related goods	14	14	14	15
Visible balance external				
trade (in Z $ millions)	166.4	99.8	88.6	349.0

Sources: Government of Zimbabwe, Statistical Yearbook 1987 (Harare: Central Statistical Office, 1987), p. 170; Government of Zimbabwe, Quarterly Digest of Statistics (Harare: Central Statistical Office, June 1989), p. 19.

increase foreign exchange to export industrial sectors by a small amount and encouraged Parliament to waive import duty and sales tax on capital equipment for approved export projects.

The government also looked to foreign investment as an answer and established an investment register to speed the approval process while studying "an appropriate investment incentive framework for both local and foreign investors in projects and programmes consistent with national development objectives."[61] In 1989 a new investment code increased profit repatriation from 50 percent to 100 percent of after-tax profits, so long as the investment was in a high-priority project. Alongside this the government signed the Multilateral Investment Guarantee Accord with the World Bank and slowly devalued the Zimbabwe dollar against major trading currencies.

These actions caused another predictable flurry of controversy, with much handwringing among leftists and reformists themselves wondering whether a period of trade liberalization could be undercut by the government budget deficit and by repatriation losses among manufacturers with less than 25 percent foreign assets, the new cutoff figure for local versus foreign ownership. It was already clear that as new foreign investment had entered Zimbabwe in the late 1980s—mainly through Mazda in Willowvale, Cluff Minerals in Freda and Rebecca gold mines,

TABLE 4.7 Zimbabwe's Principal Trading Partners[a]

Country	Exports[b]			Imports[b]		
	1981	1985	1987[c]	1981	1985	1987[c]
Belgium	32,411	51,779	69,140	16,697	21,116	14,300
United Kingdom	61,299	200,063	244,485	101,922	151,082	200,268
FRG	73,009	153,448	193,595	73,773	100,452	151,953
Netherlands	26,874	47,192	68,284	—	35,833	48,369
Italy	44,013	91,471	83,673	21,116	43,805	52,501
Switzerland	16,796	11,572	21,588	21,447	21,950	37,860
France	13,087	20,070	21,062	37,130	47,839	64,029
PRC	24,641	58,507	30,411	1,230	13,611	5,716
Czechoslovakia	—	6,726	7,793	—	6,690	10,890
GDR	—	21,068	7,409	—	16,684	3,495
Malawi	14,226	20,130	29,132	15,038	3,994	5,150
Mozambique	11,154	20,585	70,280	—	—	—
Botswana	28,678	59,592	104,859	17,362	39,113	99,201
South Africa	192,177	166,547	185,427	279,652	273,159	361,457
United States	69,770	125,807	129,455	74,423	146,728	163,538
Total[d]	888,067	1,545,343	1,892,240	1,017,694	1,446,529	1,741,763

[a]At 1987 prices, Z $1 = U.S. $.59.
[b]In thousands of Z $.
[c]At 1989 prices, Z $1 = U.S. $.46.
[d]Total trade with all countries.

Sources: Government of Zimbabwe, Quarterly Digest of Statistics (Harare: Central Statistical Office, March 1989), pp. 22–23; Government of Zimbabwe, Statistical Yearbook 1987 (Harare: Central Statistical Office, 1987), pp. 177–178.

and Delta Gold in Hartley Platinum—aged and obsolete equipment was becoming more characteristic of locally owned firms. This made factory work more dangerous. Several locally owned food-processing plants I studied in 1988 had shocking work conditions. One section of the floor in a cookie factory was covered with slimy water, and workers exposed to acids showed me their raw, unprotected hands as managers and trade union representatives looked on. Many clothing factories at the heart of Zimbabwe's export push did not issue workers protective clothing or try to ventilate workrooms thick with dust. In some cases members of workers committees were firmly in the palm of management's hand and did little to force a confrontation on these problems.

Trade and investment liberalization was coupled with reductions in state expenditures for services and the foisting of increasingly more user-payer costs on local communities. Yet the government remembered some of its promises of equity with growth. Chidzero closed his 1988 budget address with these words: "Despite all efforts and relentless search, I could find no fiscal knife sharp enough, or for that matter

TABLE 4.8   Population Estimates (in thousands)

Year	Population
1910	880
1920	1,130
1930	1,430
1940	1,940
1950	2,730
1960	3,840
1970	5,310
1975	6,280
1979	7,130
1980	7,360
1982	7,610
1984	7,950
1986	8,410
1988	8,880
1989	9,122

Source: Government of Zimbabwe, Quarterly Digest of Statistics (Harare: Central Statistical Office, June 1989), p. 1.

blunt enough, to cut down expenditures at this stage on such votes as Education, Defence and subsidies."[62] Although defense spending is not an issue of equity, education and subsidies on food and housing are, and it is in these matters that the effects of Zimbabwe's years of economic struggle on the average citizen can be clearly seen.

The Picture for the Average Zimbabwean

If we judge by letters to the Zimbabwean press and by topics raised in the 1990 election campaigns, the big economic issues for average Zimbabweans have become unemployment and low wages, transportation, and the cost of social services.

Unemployment and Low Wages. Zimbabwe's population stands at more than 9 million, and there are projections of 12.4 million people by the year 2000 if the present growth rate of 3 percent remains steady (see Table 4.8). In order to accommodate this increase, the economy must grow at 5 percent per annum at the least. Between 1980 and 1989, however, growth averaged only 3.8 percent, and the cost of creating a single job in manufacturing escalated to nearly Z $86,000 (approximately U.S. $43,000). Unemployment is the obvious consequence of these trends, and, in a twist of irony, that problem is exacerbated by Zimbabwe's spectacular successes in education.

Forty-seven percent of the population is younger than fifteen years of age and receives at least primary education, mostly at government expense. Between 1979 and 1985 school enrollments increased from

819,000 to 2.26 million, and in the 1989–1990 fiscal year alone government allocated 23 percent of the total recurrent expenditure to the Ministry of Primary and Secondary Education. Chidzero explained that this expenditure "represent[s] investment in human resources to spearhead development in the future."[63] But it was also widely acknowledged that to "redirect limited Budgetary resources to build the base for sustainable growth, efforts [would have to be] made to slow down the rate of growth of education expenditures in the Budget."[64] Education Minister Fay Chung added the caution that "one must . . . look seriously at the question of whether the investment in education and training is balanced in terms of ensuring that school-leavers will be able to find employment once they have completed their studies."[65] For the 1990–1991 fiscal year Chidzero took the plunge away from "free" primary education and reintroduced school fees, effective in 1991–1992.

Educational enrollments have outstripped teacher training and supplies: 30 to 45 percent of Zimbabwe's teachers now have only marginal training, there is a chronic shortage of textbooks and furniture, and teacher/student ratios range from one to thirty to one to thirty-three. One result is that the system has difficulty shepherding most students through British-style exams for secondary and higher education; it is not uncommon for 80 percent of students in a single district to achieve unacceptable results. The excessive failure rate limits young people's employment options. Yet it is also the case that should they pass and go on to higher levels of education, the 30 percent unemployment figure stares them in the face. Education is greatly valued as a basic human need, however, and even under these constraints the number of students at the University of Zimbabwe has doubled from the mid-1980s. A new, more technically oriented university has been planned for Bulawayo, which may help redirect student aims from hard-to-find white-collar jobs to development-oriented fields.

As it stands, car thefts are now ubiquitous in the cities, and destitute youths must get by guarding cars or finding parking places for a pleaded fee. Wage earners are in a better position but are by no means well-off. As Table 4.9 indicates, the industrial working class of mining, quarrying, and manufacturing laborers numbers nearly a quarter million and as of July 1989 averaged at least Z $210 (U.S. $100) per month in pay. The government calculated at the time that a family of six eating two meals a day with plenty of bread and one with plenty of sadza (the mealie porridge staple) could get by with Z $4 (less than U.S. $3) to spare per month.[66] Workers themselves disputed this, citing the rising costs of maintaining under- and unemployed family members.

More than one hundred thousand people continue the colonial tradition of serving as domestic laborers in the homes of the state and

TABLE 4.9   Sectoral Trends in Zimbabwean Employment

Sector	1975	1980	1985	1987
Agriculture, forestry, fishing	363,800	327,000	274,600	—
Mining, quarrying	62,600	66,200	55,200	57,400
Manufacturing	156,000	159,400	171,900	181,000
Private domestic	124,100	108,000	99,100	101,000
Public administration	48,900	71,100	89,100	91,300
Education	36,000	41,900	92,200	99,200
Health	13,500	15,200	20,500	24,300

Source: Government of Zimbabwe, Quarterly Digest of Statistics (Harare: Central Statistical Office, June 1989), p. 8.

nonstate bourgeoisies, while their families usually stay behind in rural areas. Wages for domestics rose from Z $30 in 1980 (U.S. $47) to the stipulated 1989 minimum of Z $116 (U.S. $55) per month, on top of which they were paid a monthly allowance of Z $12.50 (U.S. $6) if not provided with accommodation, transportation, utilities, and fuel. Cook-housekeepers made Z $2 (U.S. $.92) more per month, while minders of babies and the elderly made a minimum of Z $120 (U.S. $57), plus allowances. With the cost of living triple what it was at independence—mealie meal in 1989 was Z $4 (U.S. $1.84) higher than in 1988—these increases remain inadequate. The Zimbabwe Domestic and Allied Workers Union estimated that to maintain the purchasing power of the 1982 minimum wage (of Z $50 or U.S. $66) the lowest paid domestic workers needed Z $106.11 (U.S. $63.54) in 1987,[67] or Z $2 more per month than what they were paid in 1988.

The plight of the approximately 260,000 agricultural farm workers (the mostly male rural proletariat) has already been shown to be poor; most permanent workers average only a little more than domestic workers, and agro-industrial workers make a minimum of Z $191.76 (U.S. $91.28). Meanwhile, the seasonals slash soybeans, strip tobacco, or pick cotton for piecework pay with no protection from layoffs. The General Agricultural and Plantation Workers' Union (GAPWUZ) is one of the weaker unions in Zimbabwe, despite its mission to represent the bulk of Zimbabwe's workers, and it balefully solicits commercial farmers (and managers of state farms) to improve pay and to upgrade clinics and the quality of worker housing. The union's efforts are hindered by low membership—workers often complain that they rarely see benefits from their dues—and low support by a government conscious of private-sector rights and of the need to continue some discrimination in the agricultural sector in order to facilitate economic growth.[68]

Finally, even though peasant producers as a whole are doing better, their average yearly income of Z $1,410 (U.S. $875) in 1985 was considerably below the income of urban industrial workers.[69] This peasantry has been depicted as pursuing a well-defined project of restoring and safeguarding the small-scale farmer option in Zimbabwe.[70] It is isolated, however, in the sense of not having official alliances with other workers, owing in part to its geographical dispersion and to the country's poor rural communication system. There are also rural cleavages between the historically powerful Commercial Farmers' Union (CFU), its ally the Zimbabwe National Farmers' Union of former purchase area farmers, and the National Farmers' Association of Zimbabwe of communal small-holders. The latter, while it by no means represents only the interests of the 10 percent or so of substantial CA peasants, does tend to adopt the "ideology of the settler agricultural bureaucracy and the other farmers' union that CA dwellers can be divided between 'genuine farmers' and those who are not either because of absence or some purported lack of knowledge or indifference."[71] Low levels of peasant unionization and the common practice of defying boundaries separating commercial and communal lands through squatting, cutting fences, and running cattle on the neighbors' land signify that some in this large and differentiated class are semidisengaged from the state and may eventually develop more effective instruments to give voice to their complaints.

A particularly explosive issue for communal area residents may be the new national land policy, announced in 1990 after the elections and after the willing seller/willing buyer provision of the constitution had expired. Shifting its emphasis once again to resettlement, government promised to acquire five million more hectares of commercial farm land to resettle 110,000 families and introduced land price controls; payment in local, rather than foreign, currency; a tax on underused land; controls on the size of farms; and a limit of one farm per owner. Pronouncing this the second phase of resettlement—the first phase catered to landless and destitute people who usually lacked tools and farming experience as well as land—government officials emphasized that the policy would resettle productive farmers. The emphasis would thus shift to better-off farmers, and land for them would be procured in higher rainfall areas of the country.

Jocelyn Alexander argues that despite "the seemingly radical content of the new land policy and government rhetoric, the policy is likely to result in continuity rather than change,"[72] in part because budget and staff increases have not been forthcoming to ministries involved in resettlement (and are unlikely to materialize during a period of "home-grown" structural adjustment) and because the policy privileges better-off farmers at a time when high urban unemployment and continuing

impoverishment and landlessness in some CAs argue for a more comprehensive approach. In addition, the target of 110,000 new settlers
comes "simply by subtracting the number already settled from the 1982
national plan target. No attempt was made to accommodate population
growth or other changes which had occurred in the intervening eight
years."[73] Finally, the desire to obtain resettlement lands in high rainfall
areas could negatively affect Matabeleland owing to its location in a
dry region. Overall, "the new policy's principle effect on the commercial
farm sector is likely to be a proliferation of communal area encroach-
ment."[74] Poach-grazing, fence-cutting, and squatting could increase wher-
ever poor CA farmers, including women and young men, and the
unemployed see new opportunities pass them by once again, just as
they did during the days of the NLHA.

Workers in collective cooperative production are not doing well,
and women members may be doing especially poorly. Among five
collective cooperatives I studied in 1988, not one had successfully done
away with inherited practices of sexually divided labor. In one case,
male members gathered to talk to me, while women cleaned up from
breakfast. In another, wives of founding members complained that
husbands would not allow them to join the cooperative. The cooperative
spirit is also held back by weak unionization through the Organization
of Collective Cooperatives of Zimbabwe (OCCZIM). Started by ex-
combatants after independence, this union has not been able to forge
consensus on the purpose of the organization or gain visibility throughout
the countryside. OCCZIM suffers from the perception that it competes
with government for the loyalties of cooperators and for power over
cooperatives themselves. Apropos of that, representatives from fifty
women's cooperatives rejected OCCZIM's plea in 1988 to work with it
in improving marketing and supply networks; as one spokeswoman said
by way of a public retort, "OCCZIM is run by men for men and we
want marketing and supply arrangements for women."[75]

Transportation. Transportation is breaking down at an alarming and
economy-threatening rate, which influences the economic fortunes of all
Zimbabweans. In 1988 there was a severe shortage of vehicles to move
cotton from communal areas in the Midlands to the nearest Cotton
Marketing Board and elsewhere to move grains to the GMB in time to
avoid seasonal rains. Then a shortage of railroad cars and locomotives
curtailed shipments of coal from Hwange to thermal power stations. A
newspaper editorial suggested that if these problems were added to
others, "such as a shortage of consumer goods that may arise out of
failure to move imports of vital raw materials or spares, the repercussions
of the shortage become really frightening."[76]

In 1989 the Ministry of National Supplies entered barter deals with Japan, Britain, and other European countries for spare parts to fix more than one thousand government vehicles (50 percent of the fleet) and innumerable privately owned buses that were out of service. Some remaining vehicles were operating with bald tires and faulty brakes, and although the ministry asked for an annual financial allocation of Z $31 million (U.S. $14.26 million) just for government vehicles, it received only Z $4 million (U.S. $1.84 million). For a country once envied for its transport infrastructure, this has been a difficult blow to absorb. For average Zimbabweans it means long delays getting to and from work; in the case of workers from Chitungwiza township, near Harare, the delays add four hours or more to the average workday. Not surprisingly, this issue came up repeatedly in the 1990 election campaigns, and in a grand political gesture the government suddenly produced new buses for some commuter routes and resurrected plans to build a rail system connecting several commuter townships, including Chitungwiza, with Harare.

Costs of Social Services. Zimbabwean parents routinely pay more education costs than the phrase "free primary education" signifies, and once their children reach secondary school, parents pay all the fees. A 1989 report estimated that school uniforms and fees came to at least Z $300 (U.S. $143) for Form One (junior high) students attending day schools and Z $600 (U.S. $285) for boarding students. This figure included all the components noted in Table 4.10. For rural families with incomes of less than Z $800 (U.S. $400) per year, it is a tremendous hardship to come up with uniforms and fees for more than one child, let alone user-payer building fees and extras for recreation. Rural women sometimes claim they join cooperatives or farm work groups precisely to earn the extra bit that makes education possible for their children, particularly for the girls. In another of Zimbabwe's many ironies, however, such cooperatives often specialize in producing school uniforms at lower prices than most commercial companies charge, but few can obtain local school contracts.

Although other social services have improved since independence, they also carry hidden costs for average people. In the area of health care the Zimbabwe government augmented the urban-based curative approach it inherited from Rhodesia by emphasizing preventive care in rural areas, where "90% of the causes of diseases were preventable."[77] The government also undertook to improve primary health care and by 1989 had completed 450 out of a projected 681 rural health care centers. Approximately seven thousand health workers were regularly inoculating children, teaching prenatal care and nutrition, and handling almost 60 percent of births. Ahead of most African countries Zimbabwe also

TABLE 4.10 Typical Expenditures on School Uniforms in Zimbabwe, 1989

Sex of Child	Clothing Costs[a]
Boy	
Shorts	18.25
Shirt	18.15
Jersey	28.00
Blazer	55.00
Socks	4.50
Tie	5.10
Hat	4.50
Shoes	33.00
Total	166.50
Girl	
Dress	34.05
Shoes	33.00
Jersey	28.00
Blazer	55.00
Socks	3.75
Hat	10.95
Tie	5.25
Total	170.00

[a]Z $1 = U.S. $.46.

Source: Compiled from Sunday Mail, January 8, 1989, p. 1.

initiated a nationwide campaign to control the outbreak of AIDS, which now claims more than sixteen hundred victims in Zimbabwe;[78] began performing open heart surgery in Harare; and is currently developing a "test-tube" baby program.

There are several problems with the country's health programs, however, that affect access by Zimbabwe's citizens. First, the government extends free public medical service to people earning less than Z $150 (U.S. $75) per month, but because minimum wages are now above that level for many workers, the gap is filled, to the degree it is at all, by costly medical insurance. Second, as a result of poor working and living conditions, particularly on commercial farms, there is only so much a health program can do to prevent diseases such as tuberculosis; improved standards of living are needed in these cases. Third, achieving an even distribution of doctors throughout the country is problematic. The government bonds new physicians to the Ministry of Health in order to monitor this problem, but in 1988 some went on strike over conditions of service, salaries, and periods of bonding. Government was not in a position to balk at their demands in a system where more lucrative

Immunizations. Courtesy Zimbabwe Ministry of Information.

private health care already threatens the delivery of an integrated health program.[79]

In regard to housing, there are two issues: the spatial arrangement of wealthy suburbs, teeming townships, traditional rural areas, growth points, and intermediate center city flats for up-and-coming bureaucrats; and high prices. Instead of developing integrated urban and rural plans to achieve a more racially and socioeconomically balanced spatial arrangement, the government tends to reinforce inherited patterns of housing. Low-income housing is all but confined to the old Rhodesian townships and to new towns that mimic them, and both rural and urban housing programs are stymied by continually low budget allocations for the Ministry of Construction and National Housing: in 1982–1983 the ministry received Z $5.2 million (U.S. $5.7 million) more than it had requested, but in subsequent years this windfall turned into shortfalls of between Z $63 and Z $81 million below requests.

As a result, scarcity drives up prices of urban housing made worse by a construction industry slump between 1982 and 1986; by shortages of building materials, particularly cement, door frames, and electric supplies; and by ongoing problems with transport. The prices for houses in low-density suburbs often begin at Z $120,000 (near U.S. $60,000), and rents are more than Z $1,000 per month (nearly U.S. $500). While many rural dwellers continue to live in huts, the government builds inadequately small two-bedroom houses in the range of Z $15,000–20,000 (U.S. $7,500–10,000) in existing or new cement townships for the settled proletariat. Urban and rural dwellings, however, often merge when rural people come to the cities seeking employment, stay with their kin, and eke out a marginal living in the informal unwaged sector selling services or small surpluses. Extra family members add to the expenses of urban wage earners and cast shadows across government cost-of-living calculations. There is also a housing and price problem in the rural growth points, and in partial recognition of this the government announced in 1990 the introduction of titled deeds to property in those areas. Nevertheless, President Mugabe has acknowledged that "in the area of housing we are simply not making progress."[80]

CONCLUSIONS

Finance Minister Bernard Chidzero claimed in 1989 that Zimbabwe was not abandoning socialist goals. In explaining less-than-socialist policies, such as the new investment code, he said that these were "adaptations to changing circumstances in the true nature of the dialectic process."[81] The implication of this remark is that if Zimbabwe's development policies remove Marxism-Leninism from immediate concern, this does not mean that capitalist decisions made in the present will have capitalist results in the end. The possibility looms, however, that such contradictions have extended the political exercise of persuasive pretense into the economic arena and have so muddled most of Zimbabwe's policies that even basic services can no longer be carried by the state, to say nothing of the poor record on redistributing land—a productive asset—more equitably.

Chidzero seemed ready to end the dialectics in 1990, when his annual budget statement called for school fees beginning in 1991, a removal of taxes on incomes of less than Z $3,600 (U.S. $1,440), a 5 percent reduction in company taxes, and price decontrols. Although these measures seemed to herald the "return" of capitalism, they in fact represented another commingling of old and new at the point of hyphenated capitalism and socialism. This "new direction" will resonate with the Rhodesian practice of praising capitalism while simultaneously molding it into a socialism-for-whites (this time favoring investing blacks and whites). This direction will simultaneously mark a departure from the ad hoc socialism-for-blacks that has gripped rhetoric and some policies in recent years and may trumpet the new "wisdom" emanating from Eastern Europe according to which socialism-for-some-groups-only does not sustain all the rest.

At this juncture in history Zimbabwe is not alone in its search for the in-betweens of political economy that shake off the sacred shibboleths of the past and present. Its approach up to now has offered only some consolation to average Zimbabweans, who get more now in the way of education and health services but who also face nagging continuities in their personal economic circumstances.

NOTES

1. Colin Stoneman and Lionel Cliffe, *Zimbabwe: Politics, Economics and Society* (London: Pinter, 1989), p. 121.

2. X. M. Kadhani, "The Economy: Issues, Problems and Prospects," in *Zimbabwe: The Political Economy of Transition, 1980–86,* ed. Ibbo Mandaza (Dakar: Codesria, 1986), p. 105.

3. U.S. Department of Commerce, "Marketing in Zimbabwe," *Overseas Business Reports* (August 1981): 10.

4. Ministry of Economic Planning and Development, *Annual Economic Review of Zimbabwe* (Harare: Government Printer, August 1981), p. 2.

5. Ibid., p. 14.

6. Government of Zimbabwe, *Growth with Equity: An Economic Policy Statement* (Harare: Government Printer, February 1981), pp. 1–2.

7. Ibid., p. 2.

8. Government of Zimbabwe, *Transitional National Development Plan: 1982/83–1984/85,* vol. 1 (Harare: Department of Finance, Economic Planning, and Development, 1982), p. 1.

9. See Michael Bratton, "Patterns of Development and Underdevelopment," *International Studies Quarterly,* 26, no. 3 (1982): 333–372, for a discussion of nationalist development. For analyses of an alternative Zimbabwean model of development, see Peter Robinson, "Relaxing the Constraints," and Colin Stoneman, "Some Concluding Thoughts," in *Zimbabwe's Prospects: Issues of Race, Class, State and Capital in Southern Africa,* ed. Colin Stoneman (London: Macmillan, 1988), pp. 348–360, 361–368.

10. Government of Zimbabwe, *Growth with Equity,* p. 5.

11. Clever Mumbengegwi, "Continuity and Change in Agricultural Policy," in Mandaza, ed., *Zimbabwe,* pp. 203–222.

12. Stoneman and Cliffe, *Zimbabwe,* p. 130.

13. Colin Stoneman, "Agriculture," in *Zimbabwe's Inheritance,* ed. Colin Stoneman (London: Macmillan, 1981), p. 134.

14. Mumbengegwi, "Continuity and Change," p. 211.

15. Teresa Chimombe, "Foreign Capital," in Mandaza, ed., *Zimbabwe,* pp. 131–132.

16. Ray Bush and Lionel Cliffe, "Agrarian Policy in Migrant Labour Societies: Reform or Transformation in Zimbabwe?" *Review of African Political Economy,* no. 29 (1984): 93.

17. Michael Bratton, "The Comrades and the Countryside: The Politics of Agricultural Policy in Zimbabwe," *World Politics* 39, no. 2 (1987): 174–202.

18. E. H. Elwell, "An Assessment of Soil Erosion in Zimbabwe," quoted in Michael J. Drinkwater, "The State and Agrarian Change in Zimbabwe's Communal Areas: An Application of Critical Theory" (Ph.D. diss., University of East Anglia, Norwich, December 1988), p. 143.

19. Drinkwater, "The State." In support of this view, see S. Sanford, *Livestock in the Communal Areas of Zimbabwe* (London: ODI, 1982).

20. Susan Jacobs, "State, Class, and Gendered Models of Land Resettlement," in *Women and the State in Africa*, ed. Jane Parpart and Kathleen Staudt (Boulder, Colo.: Lynne Rienner, 1989), p. 170.

21. On the difficulties faced by Model B participants, see Andrew Nyathi with John Hoffman, *Tomorrow Is Built Today: Experiences of War, Colonialism and the Struggle for Collective Cooperatives in Zimbabwe* (Harare: Anvil Press, 1990).

22. See discussion in S. Moyo, "The Land Question," in Mandaza, ed., *Zimbabwe*, pp. 165–202.

23. Daniel Weiner, "Land and Agricultural Development," in Stoneman, ed., *Zimbabwe's Prospects*, p. 72.

24. Ibid., p. 73.

25. Moyo, "The Land Question," p. 188.

26. A. M. Hawkins, *Commercial Agriculture in Zimbabwe: 1985–6*, quoted in Weiner, "Land," p. 85, note 3.

27. Drinkwater, "The State," pp. 114–115.

28. Jocelyn Alexander, "The Unsettled Land: The Politics of Land Redistribution in Matabeleland, 1980–1990" (December 1990, unpublished paper), p. 32.

29. Weiner, "Land," p. 76.

30. Ibid., p. 79.

31. Joseph Hanlon, "Producer Cooperatives and the Government of Zimbabwe" (1986, unpublished paper), p. 10.

32. Jane Adams, "Economic Differentiation and Wage Labour in Rural Zimbabwe" (Paper presented at the African Studies Association meeting, October 1988); and Angela Cheater, *Idioms of Accumulation: Rural Development and Class Formation Among Freeholders in Zimbabwe* (Gweru: Mambo Press, 1984).

33. Hanlon, "Producer Cooperatives," p. 19.

34. Daniel Ndlela, "Problems of Industrialization," in Mandaza, ed., *Zimbabwe*, p. 150.

35. Kadhani, "The Economy," p. 112.

36. Ibid.

37. Nelson Moyo, "A Hostile World Economic Climate?" in Stoneman, ed., *Zimbabwe's Prospects*, p. 185.

38. Government of Zimbabwe, *Foreign Investment: Policy, Guidelines and Procedures* (Harare: Government Printer, September 1982), p. 1

39. Robert Mugabe, J. J. Heinz Company Foundation Distinguished Lecture, University of Pittsburgh, Pittsburgh, Pennsylvania, October 3, 1984.

40. Whitsun Foundation, *Rural Service Centres Development Study* (Salisbury: Witsun Foundation, 1980), pp. 60–61.

41. Des Gasper, "Rural Growth Points and Rural Industries in Zimbabwe—Ideologies and Policies," *Development and Change* 19, no. 3 (1988): 425–466.

42. M. Gottlicher, "The Influence of Rural Service Centres and Growth Points on Rural Development" (Department of Rural and Urban Planning, University of Zimbabwe, 1987, unpublished paper); and K. Wekwete, "Growth Centre Policy in Zimbabwe—A Focus on District Centres" (Department of Rural and Urban Planning, University of Zimbabwe, 1987, unpublished paper).

43. Stoneman and Cliffe, *Zimbabwe*, p. 120.

44. See discussion in Government of Zimbabwe, *Report of the Commission of Inquiry into Incomes, Prices and Conditions of Service* (Harare: Government Printer, 1981).

45. Lloyd Sachikonye, "State, Capital and Trade Unions," in Mandaza, ed., *Zimbabwe*, p. 252.

46. Robert Mugabe, quoted in *Rhodesian Herald*, March 26, 1980.

47. K. Kangai, quoted in *Rhodesian Herald*, May 30, 1980; discussed in B. Mitchell, "The State and the Workers Movement in Zimbabwe," *South African Labour Bulletin* 12, nos. 6–7 (1987).

48. See discussion in T. Shopo and S. Moyo, *Vulnerable Working Households in Zimbabwe's Segmented Labour Markets*, Working Paper no. 5 (Harare: Zimbabwe Institute of Development Studies, n.d.).

49. See discussion in Brian Wood, "Roots of Trade Union Weakness in Post-Independence Zimbabwe," *South African Labour Bulletin* 12, nos. 6–7 (1987): 69.

50. For a government perspective on these problems, see Government of Zimbabwe, *Labour and Economy: Report of the National Trade Unions Survey, Zimbabwe, 1984*, vol. 1, sect. 2 (Harare: Ministry of Labour, Manpower Planning, and Social Welfare, 1984). Also see Brian Wood, "Trade-Union Organisation and the Working Class," in Stoneman, ed., *Zimbabwe's Prospects*, pp. 284–308.

51. Senior official of ZANU(PF) as quoted by David Caute, "Mugabe Brooks No Opposition," *The Nation* 31 (August 1985): 140.

52. Compare Jeffrey Herbst's relatively upbeat analysis in *State Politics in Zimbabwe* (Berkeley and Los Angeles: University of California Press, 1990), Chapter 3, with Drinkwater, "The State," and Alexander, "The Unsettled Land."

53. Government of Zimbabwe, *First Five Year National Development Plan, 1986–1990* (Harare: Government Printer, 1986), p. 30.

54. Fay Chung, "Education: Revolution or Reform," in Stoneman, ed., *Zimbabwe's Prospects*, p. 130.

55. W. E. Eigel, "Industrial Development in Zimbabwe: The Prospects of the New Five Year National Development Plan, 1986–1990," *Social Change and Development* 16 (April 1987): 2.

56. "People Take Second Place in the Plan," *Moto Magazine*, no. 46, p. 5.

57. Bernard Chidzero, *Budget Statement, 1987* (Harare: Government Printer, July 29, 1987), p. 1.

58. Ibid., p. 5.

59. Bernard Chidzero, *Budget Statement, 1988* (Harare: Government Printer, July 28, 1988), p. 15.

60. Moyo, "A Hostile World Economic Climate?" p. 183.

61. Chidzero, *Budget Statement, 1988*, p. 7.

62. Ibid., p. 36.

63. Bernard Chidzero, *Budget Statement, 1989* (Harare: Government Printer, July 27, 1989), p. 10.

64. Ibid.

65. Chung, "Education," p. 129.

66. "COL Triples as Minimum Wages Rise Fast," *Herald*, July 3, 1989.

67. "Minimum Wage Too Low for Domestics," *Parade and Foto-Action* (May 1988): 9.

68. Interviews with GAPWUZ officials, Harare, April 1988.

69. Central Statistical Office, *The Economy of Households in Zimbabwe, 1985* (Harare: Central Statistical Office, 1988), p. 6.

70. In *Peasant Consciousness and Guerilla War in Zimbabwe* (Berkeley and Los Angeles: University of California Press, 1985), Terence Ranger refers to this project as radical in the sense of being militantly against state interference, but Marxists would consider it conservative in class terms. See discussion in Christine Sylvester, "Zimbabwe's 1985 Elections: A Search for National Mythology," *Journal of Modern African Studies* 24, no. 1 (1986): 240.

71. Stoneman and Cliffe, *Zimbabwe*, p. 113.

72. Alexander, "The Unsettled Land," pp. 52–53.

73. Ibid., p. 53.

74. Ibid., p. 58. See Robin Palmer, "Land Reform in Zimbabwe, 1980–1990," *African Affairs* 89 (1990): 163–168, for a slightly earlier and more circumspect view.

75. Statement made at the first Workshop for Women Cooperators, sponsored by the Ministry of Community and Cooperative Development and Women's Affairs, Harare, March 1988.

76. "Transport Blues," *Sunday Mail*, October 11, 1988.

77. Samuel Takarinda Agere, "Progress and Problems in the Health Care Delivery System," in Mandaza, ed., *Zimbabwe*, p. 364.

78. "Spreading of AIDS Being Monitored," *Herald*, March 20, 1990, p. 3. As of June 1988 the World Health Organization had reported only 116 AIDS cases.

79. For a discussion of these problems, see Rene Loewenson and David Sanders, "The Political Economy of Health and Nutrition," in Stoneman, ed., *Zimbabwe's Prospects*, pp. 133–152.

80. "Housing: Gvt to Act," *Chronicle*, March 26, 1990.

81. Andrew Saxon, "Public Eye," *Sunday Mail*, May 14, 1989.

5

Civil Society and State-Society Relations

The Zimbabwean government has been keen to promote political unity around ZANU PF, economic unity around the ideal of growth with equity, and racial unity around the notion of "reconciliation." The politics of personal and group identity, however, has been underscored by the many contradictions and ideological pretenses that dot the terrain of state. The result is a diverse and pluralist society manifesting simultaneous tendencies toward unity and disunity. The debates that swirl around this issue have to do with the political potencies of various disunities. Is ethnic identity inherently problematic to political unity, or is it an invention of the party-state and its opponents (and the colonial state before them) to distinguish "dissidents" from "loyalists"? Are ongoing discrepancies between the living standards of Zimbabwe's blacks and whites the result of lingering race prejudice and, in the case of elites, emulation of whites, or are the discrepancies rooted in race-linked class divisions that the state has not remedied? Is the new state emphasis on women's rights progressive or detrimental to tradition and national unity? Is religion compatible with socialism? Should art and literature serve a cause, such as anticolonialism, protradition, or national unity, or should it celebrate the diversity of responses to Zimbabwean tradition and independence?

COMPONENTS OF DIVERSITY

The most obvious points of social diversity in Zimbabwe have to do with differing ethnic and racial identities, although the black-white and Shona-Ndebele divides are often overemphasized. Objective class differences are quite pronounced, class identities are perhaps less so, and differences associated with gender and generation sometimes escape notice and other times burst into public view.

TABLE 5.1   Ethnic Groups in Zimbabwe

Group	Percent of Population
Shona	75.0
Karanga	21.0
Zezuru	17.0
Manyika	13.0
Korekore	12.0
Rozvi	9.0
Ndau	3.0
Ndebele	19.0
Ndebele	14.0
Kalanga	5.0
Tonga, Venda, Shangaan	4.0
European	1.5
Coloreds, Asians	.5

Source: Adapted from Colin Stoneman and Lionel Cliffe, Zimbabwe: Politics, Economics, and Society (London: Pinter, 1989), p. xiii.

Ethnicity, Language Groups, Regionalism, and Tribalism

What we commonly think of as ethnic identity is a complex matter in Zimbabwe. Table 5.1 indicates that the main language groups are Shona-speakers but that these comprise the subgroups Karanga, Zezuru, Manyika, Korekore, Rozvi, and Ndau, thereby indicating that "the" Shona are not one group. Similarly, Ndebele-speakers comprise the Ndebele and Kalanga language groups. In past and present history, politicians and local rural leaders have seized on superficial differences between their Shona or Ndebele language group and others as a way of mobilizing regional support for particular projects or showing disapproval of the state. (Tekere's strong 1990 showing in some Manicaland constituencies was read as mobilized Manyika alienation from national politics, even though ZUM generally did well in urban areas around the country.) In other cases the party-state has mobilized ethnic and regional identities for its own purposes; during the years of antidissidence, large administrative units of the country (Matabeleland's north and south provinces) were reduced in the minds of many to anti-Shona, anti-ZANU(PF) tribal politics because most Ndebele communities are found in what used to be a region of ZAPU strength.

Tonga, Venda, and Shangaan groups, together with the "coloreds" and Asians, make up 6 percent of the population. White Zimbabweans represent a variety of European backgrounds—English, Scottish, Irish,

Afrikaans, Greek, Italian, Portuguese, and so on—and make up less than 2 percent of the population; rarely are their differences seen as a source of ethnic conflict or tribalism.

In Zimbabwe language, ethnicity, region, and politics are often conflated, but there has been relatively little research addressing the question of precisely "how ethnic claims affect government operations."[1] Prior to the merger of ZANU and ZAPU, it was commonplace to characterize state-society relations as driven by an ethnic logic. Political scientist Masipula Sithole warned, for instance, that the tribalist and regionalist conflicts that divided and weakened the liberation movement became a tendency that could not be wished away.[2] He argued that ethnicity tends to become an important source of identity both when a liberation organization is under strain and when a period of success leads that organization to begin thinking of itself as the next government. Then the reward and punishment structure begins to center on ethnic loyalties, and the only cure is to devise regional and/or ethnic modes of representation within the liberation organization and presumably within society at large once independence is won.

The leaders of the two main political parties also depicted Zimbabwe as an ethnically torn country, each accusing the other of building political power on the back of a particular "tribal" group—the Shona in the case of ZANU(PF) and the Ndebele in the case of PF-ZAPU. The Ndebele, claimed ZANU(PF) officials, did not cooperate with the new state; some disengaged by taking refuge in the regional power of PF-ZAPU, and some went further and exited from postcolonial law and institutions altogether to become bandit dissidents. PF-ZAPU retorted that ZANU(PF) was perpetrating "dissidence" in order to break PF-ZAPU and diminish the power of the southern provinces.

The party merger in 1987 marked the beginning of the end of official tribalist accusations, and ZANU PF's 1990 election manifesto admitted that ZAPU (and, by implication, its supporters in Matabeleland) had indeed played a historic role in the struggle for Zimbabwe: "From humble beginnings and faced by almost insurmountable difficulties and obstacles, the Parties mobilised the people, won their confidence, established armed wings ZANLA and ZIPRA and after a protracted struggle lasting some sixteen years, finally won a resounding victory."[3] According to Charles Chikerema, however, the specter of ethnic division would continue to haunt the government as long as it held to a liberal nationalist course. Bluntly he says, "where racism was the philosophy of the white colonialists before independence for purposes of dividing the white and black working classes, as the case is with the apartheid rule in South Africa today, fanning ethnic hostility becomes the tactic of the black petty-bourgeoisie to keep the black working class divided in order to create favourable conditions for neocolonialism."[4]

Supplementing analyses of top-down, or government-invented, tribalism are arguments that ethnicity in Zimbabwe has a multifaceted and durable salience at both the grass-roots and state levels. Marshall Murphree finds that the Tonga, a disadvantaged minority living near Lake Kariba, use ethnicity in their encounters with Shona and Ndebele district officials as a code for economic underdevelopment. Theirs is a situation where "state interventions are seen as obstructive intrusions, to be neutralized, diverted or, if possible, to be manipulated for the benefit of individual or communal interests";[5] for example, when the state regulates fishing in Kariba, the Tonga respond that they now need drought-relief grain. In the future a more ethnically defined form of patron-clientism could emerge if the Tonga or other minorities find themselves in the position of extracting investments from elites that need ethnic groupings for survival, something Tekere's bid for leadership could have precipitated in 1990 had ZUM tried harder to break mass loyalties to ZANU PF.

However one views the ethnic dimension in contemporary Zimbabwe, there is evidence that some bridges still need to be built across real or artificial divides. At the symbolic level there is the issue of language: "None of the great classics of Ndebele have been translated into Shona and vice versa . . . [whereas] *King Solomon's Mines* has been translated into both Shona and Ndebele."[6] At the political level it could be telling that, as of July 1989, only five former ZAPU members had been given cabinet positions in the government, and two of these were at the deputy minister level. Moreover, intra-ZANU "tribalism" remains a force to be controlled. Just prior to the 1990 elections the MP from Mazowe, Chen Chimutengwende, and the ZANU-appointed governor of Mashonaland Central, Joseph Kaparadza, accused each other of fomenting differences between the Korekore and the Zezuru. Although that dispute ended in "reconciliation," to date the state remains willing to tolerate some ethnic discrimination irrespective of government calls for unity.

Race and Class

Race is also a continuing source of identity differentiation in Zimbabwe despite government efforts to promote reconciliation between whites and blacks. In cases where racial reconciliation has taken hold—mainly among the black and white bourgeoisies—traits once associated with whites often reemerge as characteristics of class.

White power is vested mostly in the small landholding and industry-owning or -controlling bourgeoisie (numbering about five thousand).

This group often keeps up a cultural-political battle against "cheeky" blacks and often expects white visitors from abroad to join a "Zimbabwe bash" based on the assumption that Africans may have won the war but cannot hold their own among "superior" cultures. Whether this is a sign of stubborn racism, merely the wail of a defeated nation, or a backlash against the government's rhetorical Marxism-Leninism is still unclear; Ian Smith simultaneously maintains, for example, that the government "chased away the country's expertise when it chased away the whites" and that ZANU PF is full of "dedicated communists."[7]

Arguably some white smugness has been fed by government statements and policies singling out commercial farmers as the backbone of growth with equity, thereby contributing to a sense that whites are indispensable to the Zimbabwean economy. That white privileges are based on class rather than race, however, becomes evident when blacks enter the ranks of the agrarian bourgeoisie. According to officials in GAPWUZ, black farm owners are apt to tolerate the same appalling conditions for their farm workers as white farmers did in colonial Rhodesia; in a few cases landowning government officials have been accused of up to three months' delinquency in paying their workers.[8]

At other levels, however, structural racism continues to support enormous and intransigent gaps in living standards between upper and proletarian-peasant classes. Whites continue to live in enclave neighborhoods with names like Mt. Pleasant, Borrowdale, Highlands, and Marlborough and to have the resources necessary to circumvent Zimbabwe's shortages. Blacks of all classes are now free to take up quarters in these and other former Rhodesian areas and to assume the bourgeois life-style. Most, however, cannot afford to do so and continue to live in urban townships, now greatly swelled by the wartime flight from rural areas, and in remote communal areas. The black state bourgeoisie, however, uses proximity to government resources, as well as status and patronage, to amass power and economic standing disproportionate to its positions as bureaucrats, managers, and technicians. But this group, unable to gain autonomy from the economic bourgeoisie or join it, try as it does, has a restricted capacity to bring about changes in society and in historical state-society relations and instead leads an existence of conspicuous consumption. While nearly 40 percent of Zimbabwe's one million work force garner only 15 percent of total incomes, state and nonstate bourgeoisies import from Europe and South Africa the televisions, watches, stereo systems, and spare tires that are at a premium in Zimbabwe.

The organizational problems among Zimbabwe's lower classes, discussed in Chapter 4, provide space for keepers of the state to define important aspects of the national agenda, notwithstanding the fact that national paradoxes, contradictions, and pretenses also provide the underclasses with opportunities to manuever. Some Zimbabwe watchers, such as Andre Astrow, see no radical future in the state's liberal petit bourgeois politics because even though this class speaks of Zimbabwe's socialist future, a vigorous move in that direction would hurt its power-accumulating, luxury-oriented, or development interests.[9] Others do not agree with this rigid view and argue that although the state bourgeoisie is in ascendance now, its neocolonialism may generate contradictions that give birth to a more progressive element from within the class.[10] Criticism of Mugabe's Willowgate pardons have been harsh, but it is instructive to note that car-seeking, accumulation-minded members of the state bourgeoisie were brought to book, to resignations, and, in one case, to suicide by "friends" from their own class. In fact, the resolution of that scandal may indicate that black color, ethnic similarities, ideological militancy, and nationalist credentials will not protect opportunists from negative scrutiny. On this there may be a certain unity of moral outlook that sets Zimbabwe apart from cases of rampant corruption, nepotism, and tribalism in Africa where "justice" can be delivered through the long arm of the military.

Class differences between blacks and whites, by contrast, rarely elicit more than angry letters to Zimbabwe's newspapers. It is only when whites are perceived as reconstructing their old political power bases that their behavior draws vehement reaction. Results of white-roll balloting in 1985 enraged members of the ZANU(PF) government and led to the heated charge that "Rhodie" ingrates had spurned the outstretched hand of reconciliation and should suffer accordingly. Yet this election perfidy did not lead to antiwhite assaults, as PF-ZAPU supporters suffered, nor did the economic status of whites decline. More recent racial outbursts have been fewer in number, and when they do occur, they seem directed more against representatives of unpopular foreign governments, such as the United States and South Africa, than against local whites.

Some racial (or more accurately, race-class) outbursts never occur. Many working-class "coloreds" of Zimbabwe, for example, resent their strange and lingering status somewhere between blacks and whites. They could vote on the white roll in the 1985 elections, and yet many say they are invisible to whites, the group with whom many identify. One woman puts it this way: "It's funny. Many Whites father Black children whom they see walking about—the children have their White father's features, yet the Whites don't seem to care or notice. White wives don't see it either, not even on the farms."[11] Zimbabwe also has a small Asian community, which in the days of Rhodesia shared with the coloreds the distinction of being unable to purchase land in either the white or black areas of Rhodesia. The status of both groups has improved since independence, but there is a sense among them of being outside the black-white cultural mainstreams of the country. This sentiment is undoubtedly shared by the few whites who take strongly Marxist positions. Theirs can be a truly lonely existence in Zimbabwe.

Gender

Issues of gender have been "hotting" up since independence. Everywhere—in households, factories, cooperatives, commercial farms, and communal areas—black women are taking seriously the government's oft-publicized commitment to promote women's equal rights with men. Meanwhile, many black men are reeling defensively from the implications of such equality, and ministries involved with community and women's affairs are suffering from some of the lowest funding and most frequently reshuffled purviews in government. Together this means that women's rights policies are earnestly debated but are implemented and heeded in fits and starts.

In traditional Shona, Ndebele, and European cultures "women" have been constituted as natural procreators and caretakers of children and male relatives. Speaking of Ndebele custom, one analyst describes gender roles this way: "While it is the man's obligation to feed, clothe and comfort his spouse, the woman is expected to cook and bear children for the man. She must prepare bedding, please the husband, remain faithful and bring up children strictly according to custom."[12] He goes on to say that a wife's subordination, and there can be more than one such subordinate in polygamous marriages, is not servitude because she contributes to the marriage bond, renders the household pleasing, and enables ancestral spirits to bestow blessings on the family. There are also important occasions when women have the opportunity to increase their personal wealth, as in the Shona custom of a daughter's husband giving *mombe youmai* (a gift of cattle to her mother) to celebrate the birth of a child and the role of the grandmother in raising a strong and healthy wife. That this gift is tied to female fertility indicates the importance of childbearing as a woman's contribution in the larger sexual division of labor.

Having children has been a crucial symbol of adulthood for men and women in societies that value the continuity of the group and that traditionally associate food and old age security with a large family. A.K.H. Weinrich reports that 56 percent of couples surveyed in the 1970s claimed to want "as many children as possible or as many as God will give them."[13] This desire was strongest in rural areas, and even poverty-stricken agricultural workers said they wanted as many children as their wages allowed. Rural Shona couples had the most children, averaging nearly five, perhaps because of the central role of agriculture in their culture, and only 3.6 percent of married women were childless. Rural Ndebele and Tonga couples averaged four children, and again few adult women were without them. Couples in urban areas, where children could be more of a liability than an economic asset in cramped housing, had smaller families, although the growth rate of the urban population was higher because of reduced infant mortality. In all cases women bore the greatest burden when their couplings failed to produce offspring. Marriages traditionally were finalized only after a child had been born. If a woman failed what was seen as mainly a female performance test, she would not secure a marriage partner, would soon be divorced by her husband, or would find herself confronting a mistress or second wife.

Some Zimbabwean analysts believe gender traditions such as this retain merit today. Joan May claims that male dominance has been more myth than reality in Zimbabwe, and Aeneas Chigwedere argues that traditional practices actually strengthen community and marriage and represent a mostly sensible sexual division of labor.[14] In this stream of thinking, tradition is not problem-free; rather, the emphasis is on the ways the villain colonialism (sometimes augmented by Christianity) distorted customary practices and rendered them dysfunctional.

In the case of fertility the argument is that traditional practice encouraged women to space children by approximately two years, sometimes under the claim "that Mwari [God] would be angry if children were born in such quick succession that the older child's life was endangered through lack of milk."[15] Traditional taboos on sexual intercourse during the nursing period weakened under colonialism among "better-off rural families, such as those of teachers and junior government employees" who "had money to buy milk powder and other baby food,"[16] and the birthrate increased. The Rhodesian government responded with a family planning campaign in the 1950s for African women only and made effective use of the mass media to further its "modern" message. By 1976 approximately fifty-five hundred women per month were requesting contraceptives from thirty government-funded clinics (sterilization was discouraged by the state in recognition that it would increase African hostility to the regime). Many did so in apparent reaction to "the shock that the traditional sexual morality of the people had suffered from the total disruption of social life," and contraceptive use may have contributed to a fall in the birthrate from 3.6 percent in 1972 to 3.4 percent in 1976.[17] As the war intensified, chiefs loyal to the Rhodesian government accused the government of giving "pills to our wives and even to our unmarried daughters who now start love affairs with many young men and we have no control over them."[18] The nationalists scored points by opposing family planning, and today Zimbabwean women are governed by restrictive abortion legislation reinforced by ZANU PF statements extolling "the decisive role of women in maintaining . . . good and stable families [as] the backbone of our society and our culture."[19] This return to tradition contributes to the high birthrate noted in Chapter 4, a factor greatly complicating national development, and leads some women to complain now about having "many children, year after year, when [we] can't afford to take care of them and [when] it gives women no free time to do anything else."[20]

Lobola, another practice defended by protraditionalists, is "the payments made by the bridegroom and his party to the father-in-law and his party to secure the services of a bride. In our traditional society, the most important of these services was the issue of children. This should be emphasized. Indeed, if *lobola* is a form of insurance at all, it is a 'children's insurance.' "[21] *Lobola*, it is commonly said, brought families together and provided a means to redistribute community resources. Colonialism, by contrast, made the pending wife's family greedy for larger payments from the wife-receiving family and generally encouraged the invention of old traditions to justify new "rules" of payment. A Shona bride, for instance, has been entitled by tradition to *kunonga*, which means a small share of a gift from the bridegroom, a portion of which she offers to the female relative most responsible for promoting the marriage negotiations; in rural areas this is usually the paternal aunt. Today it is common for brides to pick only money and, in some districts, to insist that many relatives—from aunts to sisters to parents—receive financial gifts, too. "All this," declares Chigwedere, "started with the introduction of money into the system . . . [b]ut unfortunately it is all being done in the name of tradition."[22]

To Chigwedere, it makes sense to return to the original spirit of gendered marriage and family practices, albeit with the provisions set forth by the 1983 Age of Majority Act that enable women to step out of the shadows of husbands and male relatives by marrying without family consent, retaining their own wages, gaining custody of children, opening bank accounts, and arguing their own cases in court, practices colonial officials discouraged by interpreting the traditional status of Shona and Ndebele women as akin to being minors for life. In defenses of *lobola* in a child-oriented society, little is said about the burdens falling on sterile women or on women married to sterile men.

Not all analysts are so willing to defend tradition and categorically to condemn colonial practices. Colin Stoneman and Lionel Cliffe, for instance, argue that colonialism had an impact on women in proportion to the economic situation of households. Women whose households had access to resources and cash earnings could hire laborers and thereby move out from the yoke of dependence on husbands; under those circumstances cash *lobola* payments merely augmented family income. But women-headed households were stigmatized both in traditional and colonial times and are still at the lower rungs of respectability in capitalist Zimbabwe:

> The women in them have an enormous burden of domestic, child-rearing and agricultural work, and often have the smallest holdings, may well not own or have access to oxen for ploughing and have no money to hire them. At the same time their need for cash for necessities, and for food for their families because they have neither land nor time to provide their own subsistence, drives them to find time in their overburdened lives to earn cash—by brewing, prostitution, casual labor, etc.[23]

A.K.H. Weinrich ties women's current oppression closely to colonial capitalism, emphasizing its imposition of a new sexual division of labor between male migrants and women peasants in communal areas; but she shares Stoneman's and Cliffe's skepticism about any return to falsely idealized traditions, such as the tradition of large families.[24]

As the debates continue, one practice of the past looms as particularly problematic for contemporary women's rights—patrilineal virilocality, the tradition of brides maintaining their natal group entitlements after coming to live in the village of their husbands. This custom gives women some autonomy from the wife-receiving family even after *lobola* payments have been made. At the same time, however, it renders women permanent outsiders from that family after they have borne sons for a man's lineage. When events occur that defy ready explanation, the patrilineal "insiders" can accuse the "outside" wives of being witches, thereby ensuring that women will not acquire formal power within male-dominated lineages. In Zimbabawe it is serious business to be accused of witchcraft. People say that the evil spirit inhabiting the woman forces her to go out and inflict harm on humans and domestic animals. (Such harm can be accomplished during the day when the woman has bewitched her husband so he does not notice.) If she is still at her craft after several warnings, the customary treatment of a Ndebele witch is to drive a long sharp peg into her anus or head, thereby causing her to die; today it is more likely that the "witch" will be deprived of property, assessed material damages, or sent into exile. None of this puts her family out of its misery, however, because witch spirits can be inherited.

The Zimbabwean government has taken a strong stance against witchcraft and certain other forms of divination, outlawing, decrying, and severely punishing all ritual practices that lead to "superstitious" mutilations. It also encourages education for girls and women and is

Woman in sewing cooperative. Photographer, B. Kanyama. Courtesy Zimbabwe Ministry of Information.

148

Women drawing water. Photographer, K. Kamashu. Courtesy Zimbabwe Ministry of Information.

Women agricultural workers. Photographer, Christine Sylvester.

going beyond its Age of Majority Act to rectify some of the worst abuses of traditional and colonial marriage practices. Under the Matrimonial Causes Act of 1985 a woman now has legal rights to family wealth based on her financial needs, income, family standard of living, age, and the duration of the marriage. She may divorce on the grounds of adultery, cruelty, desertion, mental illness, continued drunkenness, and irreconcilable breakdown of the marriage. This is easier to do in the cities, however, than in rural areas, where courts are often presided over by traditional leaders who resist changes in women's legal status. Moreover, property accumulated in a marriage still belongs to the husband—as long as the *lobola* was paid—and in the event of his death reverts to members of his birth family. There are countless stories in Zimbabwe of women stripped of all possessions except their cooking pots within hours of a husband's death, and children can figure into such property grabs if they are near marriage age and therefore have financial value to the man's family. The latter tradition is earmarked for review and reform within an ongoing system of male privilege.

Weinrich's work suggests that many Zimbabweans may reject or circumvent changes that appear to fly in the face of traditional wisdom. She says Zimbabweans already do this with respect to Christian rulings on marriage. The churches insist that a marriage begins at the moment of the religious ceremony. Zimbabweans have always regarded marriage as "beginning with the first acquaintance of the young people, [deepening with] the gradual involvement of their families, the transfer of bridewealth to the woman's father and the transfer of the bride to the husband's family, the birth of children and finally the establishment of a new and independent household."[25] The families Weinrich surveyed in the late 1970s delayed church weddings until all the customary signs of marriage had been observed and dismissed religious injunctions against sexual intercourse before the Christian point of marriage, for example, in favor of the time-honored tradition of testing a possible union for its fecundity before committing to it. This type of resistance may arise around state-sponsored changes for women. Agitated letters to Zimbabwean newspapers already complain that the emphasis on women's rights comes from Western "women's libbers" bent on breaking up families and lowering respect for men and tradition. Certain male members of Parliament have publicly warned women to "be careful as to how they exercise equal rights as this might create problems in some areas,"[26] a refrain one also hears from some male government officials and associates of "progressive" aid agencies. Moreover, budget time in Parliament opens the floodgates of complaints against the "special privileges" government accords women and always leads to the question of why there has been no men's ministry.

In 1989 the government tied the Ministry of Women's Affairs more closely to its own fortunes by placing it under the senior minister of political affairs. This move seems calculated less to strengthen prowomen forces in the country than to whip women's groups into political cheerleading sections for the ZANU PF government. The government also proceeds slowly and cautiously on the inflammatory issues of *lobola* and the need for family planning, seemingly in the belief, aptly summarized in Chigwedere's work, that "the status of women should be improved but total equality is a dream and will remain unattainable and any practical attempt to bring it about can only bring about disastrous upheavals to our society."[27]

Indeed, agencies of the state often work to avoid "disastrous upheavals" by maintaining traditional norms of proper womanhood. Before major international meetings in Harare, the police predictably embark on an antiprostitution campaign and round up virtually every woman they see at night in certain sections of town, irrespective of whether she is alone or accompanied by a man; professional women working later than normal business hours seem to be the special targets of these efforts. The police make no effort to locate male customers, nor does society shift any blame for prostitution onto the traditionally privileged status of men in sexual matters. Women's groups and certain members of Parliament condemn these raids, but they continue nonetheless.

Some government ambivalence on maternity leave has also arisen. The Labour Relations Act specifies that employers must provide pregnant women up to ninety days leave near the birth date of the child at three-quarters pay. In 1989, however, the Ministry of Public Service tried to cut maternity leave for civil servants from ninety to sixty days and to disallow eligibility if a woman had not worked at one job for at least one year. The ministry's argument was that the cut would "circumvent the financial difficulties which women encounter when they are compelled to take ninety days with reduced pay."[28] This veiled industry-serving paternalism was not lost on the ZCTU, the then Ministry of Community, Cooperative Development and Women's Affairs, and the *Sunday Mail*, all of which objected to the proposed change and helped to stall it.

It is also telling that there are few women in government. In 1989 only four women held ministry portfolios—one headed the women's ministry (Joyce Teurai Ropa Mujuru), one was in charge of tourism (Victoria Chitepo), Fay Chung was at Primary and Secondary Education, and Naomi Nhiwatiwa was minister of state. Three women were deputy ministers, and there were seven women MPs, not including the ministry heads. The new 1990 government reshuffled some of the players (Victoria Chitepo became minister of information, posts, and telecommunications, and Joyce Mujuru became minister of community and cooperative development after the Women's Affairs section of her ministry was "lost" to Political Affairs), but did little to retally the scorecard so that appreciably more women were in important government posts.

In civil society women are rare in "legitimate" commerce and abundant in the informal sector. They continue to predominate in peasant farming, which has become more lucrative since independence, but are also prominent among poorly paid seasonal workers on commercial farms. That they make up less than 10 percent of factory workers means they are outside one of the better paying sectors in the country. It is little wonder that some women say, "I wish I could be born again. I wouldn't get married so young and I would learn and learn until I die."[29]

Several organizations are helping women to learn their rights. The Women's Action Group publishes Speak Out, which keeps women informed about changes in Zimbabwean law, and is also returning to some of its earlier activities with women trade unionists. A privately funded women's bureau provides courses for women in income-generating projects and formal cooperatives, as do many international voluntary organizations. Local women's clubs, however, maintain the Rhodesian tradition of training women in cooking and sewing, and ZANU PF's Women's League has a reputation for promoting the power of elite women, particularly wives and other relatives of government officials.

For a few of Zimbabwe's women to learn that they have a problem at all requires them to perceive the inconsistencies that mar their unusually formidable power base. In the only matrilineal society in Zimbabwe, for instance, Tonga women customarily own immovable property, stock, and all crops reaped in their fields; moreover, they may acquire independent wealth through inheritance, dowry, or purchases.[30] Nonetheless, "Tonga men buy from their wives' brothers the right over their wives' labour and control over their children throughout their own lifetime,"[31] which stands in sharp contradiction to other practices of matrilineality. At the other end of the spectrum, white women have been long accustomed to privilege in Zimbabwe but nonetheless mute their power by upholding the custom of making men the "kings of their castles." Ruth Weiss tells the story of a typical white woman who, although bright and wealthy, never contemplated attending university and aspired only to have integrity, good manners, and restraint. Of gender equality in Zimbabwe this woman now says, "But I don't know anyone who believes in Women's Lib. We are different, aren't we, we bear children, we have this monthly thing—you know, it takes alot out of you, you can't do the same work all the time, like a man. Anyway, a woman can get all she wants from her man, if she sets about it in the right way."[32] Whether this white woman's resistance to opportunity will prevail during a period of change for black women is an open question.

The overall picture is of a state willing to make fundamental legal commitments to women's advancement in public and private spheres on an incremental basis. What Westerners understand as sexism, however, is rampant in the country, in part because social attitudes lag behind changes in the law and because the law itself addresses only the most flagrant and visible discriminations. Even then, the law's efficacy is hindered by its perceived insensitivity to traditional beliefs. As a result, the identities of many women hyphenate traditional and modern liberal dictates about women's "proper" roles in society. This means that women feel alternately empowered by the attention called to their needs and reticent about embracing new opportunities for fear that the "privileges" will bear a heavy cost in male disapproval.

Religion and Socialism

Religion has not been as divisive in Zimbabwean society as race, class, and gender, even though spiritual beliefs span traditional, Judeo-Christian, Hindu, Muslim, and Buddhist practices. The religious climate of the country has been marked mostly by debate about the role of the two dominant religions—traditional and Christian—in a society the state still claims is headed for scientific socialism.

Origin myths of Shona and the Ndebele traditional religions point to a single god who created a founding king, or chief, of the nation and to ancestors as spirit intermediaries between living humans and that god. The Shona religion includes Mwari (God), the *vadzimu* (spirits of patrilineal and matrilineal ancestors), *mashavi* (wandering spirits of people who are not necessarily related to those they influence), and *mhondoro* (spirits identified with the history of the nation). The Ndebele counterparts are uMlimu or uNkulunkulu (Spirit God, the creator) and *amadlozi* (spirits of the recent dead and those of people who died three or four generations earlier). In both versions ancestral spirits can take animal forms or can possess humans. Overall, the common rituals of these religions place considerable emphasis on the power of ancestor spirits to influence rains, droughts, harvests, household prosperity, and fertility. An important ritual in both traditions, for example, calls back the spirit of a recently dead relative to protect the family; the Ndebele call this ritual *umbuyiso*, and the Shona refer to it as *kurova guva*.[33]

European missionaries converted or semiconverted large numbers of Zimbabweans to Christian religions. This was not an easy task given the strength of tradition, and in the beginning most converts came from the group least privileged in customary religions—women. By the third decade of colonial rule, however, the Christian churches had devised effective strategies for winning over more people. The American Methodist Episcopal church "preached the gospel of the plough and aimed to turn out modern agricultural entrepreneurs."[34] Literacy was also a popular tool of conversion, as was the Roman Catholic interest in encouraging farming on the model of pious European peasant societies of the previous century. Anglicans mixed Christian doctrine with "harmless" traditional touches in church decoration. Yet there was often a tug-of-war between priests and ministers on the one side, and spirit mediums, traditional chiefs, and headmen on the other, over the issue of authority.[35]

This struggle carried over into the nationalist movement. Joshua Nkomo writes that his parents were the first among people in his ancestral village of Bango (Matabeleland) to be married in church. He had a strict Christian upbringing: "There were Bible-readings, hymns and prayers every night before bed. We were taught not to eat any food prepared for our neighbours' traditional worship, and strictly instructed never to touch liquor or tobacco."[36] He goes on to say, however, that he became attracted to traditional religion between the ages of eight and fourteen and used to sneak away with his friends to participate in customary ceremonies. Later he and others like him began to connect Christian religion with elements of colonial oppression:

> I learned that the missionary Robert Moffat had been the interpreter when the so-called agreements were made by which Cecil Rhodes claimed to have been granted rights by the last king of our country, Lobengula. I learned too that Moffat had previously said of Lobengula and his regime: "This savage kingdom must be destroyed if Christianity is to take root in this area." Lobengula and his councillors asserted that they had never agreed to the concessions that Rhodes, through Moffat as interpreter, claimed to have granted. But the only man who could say what had really transpired was Robert Moffat, and his Christian conscience.[37]

That Nkomo makes this type of connection also reflects the hard times many nationalists remember from the 1930s, when missionary encouragement of market-oriented agriculture by converts ran up against Rhodesian Depression-era policies of protecting white farmers. During those difficult years young people dropped out of established Christian churches in great numbers, and some returned to traditional religion or participated in revival movements of a millennial nature. Over the ensuing years the trend was toward greater political militancy and cultural-religious renewal, the apex coming during the armed struggle, when young guerrillas attached traditional protective fetishes to AK-47 assault rifles and in other ways accorded traditional purveyors of peasant wisdom great, although by no means total, importance.

Christian churches were also involved in the armed struggle. Some supported the guerrillas by providing them with food, medicines, and vehicles, and others informed on the guerrillas to the security forces or denounced guerrilla violence while ignoring the violence of Rhodesian Forces. Still others simply maintained a mission presence in the rural areas throughout the armed struggle and thereby became identified with the plight of local people. Toward the end of the war the leadership of the PF made it clear to churches that their support was needed and when forthcoming was valued. It admitted, however, that some missionaries had been murdered or harassed by PF forces owing to "frustrations, ill-discipline and possibly the fact that the church has, in the past, supported or accepted the system."[38] Janice McLaughlin, a noted chronicler of church history in Zimbabwe, writes that PF officials told her that "the only problem was the people who brought the Bible; they weren't following what it was saying."[39]

Today the issue is precisely how traditional religion and Christianity could fit into a "socialist" country. Virtually all of Zimbabwe's top leaders are Christian—Mugabe heads the list as a devout Roman Catholic—and so far the state has done nothing to interfere with organized religion. Some Zimbabwean Christians, however, express concern that the rhetoric of scientific socialism dismisses religion as a superstructural instrument of control by capitalists and wonder whether the day will come when a socialist government will ban it. Traditional religion can also fall into the cracks of rhetorical Marxism-Leninism. On the one hand, traditional religion predates capitalism and is therefore removed historically from the forces of oppression that concern socialists. On the other hand, by the same logic this religion is prescientific, "backward," and unnecessary for socialism.

The first president of Zimbabwe (prior to the installation of the executive presidency) was Canaan Banana, a Methodist minister who set the tone for the debate about Christianity and socialism. "Socialism," he once said, "is the legitimate child of Christianity."[40] Echoing strains of South American liberation theology, he went on to remind Zimbabweans that Christian and socialist ways of looking at the world could be hyphenated because both were concerned with struggles for order "guided by principles and values that edify man" and because both envisioned "a brave new world where man occupies the golden goal of fullness, of justice, of equality and of abundance."[41] The common enemies of right-thinking Christians and socialists, according to Banana, were racist and capitalist practices that hurt ordinary people. His message struck a chord in Zimbabwe. A seminar on Christian socialism held in

Harare in 1987 attracted approximately 250 Marxists and Christians, and when Pope John Paul visited Zimbabwe in 1989, he found a warm greeting peppered with reminders from Mugabe and others that Christian Zimbabweans were committed to struggle in South Africa, even if that struggle had to be violent (in April 1990 one of Zimbabwe's leading socialist and ANC-supporting men of God, Michael Lapsley, lost both hands and an eye to a letter bomb from South Africa).[42]

Less debate seems to swirl around the issue of how traditional religion could fit socialism, and what little is said emphasizes the community orientation of tradition and its basic compatibility with the collectivism of socialism. In contrast to state engagement with Christian thinking, only tacit and superficial support for traditional religion emanates from official quarters. The state fetes all visiting dignitaries with a display both of modern military smartness and traditional dance, the latter deriving from customary religious rituals, but "modernity" takes preference over tradition in normal state-society relations. Illustrative of this order of priorities is the story of a spirit medium of Nehanda named Sophia Tsvatayi. The medium recruited and advised guerrillas during the war and then returned to her original place of dwelling at Great Zimbabwe. The local police disapproved of her residence there and continually harassed her, whereupon guerrillas at a nearby assembly point vowed to relay her gallant story to the new government. En route to Harare, however, they killed two white farmers, and this resulted in even more harassment of the medium:

> Once guerillas were known to be with her her home was stormed by the police, several people were shot and killed by them and all the remainder, including Sophia, were arrested. Her children, aged twelve and fourteen, were assaulted, held in Police custody for nine months, and threatened with death. . . . She was tried in December 1981 for the settlers' murders, convicted, and sentenced to death.[43]

In 1988 traditional spiritualists formed the Association of Zimbabwe Spirit Mediums to protect customary knowledge from modern assaults; one of their campaigns has been to restore traditional expertise in matters of rural conservation. This association has brought spirit mediums more directly into the political process and is part of a general resurgence of traditional authority that has been under way since the mid-1980s. But it seems nevertheless that the state incorporates Christian religions as political allies, playing up the rhetorical-ideological aspects of equitable development, and leaves traditional religion to the realm of "culture."

Culture

Efforts have been made since independence to define distinctly Zimbabwean histories, ways of life, and modes of expression in a Rhodesia-aware society. The scope of this task has been monumental, and its execution has been marked by considerable debate about who controls culture and what is authentic and what is invented tradition.

The Zimbabwe Federation of Education with Production (ZIMFEP) argued at a Harare cultural seminar in 1987 that "the total arrangement of life and production is what produces a definite pattern of life which we call culture, and is manifested through various forms of expression such as life styles (i.e., classes, quality and standard of living), technology, politics, music, dance and drama."[44] To this rather formidable list of cultural expressions others explicitly add education and gender concerns,[45] and for each of these areas critics point out that Zimbabwean society and state have been slow to rectify the cultural inequities inherited from the colonial era.

ZIMFEP takes the state to task for allowing the transnational company to mediate Zimbabwean culture and to brag "proudly that its products and services have affected the quality of life of the Zimbabwean."[46] Sculptor David Mutasa pointedly accuses these middlemen of debasing African art, calling it "primitive art," and seeking to make financial gains at the expense of the African artist.[47] Education-minded analysts such as Peter Garlake saw "no sense of movement in Zimbabwe towards a re-examination of the precolonial past during the early days of independence, and endeavored to correct this problem by preparing revisionist history texts."[48] More recently, Jane Parpart has argued that gender has slipped off the agenda at the level of ideology and culture in Zimbabwe, and Laiwan Chung adds that when women try to contribute to the creative arts, men say, "It's against our culture."[49]

These critiques can be seen in debates about the so-called Shona stone carvings that grace the sculpture garden at the National Gallery of Zimbabwe in Harare and figure prominently in the country's tourist markets (along with batiks, bead jewelry, baskets, musical instruments, and clay animals). "Middlemen" promoters, claims Mutasa, sell the sculptures on the basis of trumped-up notions of Shona authenticity in art. Art critics and some sculptors claim that pieces depicting family members in tight proximity to each other and sacred animals in surrealistic spirit forms are "not linked to the demands of any established tradition."[50] They argue that the work of Zimbabwe's most popular sculptors, such as Bernard Matemera and John Takawira, reflects fusion styles of a stone-carving community "in which the old order and the new idea, tradition and experiment exist without rancour and conflict of interest and con-

Zimbabwean stone sculpture. Courtesy Zimbabwe Ministry of Information.

tribute to ongoing development."[51] Some women sculptors, notably Agnes Nyanhongo and Locadia Ndadarika, maintain that the themes of the sculpture form a link with the community's past. Says Nyanhongo, "I want my sculpture to send messages to my children and to my grandchildren so that they will never forget our culture."[52]

Literature is another area in which debate about past and present culture rages. During UDI years Zimbabwe's writers had to be mindful of state censors and work without benefit of international contacts. In 1983 Zimbabwe sent a dramatic signal to the world that its days of cultural isolation were over by hosting the Bookweek Africa exhibition in Harare. This event has now become an annual celebration of African and socialist writings, featuring lectures, writing workshops, and dozens of book displays. It provides a venue for Zimbabwean writers to polish their work by rubbing shoulders with such prominent African authors as Chinua Achebe and Ngugi wa Thiong'o and adds Zimbabwean voices to debates about whether to write in the vernacular or in a European language, whether to focus specifically on political and economic themes, or whether to develop whatever voice one wants without fear of being called a traitor to revolutionary Zimbabwe.

For novelists who missed the African renaissance of the 1960s, the comeback has been impressive: Dambudzo Marechera, Chenjerai Hove, Charles Mungoshi, and Musaemura Zimunya, among the male writers

of poetry and short stories, and Tsitsi Dangarembga, Freedom Nyamu-
baya, and Sekai Nzenza, among the female writers of novels, poetry,
and autobiographies are leading the way. Hove's recent novel *Bones*, an
evocation of a woman farm worker during Zimbabwe's armed struggle,
won the 1989 Noma award for African literature, and Dangarembga's
Nervous Conditions has drawn considerable attention as a powerful story
of a rural teenage girl who finds double-edged success when her wealthy
uncle sponsors her education at a mission school during the 1960s.
Other works that form the core of Zimbabwean literature include Marechera's *House of Hunger* and *Mindblast*, Mungoshi's *Coming of the Dry
Season* and *Waiting for the Rain*, and, from an earlier era, Doris Lessing's
The Grass Is Singing and *Going Home*.

Hove, the author of *Bones*, notices that Zimbabwean writers are
deeply in search of the " 'bones' of their society's conscience on the
historical road traveled thus far," have "already started feeling the pain
of frustration that resulted from all the politicians' unfulfilled promises,"
and have "stopped celebrating and chanting slogans of independence."[53]
(The now deceased Marechera, however, was always critical of independence—as well as war and those who were against war—because
he saw independent Zimbabwe as a continuation of the House of Hunger
he experienced as a child in the Rusape area and then depicted in his
novel of the same name.)

Drama also figures into Zimbabwe's cultural and social awakening.
The National Theatre Organisation and the Harare drama group named
Reps are still under the control of whites and continue to favor European
and American plays, as one involved member told me in 1988, because
"blacks have no background or interest in drama." ZIMFEP's Community
Based Theatre Project and the Zimbabwe Association of Community
Theater work to correct this misperception and thematic imbalance by
promoting drama groups in Harare's high-density suburbs. The Canadian
University Service Overseas also sees theater as an important aid in
development and specifically supports a Bulawayo drama group called
Iluba Elimnyama, which writes and performs plays about such issues as
sexual harassment, unemployment, and nepotism. A Zimbabwean drama
troupe called the Meridian Group won honors at the 1990 Edinburgh
festival for its production, "Rise and Shine of Comrade Fiasco," a play
about a guerrilla who stayed in hiding until 1988 and was then treated
badly for criticizing the "new" Zimbabwe. Outside the arena of formal
theater, drama figures into programs of the Ministry of Community·and
Cooperative Development as a way of communicating ideas on partici-
patory democracy and crops up in a variety of other teaching situations;
a 1990 conference on farm worker rights, sponsored by GAPWUZ, featured participants devising impromptu plays to illustrate strategies for

resolving conflict between a farm manager and a worker accused of drinking on the job.

Zimbabwe's popular music industry is also thriving. One local performer, Thomas Mapfumo, drew considerable attention by penning a song called "Corruption" in the midst of the Willowgate scandal and then figured prominently with other Zimbabwean performers in Glasgow's 1990 Mayfest, a celebration of international culture. Other popular local groups include the Bhundu Boys, Runn Family, Transit, Ilanga, John Chibadura, and the Marxist Brothers, and there are many individual singers who have large followings, among them Stella Chiweshe and Leonard Dembo. Audiences that once languished under UDI isolation now fill local stadiums for Paul Simon and his Graceland tour, Eric Clapton, and Harry Belafonte's fund-raising efforts for the Child Survival organization. Performances once marred by booking and staging problems now run more smoothly under the watchful eye of the Ministry of Culture. (In one infamous case a black girls' choir from South Africa was nearly deported because its agent refused to honor the performance schedule until more money was forthcoming; he checked the group into a local hotel for the duration of the negotiations and threatened to leave without paying the bill.) Local women singers, such as Susan Mapfumo, however, complain that a male-dominated industry treats women performers as prostitutes, which puts severe constraints on the development of women artists. Research by Angela Impey at the Zimbabwe College of Music shows that women performers who choose to marry often sacrifice solo singing careers and work instead as background singers. Women who do sing solo usually bypass marriage so as to ensure that they are not accused of having low morals as they would be by their husbands' families.[54]

Social diversity is also represented in Zimbabwean music by lingering interest in the classical traditions of Europe and in the mbira sounds of traditional music. In postindependence Zimbabwe classical music is strongly supported by the diplomatic community and by training programs at Mount Hampden Training Centre, the University of Zimbabwe, and the Zimbabwe College of Music. No similar institutionalization of traditional music exists. Mbiras—which have a wooden keyboard and a set of tuned keys within a resonating chamber made from a gourd and surrounded by pebbles, snail shells, or even bottle tops that rattle—are associated with spirits and are making a comeback at a time of renewed interest in tradition.

Film encapsulates many of the ambivalences in Zimbabwe's cultural milieu. Most films shown in Zimbabwe are made outside the region— in the United States and Europe—and display life-styles that cultural nationalists decry as decadent: "The Western culture of love-making on the screen is being instilled in us through the most powerful medium of communication—motion picture[s]. We then have baby dumping and blame our children for lack of discipline and culture. These are repercussions of the consumer culture which has been promoted during colonial days and after independence."[55] To date, however, Zimbabwe has had difficulty competing with the marketing, promotion, and distribution networks of the West in order to provide alternative films for local audiences. The Zimbabwe Film and Video Association is collecting films from other African countries and promoting the work of local producers such as Simon Bright, whose efforts with Ingrid Sinclair on the documentaries *Corridors of Freedom* (1988) and *Limpopo Line* (1990) depict struggles to reap the benefits of cooperation between countries of southern Africa, and Olley Maruma, who masterminded the first feature film made entirely by Zimbabweans, *Consequences* (1989), which deals with teenage relationships that result in unwanted pregnancies. Zimbabwe has been more successful in marketing its scenery. The films *Cry Freedom*, *A Dry White Season*, and *A World Apart* were shot wholly or partially in Zimbabwe, as was a critically panned rendition of *King Solomon's Mines*. But unfortunately for Zimbabweans, international filmmakers do little to train locals in the skills of the industry. Says actress Shuvai Chikombah, "Foreign crew handle the cameras while local crew hold the clapper. . . . They apply the make-up and we hold the make-up kits. I wonder how we'll gain experience this way."[56]

In a situation marked by efforts to correct the cultural monopoly of the West, the Zimbabwean state has walked a fine line between respecting artistic license en toto and imposing some restrictions at the margins of choice and artistic identity. It has, for example, turned the old Rhodesian Censor Board into a vehicle for identifying and axing portions of new plays that insult black integrity, and in 1985 it banned the violent film *Rambo: First Blood*. In other cultural arenas government influence has been more subtle. Speaking at 1989 graduation ceremonies at Mutare Teachers' College, the minister of state for national scholarships, Joseph Culverwell, told the new teachers, "It is imperative that you constantly update your knowledge of scientific socialism while keeping abreast with developments in every sphere."[57] So far the balance has tipped in the favor of tolerance, and despite critiques leveled against the state's many false promises in other realms of political economy, an artist such as David Mutasa has no qualms in saying, "I now feel more free and unfettered to produce work than I ever did prior to the Independence of Zimbabwe in 1980."[58]

CONCLUSIONS

Zimbabweans are experiencing pressures to assert and at times to invent cultural authenticity through ethnic identification, traditional religion, racial politics, and artistic themes. Ironically, this is an aspect of modernity's engulfment of difference by submerging it in a discourse of integration, unity, and commonality. Yet positions in between and marginal to old and new also struggle for space in Zimbabwe's inherited matrix of identities, as does a state that is itself multicentered and cross-pressured.

"The way we used to do things" can mean the ways some men and certain forms of knowledge commanded things be done. Thus, a woman, a member of a minority ethnic group or subgroup, or a person with an illness that cannot be cured by a traditional healer can be held back by tradition. But an unbridled modernism is also no panacea, in part because it distorts tradition and in part, as socialist-Christians and some contemporary writers point out, because it promotes individualistic differentiation. With racial cleavages still invading the Africanizing bourgeoisies, gender differences rising to the fore, and artistic impulses struggling for resources, Zimbabwe's calls for "unity" are simultaneously chimerical, antidemocratic, and potentially celebratory of common identity within a context of respected differences.

NOTES

1. Jeffrey Herbst, *State Politics in Zimbabwe* (Berkeley and Los Angeles: University of California Press, 1990), p. 168.

2. Masipula Sithole, *Zimbabwe: Struggles Within the Struggle* (Salisbury: Rujeko, 1979).

3. ZANU, *ZANU PF Election Manifesto, 1990* (Harare: Jongwe Press, 1990), p. 1.

4. Charles Chikerema, "Journalists and National Unity: What Role?" *Social Change and Development* 17 (1987): 6.

5. Marshall Murphree, "The Salience of Ethnicity in African States: A Zimbabwean Case Study," *Ethnic and Racial Studies* 11, no. 2 (1988): 132.

6. Musa Zimunya, "Writing for National Unity," *Social Change and Development* 17 (1987): 12.

7. Interview with Ian Smith, Harare, March 27, 1990.

8. Interviews with GAPWUZ officials, Harare, April 1988.

9. Andre Astrow, *Zimbabwe: A Revolution That Lost Its Way?* (London: Zed Press, 1983).

10. Ibbo Mandaza, "The State and Politics in the Post–White Settler Colonial Situation," in *The Political Economy of Transition, 1980–86*, ed. Ibbo Mandaza (Dakar: Codesria, 1986), pp. 21–74.

11. Shelagh, quoted in Ruth Weiss, *The Women of Zimbabwe* (London: Kesho, 1986), p. 52.

12. Wallace Bozongwana, *Ndebele Religion and Customs* (Gweru: Mambo Press, 1983), p. 8.

13. A.K.H. Weinrich, *African Marriage in Zimbabwe: And the Impact of Christianity* (Gweru: Mambo Press, 1982), p. 110.

14. Joan May, *Zimbabwean Women in Customary and Colonial Law* (Gweru: Mambo Press, 1983); and Aeneas Chigwedere, *Lobola: The Pros and Cons* (Harare: Books for Africa, 1982).

15. Weinrich, *African Marriage*, p. 119.

16. Ibid.

17. Ibid., pp. 122–123.

18. Ibid., p. 130.

19. *ZANU PF Election Manifesto 1990*, p. 21.

20. Zimbabwe Women's Bureau, *We Carry a Heavy Load: Rural Women in Zimbabwe Speak Out* (Harare: Zimbabwe Women's Bureau, 1981), p. 14.

21. Chigwedere, *Lobola*, p. 2.

22. Ibid., p. 8.

23. Colin Stoneman and Lionel Cliffe, *Zimbabwe: Politics, Economics and Society* (London: Pinter, 1989), p. 73.

24. A.K.H. Weinrich, *Women and Racial Discrimination in Rhodesia* (Paris: UNESCO, 1979). Elizabeth Schmidt argues that colonialism often worked hand in glove with patriarchal tendencies in African society ("Negotiated Spaces and Contested Terrain: Men, Women, and the Law in Colonial Zimbabwe, 1890–1939 [Paper presented at the annual meeting of the African Studies Association, Atlanta, Georgia, 1989]).

25. Weinrich, *African Marriage*, p. 43. Interesting and instructive stories about marriage are also featured in Irene Staunton, ed., *Mothers of the Revolution* (Harare: Baobob Books, 1990).

26. J. T. Chinyati, quoted in *Hansard*, July 5, 1988.

27. Chigwedere, *Lobola*, p. 51. On go-slow approaches to women in Zimbabwe, see Gay Seidman, "Women in Zimbabwe: Postindependence Struggles," *Feminist Studies* 10, no. 3 (1984): 419–440. On legal hurdles, see Alice Armstrong, ed., *Women and Law in Southern Africa* (Harare: Zimbabwe Publishing House, 1987).

28. Chris Andersen, cited in "Leave Cut Designed to Serve Women," *Sunday Mail*, March 5, 1989.

29. Zimbabwe Women's Bureau, *We Carry a Heavy Load*, p. 10.

30. H. Childs, *The History and Extent of Recognition of Tribal Law in Rhodesia* (Salisbury: Ministry of Internal Affairs, 1976).

31. Weinrich, *African Marriage*, p. 40.

32. Catherine, quoted in Weiss, *The Women of Zimbabwe*, p. 63.

33. For discussions of traditional religion, see David Lan, *Guns and Rain: Guerrillas and Spirit Mediums in Zimbabwe* (Berkeley and Los Angeles: University of California Press, 1985); Michael Bourdillon *The Shona People* (Gweru: Mambo Press, 1987); Herbert Aschwanden, *Symbols of Life: An Analysis of the Consciousness of the Karanga* (Gweru: Mambo Press, 1982); Herbert Aschwanden, *Symbols of Death: An Analysis of the Consciousness of the Karanga* (Gweru: Mambo Press, 1987); Michael Gelfand, *The Spiritual Beliefs of the Shona* (Gwelo: Mambo Press, 1977); N.M.B. Bhebe, "The Ndebele and Mwari before 1893," in *Guardians of*

the Land, ed. J. M. Schoffeleers (Gwelo: Mambo Press, 1979); Terence Ranger, *Revolt in Southern Rhodesia, 1896–7* (London: Heinemann, 1979); and Terence Ranger, *Voices From the Rocks* (forthcoming).

34. Terence Ranger, *Peasant Consciousness and Guerilla War in Zimbabwe* (Berkeley and Los Angeles: University of California Press, 1985), p. 43.

35. For discussions of the rise of Christianity in Zimbabwe see J. A. Dachs, ed., *Christianity South of the Zambezi*, vol. 1 (Gwelo: Mambo Press, 1973); and Michael Bourdillon, ed., *Christianity South of the Zambezi*, vol. 2 (Gwelo: Mambo Press, 1977). Also see N. Bhebe, *Christianity and Traditional Religion in Western Zimbabwe, 1859–1923* (London: Longman, 1979).

36. Joshua Nkomo, *Nkomo: The Story of My Life* (London: Methuen, 1984), pp. 10–11.

37. Ibid., p. 13.

38. Janice McLaughlin, " 'We Did It for Love': Refugees and Religion in the Camps in Mozambique and Zambia During Zimbabwe's Liberation Struggle," in *Church and State in Zimbabwe*, ed. Carl Hallencreutz and Ambrose Moyo (Gweru: Mambo Press, 1988), p. 140. The role of various religious beliefs and practices in the armed struggle are detailed in Lan, *Guns and Rain*; Ranger, *Peasant Consciousness*; Hallencreutz and Moyo, eds., *Church and State*, Part I; and David Maxwell, "Religion and the War in Northern Nyanga" (Work in progress for the D.Phil., 1990, St. Antony's College, Oxford University).

39. McLaughlin, " 'We Did It for Love,' " p. 141.

40. "Socialism—the Legitimate Child of Christianity," *Moto Magazine*, no. 54, p. 3.

41. Ibid.

42. Among many books on the subject of Christianity in "socialist" Zimbabwe, see Hallencreutz and Moyo, eds., *Church and State*, Part 3, and Canaan Banana, *Towards a Socialist Ethos* (Harare: College Press, 1987).

43. Peter Garlake, "Prehistory and Ideology in Zimbabwe," *Africa* 52, no. 3 (1982): 17. There were rumors in 1989 that she had finally been released. Her case also illustrates the party-state's tendency to define civil society as a field of danger that must be controlled.

44. ZIMFEP, *Community Arts and the Question of Culture in the City of Harare* (Harare: ZIMFEP, 1987), p. 1.

45. Garlake, "Prehistory and Ideology"; Jane Parpart, "Putting Gender on the Agenda," *Southern Africa* 3, no. 6 (1990): 34–35.

46. *Community Arts*, p. 2.

47. See David Mutasa, "Artists Statement" (London, September 1988, xerox), which he elaborated at a workshop on art and the liberation struggle held by the Britain Zimbabwe Society at its 1990 Dayschool on Presenting Zimbabwe—Popular Culture on the Front Line, London, April 28, 1990.

48. Garlake, "Prehistory and Ideology," p. 17. See Peter Garlake, *People Making History*, Book 1 (Harare: Zimbabwe Publishing House, 1985); Peter Garlake, *Life at Great Zimbabwe* (Gweru: Mambo Press, 1982); and Peter Garlake, *Early Zimbabwe: From the Matopos to Inyanga* (Gweru: Mambo Press, 1982–1983). Also see Kathy Bond-Stewart, *Women's Problems* (Harare: Zimbabwe Publishing

House, 1984); and Kathy Bond-Stewart, *Capitalism, Socialism and Development* (Gweru: Mambo Press, 1986).

49. Parpart, "Putting Gender on the Agenda," p. 25; Laiwan Chung, "Carving Out a Role: Women and Contemporary Culture in Zimbabwe," *Africa South*, no. 4 (March–April 1990): 39.

50. *Zimbabwe Heritage: Contemporary Visual Arts* (Harare: National Gallery of Zimbabwe, 1986), p. 25.

51. Celia Winter-Irving, Catalog for "African Metamorphosis," an exhibit of Bernard Matemera at the Zimbabwe National Gallery, Harare, December 15–January 18, 1988, p. 2.

52. Quoted in Fiona Lloyd, "Storytellers in Stone," *Africa South*, no. 4 (March–April 1990): 43.

53. Chenjerai Hove, "Writers Continue to Reap Literary 'Harvest of Thorns' in Their Pages," *The Guardian*, April 20, 1990, p. 18. The novels mentioned here are mostly available through the Zimbabwe Publishing House Writers Series (Harare). *Bones* is published by Baobob Books (Harare, 1988), Lessing publishes with Grafton Books (London), Nzenza's *Zimbabwean Woman* is available through Karia Press (London, 1988), and *Nervous Conditions* is published by the Women's Press (London, 1988).

54. Chung, "Carving Out a Role," pp. 38–39. For a discussion of the sources of contemporary Zimbabwean music, see F. Zindi, *Roots Rocking in Zimbabwe* (Gweru: Mambo Press, 1985).

55. *Community Arts*, p. 6.

56. Quoted in Fiona Lloyd, "Women in Theatre, Jan. 1990 Harare: Celebration and Surprise," *Africa South*, no. 4 (March–April 1990): 41.

57. "Teachers Told to Focus on Socialism," *Sunday Mail*, May 14, 1989. It is ironic that the Ministry of Education efforts to teach secondary school teachers Marxist-Leninist political economy in 1987–1988 were quickly abandoned. I am grateful to David Maxwell for bringing this to my attention.

58. Mutasa, "Artists Statement," p. 1. Some musicians and artists, however, have complained about low levels of state support for the arts and about radio programs that mostly feature international music.

6

Zimbabwe's International Profile

Zimbabwe has a high-activity profile in foreign affairs that stands in sharp contrast to the surreptitious cast of Rhodesian diplomacy during the UDI years. That period of intensifying struggle saw combatants and strategists in contact with international allies for diplomatic support and for economic and military assistance. Often, however, those contacts had to be quiet, if not actually covert, or Rhodesia would risk exposing its sanctions-busting efforts and nationalists their supply routes and training bases. Today Harare is the veritable hub of southern African international relations and an important center of Third World politics.

Zimbabwe has assisted the Mozambique government against MNR insurgents. It has become a staunch supporter of the Southern African Development Coordinating Conference (SADCC) and an equally strong advocate of majority rights and rule in South Africa; Nelson Mandela made Harare one of his first stops after release from prison in 1990. Zimbabwe has hosted meetings on child survival, nonalignment, and international socialism and has also feted numerous dignitaries, among them Margaret Thatcher, ANC official Oliver Tambo, Sam Nujoma of neighboring Namibia, Japanese commercial delegations, Reverend Jesse Jackson, Muammar Qaddafi, and the pope. A simple headline from the British paper *The Guardian* catches this cosmopolitan spirit: "Harare, a valued point of contact for East, West—and South."[1]

In style the ZANU PF government has the reputation of being alternately uncompromising and reasonable. Mugabe, one commentator says, can walk right out to the precipice, look over the edge, and then back away, particularly when action would put him on a collision course with South Africa.[2] He has looked over the edge and not backed away from a series of difficult dealings with the United States; these started with "innocent" criticisms of U.S. foreign policy and led to a vengeful aid cut, Harare holding firm against superpower intimidation, and

165

renewed aid. Zimbabwe can blunder, too, as it did in lauding the "progressive" Ceauceşcus of Romania in the years preceding their demise. Remarkably, there have been few debates about Zimbabwe's foreign policies, although concerns have been raised about the country's potential to dominate SADCC and about Zimbabwe's military support for the FRELIMO government of Mozambique. Questions are just now being framed about Zimbabwe's future relations with South Africa.

NATIONALIST AND RHODESIAN CONTACTS DURING THE WAR YEARS

The nationalists and Rhodesians alike made extensive use of international networks during the war. Joshua Nkomo's travels on behalf of the nationalist cause by now are legendary, but he was by no means the only devotee of external relations: Nathan Shamuyarira (of ZANU, then Front for the Liberation of Zimbabwe, and then ZANU), taught for awhile at Princeton University, and Eddison Zvogbo studied law at Harvard. During these travels both men took a keen interest in the struggle at home and represented the nationalist cause at various international meetings. Other nationalists went abroad to secure training facilities and war matériel for the guerrillas from the PRC, the Soviet Union, the German Democratic Republic (GDR), Romania, and North Korea. All maintained ties with Great Britain throughout because as long as Britain retained its colonial portfolio on Rhodesia, it was an actor to contend with.

The Rhodesians courted the Portuguese colonists in Angola and Mozambique (until the mid-1970s) and the National Party in South Africa and sought markets in France, the FRG, Japan, and, to some extent, the United States. The Rhodesians then became diplomatically involved in negotiations for a Rhodesian settlement, first with selected Zimbabwean nationalists and representatives of neighboring Frontline States and later with South Africa, Britain, and the United States. Meanwhile, Rhodesia was officially anathema at the United Nations and the Organization of African Unity.

Neighboring countries were also involved in Zimbabwe's nationalist conflict. Zambia provided sanctuaries for ZIPRA soldiers—although not without interfering with their politics—and staunchly adhered to sanctions that hurt its economy more than Rhodesia's. Tanzanian development was siphoned off through defense spending and through its efforts to complete the Tazara railroad as a route for Zambian goods. Botswana, surrounded by hostile armies in Rhodesia, Namibia, and South Africa, could ill afford to make direct contributions to the struggle; nevertheless, it did provide camps for Zimbabwean refugees and in retaliation was bombed by Rhodesians. As for newly independent Mozambique, ZANU's most stalwart ally, the war retarded development by adding considerable "direct costs to the government without providing much in alternative revenue or production."[3] All these actors would have lingering claims on the new state.

ZIMBABWE AND THE SOUTHERN AFRICAN REGION SINCE 1980

South African hopes for a moderate settlement in Zimbabwe were dashed by the election victory of ZANU(PF). South Africa had invested U.S. $300 million in the Rhodesian war against the nationalists and $2 million in the election campaign against ZANU, subsidizing Muzorewa's campaign in particular.[4] It had also floated the idea of a grand constellation of Southern African states (CONSAS) conjoining the Frontline members with South Africa and its Bantustans. This organization would enable South African corporations to be at the center of regional technical and development plans and help South Africa retain political leverage in the region and economic dependence on its rail routes, ports, and high-technology goods. To work, however, CONSAS required a cooperative government in Zimbabwe and an enlarged Customs Union to include Mozambique, Angola, and Zimbabwe as well as its current members— Botswana, Lesotho, and Swaziland.

South Africa already had a formidable presence in the Zimbabwean economy on which to build new ties. It had become Zimbabwe's principal trading partner in the years following UDI sanctions, and there were at least forty-three firms of South African origin in Zimbabwe and many British firms with South African subsidiaries or directorships;[5] indeed, five of Zimbabwe's top ten industries were affiliated in some way with South African companies, including Zimbabwe Breweries, Hippo Valley, Premier Portland Cement, Plate Glass, and BAT. Derrick Chitala estimates that "in 1976 the total South African investment commitment in Zimbabwe was . . . £200 million which rose to £478 million in 1979."[6] With these controls on technology, management, and marketing in place, a friendly Zimbabwe woven into a South Africa–controlled organization of states would surely have enhanced South African capability and increased Zimbabwe's landlocked dependence on South African transportation routes to the sea over the ports of Mozambique damaged during that country's liberation struggle.

Zimbabwe and the other Frontline States, however, had a different cooperative scheme in mind and began working on it even before Zimbabwe acceded to formal independence. Regional planning meetings in 1979 and 1980 gave hints of a highly innovative, promising, and

South Africa–excluding scheme to be known as SADCC. It would be based not on the familiar model of a customs union or common market but on regional cooperation in the development of economic infrastructures. It would circumvent the trade routes, technological reliance, and development plans South Africa sought to solidify around itself and thereby preserve the independence and sovereignty of all signatories and reduce redundancy in separate national development efforts.[7] Over a long period of time it was hoped that SADCC would encourage regional investments and enable member states to reduce their reliance on South African firms and on the economies of the advanced industrialized countries.

Zimbabwe, SADCC, and the Preferential Trade Area (PTA)

SADCC formally came into existence after Zimbabwe's independence, and each participating member—Angola, Botswana, Lesotho, Malawi, Mozambique, Swaziland, Tanzania, Zambia, Zimbabwe (and now Namibia)—agreed to take responsibility for coordinating development in one major infrastructural sector. Zimbabwe became the overseer of food security, and its tasks came to include developing data banks and an early warning system on droughts; building up a regional food reserve; coordinating studies on postharvest food loss reduction, food-processing technology, and the infrastructures of food marketing; and helping plan for food aid in the region. That Zimbabwe was asked to assume these tasks came as no surprise given its impressive history of agricultural performance prior to independence. How that sector would perform after independence was an unknown.

It is generally acknowledged today that Zimbabwe is a good SADCC partner. The country has lived up to its commitments in food security and agricultural research and has been known to extend assistance over and beyond its formal SADCC obligations. It has been particularly successful in increasing food reserves for regional emergencies; for instance, after the 1986–1987 harvest it had "about two years' supply of maize despite shipping grain to Botswana, Mozambique, Zambia, Angola, and to South Africa (over 250,000 tonnes)."[8] Zimbabwe also assisted Mozambique with agricultural rehabilitation and undertook to test and promote sorghum and millet crops in the region. Partly in response to Zimbabwe's seriousness of purpose within SADCC, Mugabe was awarded the U.S.-based Africa Prize for Leadership for the Sustainable End to Hunger in 1988.

Despite this stellar record in food security, certain of Zimbabwe's internal development decisions seemed to run counter to the spirit of SADCC cooperation. To enhance self-sufficiency in energy, for instance,

Zimbabwe installed new thermal electrical power units at Wankie. This action in effect snubbed SADCC goals for regional energy integration and ignored energy-providing capabilities already in place in Zambia and Mozambique (in retrospect there may have been some wisdom in this decision given that a 1989 fire at Zambia's Kafue station caused electricity to be rationed in Zimbabwe). Zimbabwe also transgressed the spirit of SADCC in the early 1980s by restricting imports of textiles from Botswana in order to protect domestic industry (an improved trade agreement was negotiated late in 1988). In 1983 Zimbabwe signed on with North Korea for rice and overlooked Malawi as a cheaper source because of President Banda's support for the Mozambican insurgents. Zimbabwe also annoyed the Tanzanians by internally duplicating a SADCC project for a chemical pulp and paper mill. Overall, Zimbabwe continues to export more to its SADCC cohorts than it imports from them.

Zimbabwe's recent economic liberalization efforts may herald new problems of coordination with SADCC. Signatories agree that would-be foreign investors must negotiate business terms both with the country where they will locate and with the relevant SADCC commission. Zimbabwe's 1989 investment code, however, promises ninety-day processing of investment applications through the new Investment Centre and offers more inviting repatriation terms for firms willing to invest in high-priority areas. Zimbabwe is already the most highly developed member of SADCC, and its liberalization policies could attract a good proportion of all new investments in the region. This would put Zimbabwe in conflict with regional commitments and expose its "apparent aim of self-sufficiency extending to almost every product that the region might be able to sell to it."[9] Zimbabwe is in the enviable position, however, of having the most to gain from an enlarged export market and from semiautarchy.[10]

Zimbabwe is also a member of PTA, an organization far larger in membership (fifteen countries) and more diverse than SADCC that promotes trade under liberal practices of reciprocity in agreements and reduced tariffs.[11] Within PTA, Zimbabwe administers the Multilateral Clearing Facility, but it also takes advantage of cracks between SADCC and PTA to offer certain nonmember neighbors (such as Mozambique) the preferential quotas disallowed among PTA members.

The crucial question, however, is whether efforts to circumvent South Africa, such as SADCC and the PTA, make economic sense amid the rising tide of South African reform. A one-day symposium on this question held in Harare in April 1990 vented warnings that the region may be approving projects that stand in the way of normal relations with a postapartheid South Africa. Nevertheless, "it is not clear that once the political factor [of South Africa] is out of the way there will be a common SADCC interest."[12] There is also the question of Zimbabwe's new trade relations with Namibia. "A Harare based trade consultant thinks the present value of trade between the two countries is between Z $500,000 and Z $1 million (U.S. $225,000–450,000) . . . mainly in pottery, metal products and textiles."[13] The idea is to ease Namibia away from its strong trade reliance on South Africa. It is a sign of Zimbabwe's aggressive interest in prying apart that link that it initiated direct air service to Windhoek within a month of Namibia's independence.

The South African Nemesis

As Zimbabwe pursued the SADCC strategy of circumventing South Africa infrastructurally, it simultaneously came into more direct confrontation with the government of South Africa and some of its regional clients in two ways. First, it became a mainstay of Zimbabwe's foreign policy to protect the FRELIMO government in Mozambique against the MNR forces of insurgency that Rhodesia created for its own war in the 1970s and that South Africa then took over to make life difficult for Marxist Mozambique. Zimbabwe spent up to Z $1 million (U.S. $500,000) a day throughout the middle to late 1980s supporting between ten thousand and twelve thousand Zimbabwean troops in their efforts to clear out MNR sanctuaries and protect the SADCC-revitalized Beira port and the Benguela rail route through Mozambique. Shortly before Samora Machel's death in 1986, Mugabe, Machel, and Kaunda journeyed to Malawi and presented President Banda with a veritable ultimatum: "Either Malawi stops supporting the gunmen of the South-African–backed MNR, or the Frontline may decide to throttle the Malawian economy."[14]

Zimbabwe's well-equipped, well-motivated, and highly trained troops frequently made the difference in Mozambique between MNR victories and defeats, and the MNR responded, somewhat ludicrously, by declaring war against Zimbabwe. Far more seriously, it began raiding Zimbabwean farms and villages in border areas and by 1990 had contributed to the deaths of approximately 370 Zimbabwean civilians. As the war continued, the costs became increasingly difficult for Zimbabwe's citizens to bear, what with urbanites riding dilapidated buses to work and businesses complaining about foreign exchange constraints. Edgar Tekere, whose Manicaland home area suffered the preponderance of MNR attacks, made much of what he called Mugabe's misguided Mozambican priority during the 1990 election campaign and vowed to withdraw Zimbabwean troops if elected president. In this he dared break the taboo on speaking against boundless aid to ZANU PF's wartime ally, and his views were echoed in letters to Zimbabwe's print media complaining that Zimbabwe's army could not be counted on to protect citizens on the Zimbabwe-Mozambique border.

In mid-1988 I publicly asked the minister of foreign affairs, Nathan Shamuyarira, how far the Zimbabwean government was prepared to go to defend Mozambique. His oblique answer in a nutshell was, "We will go far." Yet in response to the costs and apparent unwinnability of the war in Mozambique, Mugabe came out in support of a negotiated settlement of the conflict in 1989 and offered his services as a mediator. Mugabe tried to broker the conflict by maintaining the Zimbabwean military in Mozambique, encouraging negotiations, and making it clear that a settlement must respect the integrity of the FRELIMO government and include discussions with and hard-hitting terms for the MNR's South African backers.

But the process has not gone smoothly. Even after the de Klerk government embarked on its historic efforts to normalize South Africa's internal politics, the MNR stepped up its attacks on Zimbabwe, massacring four children and three adults in the Mount Darwin area in February 1990. Writing in *Africa South*, Steve Askin and Jose Manuel Das Fontes warn that "the continuing carnage illustrates that stopping the wars South Africa unleashed against the Frontline States will be a slow and painful process."[15] They also caution that

> past experience may even encourage continued low-intensity regional war by the South African security establishment, as such a strategy partly "worked" for whites during the talks which turned Rhodesia into Zimbabwe. The worst Rhodesian incursions against neighbours came after the first talks between Ian Smith and his black adversaries. . . . Even if Pretoria pulls back from destabilisation, it will leave a deadly legacy of regionwide disruption. No resources will be enough to rebuild the farms and factories and transport lines ruined in the past decade.[16]

In June 1990 direct peace talks scheduled to take place in Malawi were postponed, in part owing to "difficulties" expressed by the MNR team.[17] The first round of talks was held in Rome on July 11, 1990.

Mugabe's second confrontational approach to South Africa revolved around efforts to talk regional leaders into imposing mandatory and wide-ranging sanctions against the white redoubt in the years before the 1990 changes. Zimbabwe, as noted in Chapter 3, had itself suffered from a variety of South African sanctions in the early years of independence, to say nothing of the earlier sanctions brought against Rhodesia, and therefore knew from experience that this tool could deliver a nasty cut. When the Botha government imposed an internal state of emergency in 1986 and cracked down on antiapartheid organizations and activities of young "comrades" in the townships, Mugabe took up the sanctions issue with special vigor.

With Kaunda's assistance Mugabe forcefully presented the case for comprehensive regional sanctions, including the termination of air links with South Africa. The other regional states, however, made it equally clear that they simply could not afford the economic consequences—in the forms of lost revenues or retaliation—that this move would engender. The point was also made that terminating transport links with South Africa would put undue pressures on MNR-threatened Mozambican ports and all but invite an escalation of South Africa's already nasty policy of regional destabilization, which in May 1985 included bombing raids on Gabarone and Lusaka and the destruction of an ANC-linked building in Harare. Botswana and Mozambique in particular wanted the Frontline States to pressure Britain and EEC countries to enact harsh sanctions, arguing that these countries could well afford the economic shortfalls they might thereby incur. Mugabe and Kaunda, however, pressed on and brought up the issue once again at a Commonwealth meeting. By July 1987, however, the regional sanctions issue had clearly landed as a nonstarter. With the ZCTU worriedly starting a fund to protect workers against anticipated sanctions-related layoffs and signs in Harare shops heralding presanctions sales, Mugabe and Kaunda stepped off the regional sanctions track, and Mugabe threatened instead to impose a ban on all South African imports, which proved unpopular in Zimbabwe and untenable.

The sanctions issue subsequently became less visible and pressing as the South African government took dramatic steps to unban the ANC and move toward negotiated constitutional change. When Nelson Mandela spoke in Harare in March 1990, he assured whites in South Africa that black South Africans understood the suffering racism had caused and would not turn the tables on their oppressors any more than Mugabe had done in Zimbabwe. Yet the letter bomb sent to Reverend Michael Lapsley demonstrated only a month later that South Africa expected Zimbabwe to continue abiding by its old gentlemen's agreement to refrain from harboring ANC guerrillas on its soil, in return for which South Africa would not conduct serious military actions against Zimbabwe. Now, however, there was the added message that ANC supporters should not prematurely revel in victory.[18]

ZIMBABWE'S INTERNATIONAL PROFILE IN A GLOBAL CONTEXT

Zimbabwe's hard-line posture on South Africa greatly influenced the agenda of the Non-Aligned Movement (NAM) between 1986 and

1989, when Mugabe served as its chair. In an organization more critical of Western imperialism than of communism, Mugabe used his prestige to hammer away at the West for not doing enough to bring down the apartheid regime. NAM members supported his especially strong attacks on the United States for using the policy of constructive engagement with the South African government to continue the pro–South African policies all administrations since Kennedy had pursued. The 1988 NAM gathering lambasted Washington for hosting Jonas Savimbi, head of the National Union for the Total Independence of Angola, which was seeking to topple the Popular Movement for the Liberation of Angola government; for financing the Nicaraguan contras; and for linking removal of Cuban troops in Angola, called in by the MPLA government as protection from South Africa, with independence for Namibia (subsequent developments in Namibian independence then rendered the last criticism passé).

Zimbabwe was visible but less active in other international arenas. It became the fiftieth member of the Organization of African Unity and a firm supporter of its liberation committee. Mugabe also personally took Zimbabwe's seat in the United Nations in August 1980 and committed Zimbabwe to Afro-Arab solidarity and Palestinian self-determination. In 1990 Zimbabwe condemned Iraq's invasion of Kuwait but did not otherwise become involved. Zimbabwe focused most of its attention on the international relations of its region.

Zimbabwe-U.S. Relations

Under Jimmy Carter the United States was the first country to establish a diplomatic presence in Zimbabwe after independence, immediately pledging U.S. $2 million to rehabilitate war-damaged medical clinics. Mugabe then paid a state visit to Washington in August 1980, and by the following year the U.S. government had pledged U.S. $276 million in aid, mostly for a commodity import program and food security projects.

Relations soured, however, when Zimbabwe proved too outspoken about constructive engagement with South Africa and U.S. imperialism in the Third World for Ronald Reagan's hard-line temperament. When Zimbabwe refused to condemn the Soviet Union for shooting down a Korean passenger plane, the United States halved its aid, and this cost Zimbabwe U.S. $40 million. In 1986 former president Carter happened to be present in Harare for U.S. embassy Fourth of July celebrations and walked out on a speech, read by an official from the Mugabe government, that criticized the United States for ignoring parallels between its revolution and the one blacks were waging in South Africa. Mugabe apologized to Carter for the personal affront but refused to eat humble pie on the more general criticism. The Reagan administration responded by terminating all government-to-government aid to Zimbabwe remaining in the 1985–1986 program, and this cost Zimbabwe U.S. $5 million for an agricultural commodity and support program and U.S. $4.8 million in unallocated funds.[19]

In 1988 it was Zimbabwe's turn to be incensed by the United States. Headlines screamed across New York newspapers that a Zimbabwean diplomat at the United Nations was abusing his child and that the New York City Welfare Division was refusing to bring Zimbabwean authorities in on the case. The Welfare Division claimed it had no particular reason to believe the child would be safe in Zimbabwe, and the Zimbabwean government criticized the constant suggestion that the child was safer in the hands of New York social workers and psychiatrists than he could ever be in Africa. More than one Zimbabwean suggested to me at the time that a diplomat from France or England would never be subjected to such humiliation, nor would it be thinkable to deny those countries their right to handle the matter. "People like to think," observed one Zimbabwean, "that African countries are barbaric and cannot be trusted to treat a child properly." Indeed, when the U.S. courts ruled that the child could not be held any longer in U.S. foster care, he returned home in the company of a Zimbabwean social worker and a psychiatrist assigned by the U.S. State Department to monitor his progress.

These incidents marked a particularly low period in U.S.-Zimbabwean relations. Yet when the Reagan ambassadorial appointee to Zimbabwe left his post in March 1989, he could say that relations between the two countries had improved dramatically. Thanks to an ice-breaking new round of aid from the United States, that was true. The United States made a U.S. $17 million grant available to Zimbabwe as of August 1988 to stimulate rural development and private business. According to the terms of the grant, Zimbabwe would initially receive $5 million, and the remainder would follow over the next two years, apparently if Harare minded its manners. Despite the possibility of delayed disbursements, Minister Bernard Chidzero called the aid package "a giant step in strengthening relations between our two countries,"[20] and to date there has been no further disruption of relations between them.

Zimbabwe–Eastern Bloc Relations

Zimbabwe's years of anti-U.S. rhetoric did not result in especially close relations between Harare and the Soviet Union. It was more than a year after independence before Harare opened formal diplomatic channels with Moscow, owing to the latter's support for ZAPU nationalists during the war, and Harare thereafter criticized the USSR for its actions in Afghanistan. Soviet diplomats and journalists tell of leading a cloistered existence at their embassy and of maintaining proper manners with the Zimbabwean government.

The smaller Eastern European countries fared better. Mugabe made a point of visiting several socialist countries in 1981, among them Yugoslavia, where Mugabe negotiated training for mass communications; Romania, where Zimbabwe was offered assistance in agriculture; and Bulgaria, which offered Mugabe help in cooperative farming. Zimbabwe also established good relations with the GDR, another wartime ZAPU supporter, but only Romania and Yugoslavia represented the Eastern bloc at ZIMCORD. Years later Zimbabwe's growing interest in countertrade led to aid of a different type from Hungary—light bulbs, industrial raw materials, chemicals, motor spares, and mining machinery in return for a portion of Zimbabwe's 1986 tobacco crop.

As social movements unseated one after another Eastern European government in the momentous year of 1989, Mugabe took the hard-line view that these were only temporary aberrations in the historical movement toward socialism and that, even so, the type of program ZANU PF envisaged for Zimbabwe would little resemble the practices now being toppled. Zimbabwean socialism, he said, would reflect local African values and would not be imposed on the people by the state. The magazine *Social Change and Development*, publishing once again in 1990 after financial problems caused it to close down in September 1988, offered a spirited defense of Mugabe's position, arguing that Eastern European socialist "peoples are finding their voice and, while they may object to some things that have been done by socialist governments, they want freedom, not new exploitation under capitalism."[21] Not everyone concurred with the apologias, however, and Jonasi for one, a columnist for *Moto Magazine*, said bluntly that "despite their protestations our leaders are heading in the same direction Eastern Europe is moving away from,"[22] implying that they were socialists with no commitment to socialist practice.

Even before the upheavals in the Eastern bloc, there were signs that in some ways the Zimbabwean state's view of Eastern European socialism was only rhetorically laudatory. Visiting academics from some of these "fraternal" countries complained that the Zimbabwean government was particularly slow to process their temporary employment permits and prone to turn down their services altogether in favor of people with Western qualifications. A member of Zimbabwe's Parliament also expressed disappointment in 1988 "at the way that some of the students who completed [degrees] in socialist countries have been handled," going on to say that he knew of cases in which Zimbabwean students returning from Bulgaria and Czechoslovakia "were actually discriminated against when they got into this country because those who had obtained western degrees thought they had superior degrees to those obtained by their counterparts."[23]

Zimbabwe also retained the loyalty and ties to the PRC that ZANU's wartime experiences had generated. Mugabe was quick to visit Beijing in 1981, the Chinese were forthcoming in assisting the government to build a large sports stadium in Harare, and the two countries entered into numerous cultural and trade agreements. During the 1989 democracy campaign in China, the Zimbabwean press downplayed challenges to the PRC government posed by student protesters and then refrained from debating the consequences of armed reprisal against the unarmed students, undoubtedly because Zimbabwe was itself experiencing problems with university students and feeling the challenge of a new political party.

North Korea also figured prominently in Zimbabwe's loyalties. The government's infamous Fifth Brigade, sent to quell dissidence in Matabeleland in 1983, was North Korean trained, and its harsh military methods caused some concern within and outside Zimbabwe about increasing movement toward North Korea's authoritarian model.[24] North Koreans also contributed the socialist realist sculpture of Zimbabwean guerrillas that occupies a prime position at the National Hero's Acre in Harare; this was a commission for which local Zimbabwean sculptors were not asked to bid.

Zimbabwe's Relations with
International Lending and Aid Agencies

If Zimbabwe has been adept at pursuing several seemingly contradictory paths simultaneously, such that, in the words of Nathan Shamuyarira in 1982, neither superpower "can rely on any automatic support from us because we support specific issues rather than general alliances,"[25] it is nonetheless clear that Zimbabwe tips its trade and aid hat in the capitalist direction. Zimbabwe has extensive and mostly good relations with a variety of international training and aid organizations and with private foundations from the West. After years of aid cutoffs under UDI, the influx of such organizations—in 1985 there were more than thirty international agencies gearing their Zimbabwe programs at least in part to cooperatives alone[26]—has taken many Zimbabweans by pleasant surprise. It has also, however, raised the specter of donor-directed development.

The EEC, for instance, has a microprojects program in Zimbabwe under terms of the Lome Convention of 1984. The objective of the program is to support self-help projects for rural development that meet certain conditions, including technical, financial, and economic feasibility; 50 percent cost sharing between the EEC and local community and government services; and assurances that ultimate running costs will be locally available. The projects must also fall into one of several specific categories of priority, such as rural water supplies for domestic consumption, storage and processing of agricultural inputs and outputs, or productive communal self-help schemes such as orchards, woodlots, vegetable gardens, and irrigation projects. Potential aid receivers submit formal, written grant requests that include descriptions of the project, its location, layout, size, levels of responsibility in personnel, planned results (quantified if possible), cost estimates, details of cost-sharing schemes, prices and costs per item of materials, equipment, labor, technical supervision, and signatures of three persons from local community and provincial-level departments responsible for financial and technical implementation of the project.[27] For this a project can garner support of between U.S. $500 and U.S. $100,000.

EEC representatives say that stringent conditions are the key to actual profit generation in small Third World businesses. By contrast, Oxfam America had to cut its program in Zimbabwe drastically after finding that showcase projects, principally the Batsiranai collective cooperative, were either misusing donor funds or simply failing to achieve surpluses. The problem with stringent conditions, however, is that many rural people in Zimbabwe are illiterate and can submit project proposals only if they find patrons familiar with Western accounting procedures. Thus, there is often a white Zimbabwean or European virtually leading project members through the process and thereby creating a position for herself or himself as a "consultant." This dilemma, plus the fact that guidelines reward capitalist thinking in a country of socialist sloganeering, can result in projects simultaneously at cross-purposes with stated principles and consonant with unfolding realities at the policy level.

At the macro level of international lending, Zimbabwe "strongly denies implementing International Monetary Fund type[s] of structural adjustment"[28] and claims instead to be following its own independent course of adjustment in response to its own needs, albeit one that is close to IMF guidelines. The Canadian International Development Agency (CIDA) recognizes Zimbabwe's sensitivity to outside direction and lays more stress on positive inducements for Zimbabwean policies deemed effective than on punitive actions à la the IMF and the EEC. One of CIDA's major contributions lies in providing Zimbabwe with foreign exchange for imported inputs, which the government desperately needs, and disbursing grants rather than loans. This is not to say that CIDA's approach is totally magnanimous, but Canada's concerns to promote economic liberalization through its grants do match Zimbabwe's 1990 priorities.[29]

CONCLUSIONS

Zimbabwe's high-activity profile in international relations has its pluses and minuses. On the plus side, there is no doubt that Zimbabwe's leadership of NAM and activist approach in the southern African region have brought considerable stature to the country and to Robert Mugabe, who has emerged as a key spokesperson for the Third World in the late twentieth century. On the down side, there are only so many actions Zimbabwe can take to counter the reality that even as South Africa changes, it continues to loom as the giant among all the region's relative Lilliputians, with tentacles reaching well into Zimbabwe's economy. Zimbabwe's improving relations with a liberated South Africa could provide relief from high military expenditures and from concern about export and transport reliance on an apartheid government, although not necessarily from high levels of South African capital in the economy. But specific relations between the two countries will depend on South Africa's internal stability and on the direction its economy takes. There is less Zimbabwe can do to erase power differentials between itself and the West other than to stand tall on its principles and support SADCC. Yet Zimbabwe can muddy the waters of regional cooperation by violating its own commitments to south-south trade when these run up against possibilities for self-reliance, another preoccupation that may ease if landlocked Zimbabwe develops trustworthy relations with South Africa.

That Zimbabwe's current foreign policies are ambivalent and contradictory should come as no surprise given that the same qualities characterize its domestic political, social, and economic policies. Nevertheless, Zimbabwe stepped firmly out of the Rhodesian shadow by assuming a posture of prosocialist nonalignment in international political affairs, and on matters of trade and finance it at least insists on doing things its own way—for good, for ill, or for some fate between those points.

NOTES

1. Peter Murray, "Harare: A Valued Point of Contact for East, West—and South," *The Guardian*, May 12, 1989, p. 14.

2. Kurt M. Campbell, "Unfinished Business: Zimbabwe One Year After Unity," *New Leader* 81, no. 21 (1988): 17.

3. Carol B. Thompson, *Challenge to Imperialism: The Frontline States in the Liberation of Zimbabwe* (Boulder, Colo.: Westview Press, 1985), p. 78. Much of my subsequent discussion relies on this source.

4. David Martin and Phyllis Johnson, "Zimbabwe: Apartheid's Dilemma," in *Destructive Engagement: Southern Africa at War*, ed. Phyllis Johnson and David Martin (Harare: Zimbabwe Publishing House, 1986), p. 44.

5. Duncan C. Clarke, *Foreign Companies and International Investment in Zimbabwe* (Gwelo: Mambo Press, 1980), Chapter 3.

6. Derrick Chitala, "The Political Economy of SADCC and Imperialism's Response," in *SADCC: Prospects for Disengagement and Development in Southern Africa*, ed. Samir Amin, D. Chitala, and Ibbo Mandaza (London: Zed Press, 1987), pp. 25–26.

7. For discussions of SADCC, see Thompson, *Challenge to Imperialism;* and Carol B. Thompson, "Zimbabwe in SADCC: A Question of Dominance?" in *Zimbabwe's Prospects: Issues of Race, Class, State and Capital in Southern Africa*, ed. Colin Stoneman (London: Macmillan, 1988), pp. 238–256; Stephen Lewis, Jr., *Economic Realities in Southern Africa (Or, One Hundred Million Futures)*, Discussion Paper 232 (Sussex: Institute of Development Studies, Sussex University, June 1987); John Hanlon, *SADCC: Progress, Projects and Prospects* (London: Economist Intelligence Unit, 1984); Amin et al., eds., *SADCC*.

8. Thompson, "Zimbabwe in SADCC," p. 245. This reserve has subsequently fluctuated, depending on drought conditions.

9. Colin Stoneman and Lionel Cliffe, *Zimbabwe: Politics, Economics and Society* (London: Pinter, 1989), p. 186.

10. For a discussion of semiautarchy, see Peter Robinson, "Relaxing the Constraints," in Stoneman, ed., *Zimbabwe's Prospects*, pp. 348–360.

11. Carol B. Thompson, "Zimbabwe in Southern Africa: From Dependent Development to Dominance or Cooperation?" in *The Political Economy of Zimbabwe*, ed. Michael Schatzberg (New York: Praeger, 1984), pp. 197–217.

12. "SADCC and SA: The Road Ahead," *Southern African Economist* 3, no. 5 (1990): 5.

13. "Namibia Looks North," *Southern African Economist* 3, no. 1 (1990): 34.

14. "Why Frontline Lost Patience with Banda's Double Game," *Moto Magazine*, no. 49, p. 13.

15. Steve Askin and Jose Manuel Das Fontes, "Pretoria's Deadly Virus Rages On," *Africa South* (March–April 1990): 12.

16. Ibid.

17. "Peace Talks Put Off," *Herald*, June 14, 1990.

18. Andrew Meldrum, "Apartheid's Long Arm," *Africa Report* 35, no. 3 (1990): 25–27.

19. For discussions of U.S. aid to Zimbabwe, see Theresa Chimombe, "Foreign Capital," in *Zimbabwe: The Political Economy of Transition, 1980–86*, ed. Ibbo Mandaza (Dakar: Codesria, 1986), pp. 123–140; Arnold Sibanda, "The Political Situation," in Stoneman, ed., *Zimbabwe's Prospects*, pp. 257–283; and Economist Intelligence Unit, *Country Reports for Zimbabwe and Malawi* (London: Economist Intelligence Unit, 1982–present).

20. "U.S. Ends Zimbabwe Aid Freeze," *New York Times*, September 1, 1988.

21. "Human Rights—West and East," *Social Change and Development* 22 (1990): 14.

22. Jonasi, "Tread Carefully," *Moto Magazine*, no. 85 (February 1990): 17.

23. S. D. Malunga, *Hansard*, July 6, 1988.

24. Economist Intelligence Unit, *Quarterly Economic Review of Zimbabwe and Malawi*, no. 2 (London: Economist Intelligence Unit, 1983).

25. Christine Sylvester, "An Interview with Nathan Shamuyarira and Comment on the Zimbabwean Situation," *Alternatives* 8, no. 3 (1982–1983): 491.

26. Francis Chinemana, *Inventory of Resources for Co-Operatives* (Harare: Canadian University Service Organization, 1985).

27. Government-EEC Microprojects Programme of Lome II, "Guidelines for Projects" (xerox).

28. R. S. Maya, *Structural Adjustment in Zimbabwe: Its Impact on Women* (Harare: Zimbabwe Institute of Development Studies, 1989), p. 1.

29. This section is informed by discussions with Timothy Shaw, Dalhousie University.

7

A Less Contradictory Future?

As Zimbabwe enters its second decade of independence, it also enters a netherworld of expectations. It is a new country, enjoying some of the good faith that accompanies this status, and in an era of accelerating history, Zimbabwe is sufficiently established for its patterns of political economy to be available for critique. In evaluating Zimbabwe's prospects—an undertaking that must be approached cautiously—let us first consider the types of queries raised about Zimbabwe's future during its first six years of existence. What were the biases inherent in these questions, and can we correct them at this juncture in Zimbabwean history? Then let us consider new and old constraints and opportunities bearing on the country's choices and the important matter of what ordinary Zimbabweans expect from their state and economy.

FIRST-WAVE QUESTIONS

From the day Britain lowered its imperial flag, Rhodesians vacated positions of political power, and a new symbol of Zimbabwe was hoisted that combined the black, green, and yellow of the modern liberation struggle and the Zimbabwe bird of yesteryear, analysts were preoccupied with such questions as, what is the nature of Zimbabwe's transition? More specifically, is socialism a likely prospect, or is Zimbabwe a chip off the old Rhodesian block? If socialism is on the agenda, what type are we talking about, what are the leading social forces in the transition, and which members of Zimbabwe's diverse and complex society are most likely to benefit from a socialist future? If socialism is unlikely, why is this so? Where are the bottlenecks, and will, or should, progress be made to surmount them?

These questions tended to be stated in either/or terms. The parameters of the country's future were matters of Marxist socialism versus

181

something else, absolute benefits versus absolute losses, "good" futures
versus "bad" futures. How one defined "good" and "bad" depended
on ideological proclivities, but in any case the parameters were often
so narrow that they left out a tremendous number of in-betweens. Of
course, this tendency understandably reflected the commitment to socialism that characterized much first-wave analysis[1] as well as the
contradictions unleashed when the government unrelentingly proclaimed
Zimbabwe "Marxist-socialist" and just as repeatedly steered or tolerated
courses of action that made a mockery of that proclamation.

Another type of analysis has begun to correct the preoccupation
with polarized outcomes. This analysis frames discussions of continuities
and discontinuities in Zimbabwe within a "whole series of multiple and
indefinite power relations"[2] that trigger, complement, and refute the
official contradictions. It now seems reasonable to suggest, for example,
that when faced with organized political challenges or with ordinary
people clamoring vociferously for greater redistribution, the party-state
has taken refuge in the Rhodesian tradition of assigning one group the
label of "indispensability" and accusing others of tribalism, selfishness,
or treason. Thus, against the electoral-dissident challenge posed by ZAPU
and more conventionally by ZUM, ZANU PF overrepresented itself as
the indispensable tool of an indispensable unity while simultaneously
engaging in actions that smacked of colonial authoritarianism. The Fifth
Brigade in Matabeleland gave vent to that tendency, as did government
detentions of ZUM supporters in 1990 and ZANU PF's extraordinary
efforts to prevent favored candidates from primary defeat at the hands
of "the people." At the local level the state has displayed its indispensability by creating local institutions that are controlled at the top
or that continue the tradition of patriarchal indispensability. In times
such as these, the government has gotten stuck between its promises
to the (whole) people and its concern "to protect the economic interests
of insiders from the challenge of outsiders."[3]

The party-state also possesses a "pragmatic" tendency to mix the
metaphors of "good" and "bad" people—of insiders and outsiders—for
political effect. White Zimbabweans are alternately presented to the
people as indispensable, skilled workers and as treacherous reactionaries.
During the 1990 election ZANU PF politicians continued to use this
tactic by promising to take away some white land while simultaneously
reassuring the CFU it would be consulted on all matters of land reform.
Once the heat of the election passed, the urgency of singling out whites
for public disapproval passed as well, and the government moved against
the "insider" teachers it had assiduously wooed during the campaign,
refusing wage increases for certain categories of teachers and then firing
those who subsequently struck against the government. Also, inside

members of the government own large tracts of commercial farmland at the expense of the land-hungry implicitly left outside a system that frequently touts "the people" as the insiders.

In areas where the government has perceived itself as relatively free from political challenge, it has more genuinely tried to strike a conciliatory balance among the competing demands of organized groups. This comes through in efforts to promote land reform and cooperatives while simultaneously liberalizing the investment climate for large capitalists. It shows in reform efforts on behalf of women that stop just short of actions that would cause men to go on a rampage. Reinflating the sagging balloon of Marxism-Leninism seems part and parcel of this balancing act. There are mixed messages in rhetorical Marxism about precisely who are the indispensable referees of the future, the judging sovereigns, the shapers of a future *perestroika* (restructuring), if need be, whose verdicts on exploiters will be harsh. That Marxism-Leninism is having a rough ride elsewhere these days may simply be irrelevant to Mugabe's use of it to discourage excess (without appearing too personally dictatorial), in order to keep "the people" on his side. The irony is that many of Zimbabwe's peasants want radical land reform in the sense of a marked change from past practices but not in the sense of a radical Marxist-Leninist collectivization. Given that Zimbabwe's workers are already divided in their loyalties to ZANU PF,[4] one wonders whom the fading Marxist-Leninist rhetoric is meant to please.

At the base of these cross-cutting trends lies a liberal-corporatist-populist-welfare economy that, despite stresses, strains, bottlenecks, and adjustments, remains decidedly capitalist, seemingly on purpose. Most members of the government and ruling party are comfortable with this economic hyphenation and prefer it to (what appears to be) Mugabe's solitary quest for a more radical political economy. Knowing this, we can still speak of a political economy undergoing transition, but the processes are longer, more transhistorical, and less malleable in the short term than the first-wave debate about transition in Zimbabwe suggested. If more imminent discontinuity is in the cards, it will probably come about as a second- or third-order set of changes unleashed, more than shaped, by social backlashes against mounting inequities and economic bottlenecks.[5]

Zimbabwe is not an example of unfettered capitalism, however, and it is not beholden to international lending agencies to the degree that it has lost the capacity for semiautarchy. Zimbabwe, like Rhodesia before it, is somewhere in between socialist and capitalist parameters. Large capitalists can win in this system; yet the government has had a difficult time attracting foreign investment, a problem Rhodesia faced after UDI but for different reasons. Peasants lose out in a competitive match with commercial farmers, just as they did during colonial rule; yet peasant production has increased since independence, albeit with disparities among peasant cultivators owing to the state's tendency to reintroduce NLHA-era schemes. Nevertheless, the real wages of urban workers have fallen since independence, as they often did during the colonial period, and interviews conducted by the *Financial Gazette* on the eve of Zimbabwe's tenth anniversary suggest that "ordinary Zimbabwean citizens have more complaints than reasons for contentment with the way their lives are being affected by the prevailing economic situation."[6] This view is reinforced by the news magazine *Africa South*, which calls the Zimbabwean hyphenation "the undecided economy" and which in related stories recounts many instances of local nervousness about government refusal "to address the socio-economic results of Zimbabwe's capitalist development,"[7] especially as liberalization becomes the catchword of the day.

Two final points on these state-focused contradictions deserve mention. First, the Zimbabwean state manages its overlapping tendencies with less oppression and hunger than most African states can claim. Moreover, the state-led liberal nationalist here and now improves on the political economy of Rhodesia. In that eighty-year span of colonial history, the state took a strongly interventionist position within the economy without providing political equality, social services to speak of, or income distribution for blacks. The Zimbabwean political economy, by contrast, has full adult suffrage, considerable education and health benefits for the majority population, and some redistributed marginal assets and incomes through new land, wage, and housing policies. Virtually every important document on development planning, including the 1989 investment code, repeats the pledge to protect Zimbabwe's poor from economic dislocations and maintain policies sensitive to issues of equity. So far the promises have been bereft of bite, and thus the country's poor still await Zimbabwe's *perestroika*.

Second, until the Zimbabwean government allowed the twenty-five year state of emergency to lapse in July 1990, there was also little in the way of a sustained *glasnost* (openness). Jonathon Moyo of the University of Zimbabwe's Political Science Department argued that "without a free political system, the free market won't operate effectively." But small industrialist Garth Heathcote said a one-party state would "be good for business in the short-term, especially if unpopular moves are necessary, like imposing a recession through tough Reserve Ban policies." Even he believed that "in the long-term, though, it will breed authoritarianism," and others said that "those fighting for a different Zimbabwe—redistribution of wealth, labour intensive production, balanced growth, more rudimentary consumer goods for the povo [people]—

had better prepare for a rough ride."[8] Now the one-party issue seems to be a dead point, thereby rendering the polarized either/or outcomes envisaged in the first wave of Zimbabwe analysis appealingly simple or sentimentally old-fashioned.

NEW AND OLD QUESTIONS, CONSTRAINTS, AND OPPORTUNITIES

The world economy is a double-edged constraint/opportunity in its simultaneous offer of possibilities for expanded trade and for greater export dependence. Zimbabwe's neighbor to the south is another two-sided challenge that offers the old face of economic and political threat and a new face of internal accommodation and externally normalized relations. New and old considerations, therefore, conjoin around a different set of questions from wave one: Will the investors Zimbabwe hopes to attract through trade liberalization policies simply head south to a more developed and soon-to-be-respectable South Africa? Will investors bypass the region altogether in a headlong rush to Eastern Europe? Will SADCC change its original raison d'être and welcome its erstwhile enemy into the fold, thereby boosting the regional market? Will Zimbabwe's fears of a militarily and economically superior South Africa disappear with normalization? Will Zimbabwe's reliance on South African firms such as Anglo-American, Delta Corporation, and National Foods become more acceptable when South Africa is liberated? And if reform to the south goes off track and another "emergency" is called, will Zimbabwe stand in the middle of a new cross-fire, or will it (indeed, can it) plunge into the fray? A South Africa that continues to be powerful (presuming it does) even as it turns into a friend is such a newly salient possibility that we dare only raise these questions at this time; from the vantage point of early 1991 there is, after all, still much ground to cover before the shape of South Africa comes into focus.

Similarly, continuing engagement in the world capitalist system presents some uncertainties, particularly concerning prices and markets for Zimbabwe's commodity and manufacturing exports and supplies of imported oil. Unlike the Zimbabwean–South African relationship, however, there are ready-made "answers" to questions of Zimbabwean–world economy relations as dispensed by the IMF, the World Bank, other bilateral and multilateral sources of development aid, and private voluntary agencies. Zimbabwe is currently reaching for, and claiming as its own insight, the structural adjustment "answer" to a sagging economy, but whether this will be "the" answer in the future is a matter of speculation.

Other constraints and opportunities are lodged deep in the heart(s) of Zimbabwean society. Relatively few first-wave analyses of Zimbabwe took as their starting point the wishes and preferred futures of factory workers, domestic laborers, cooperative participants, trade unions, agricultural workers, children, housewives, and so on. Notable exceptions were works by Terence Ranger and David Lan on aspects of state-peasant relations during and immediately following the armed struggle and Colin Stoneman's and Lionel Cliffe's more recent reminder that social struggles in Zimbabwe are by no means over.[9] To turn their eyes from the state, as many analysts cited in this book are now doing, is not tantamount to ignoring politics or the international arena. Rather, it is to give pride of place to capillary centers of power and to ask such questions as, how many simultaneous revolutions are reshaping the political and economic "rules" of state in Zimbabwe?[10] A question of this type draws attention to groups in opposition to or in complicity with certain state and capital policies and notes their locations, their internal disagreements, and the extent to which separate struggles are contradictory or unified or both. At issue is what Zimbabwe's ordinary people want from government and along what class, gender, generational, ethnic, or racial lines their demands emanate. From this perspective, the fact that Zimbabwe is a hard-won nation and also a bastion of Rhodesian and pre-Rhodesian particularisms means that unity can be stubbornly elusive, terribly abstract, the right hand of authoritarianism, or already present in pockets of opposition to official "unity."[11]

This emphasis on simultaneous constraints and opportunities, on society as well as state, derives from increasing awareness that lingering certainties about the "proper" location of effective power are being challenged by popular doubts about the uses to which states, bureaucracies, and parties put their monopoly of force and their representational "wisdom." This is one reason Zimbabwe appears to be such a dialectician's dream.[12] Alongside the country's objective situation as a landlocked postwhite colonial state, and concomitant with the choices and decisions the government makes or fails to make, ideological cross-currents, hyphenated identities, and policy skepticisms abound, thereby making choices more difficult, more loaded, and more double-edged. Consensus—to the degree it ever existed—fractures, and knowledge becomes partial rather than totalizing. A state facing such disunity can attempt to "take command," make a choice, opt for an answer, or designate a development path that resonates with the wisdom of modernity; ergo Mugabe's steadfast appeal to an era of one-party unity in Africa that arguably never really existed anyway. Yet social struggles and contestations can hold precipitous decisionmaking in abeyance. Tendencies toward and away from popular contestation, toward and away from state control, have unfolded together in Eastern European countries, and a similar type of process, although different in its particular manifestations, may be transpiring in Zimbabwe.[13]

There are some decisions that Zimbabweans cannot delay making and some policies that citizens and analysts cannot afford to deconstruct into oblivion. Urban workers need better transportation and housing. The unemployed need work. Rural areas need better roads, facilities, and development policies. The population growth rate of more than 3 percent per year requires attention, and frequent droughts must be anticipated. Many issues on the Zimbabwean agenda, however, have to do with how and for whom to organize agricultural production, whether producer cooperatives should have a higher priority, whether *lobola* is a useful and fair social convention, whether investment guidelines promote the type of balanced development the state seeks, whether Zimbabwe's natural resources (which are the envy of many countries) are used to benefit its poorest citizens, whether a multiparty system is better for whom, and whether single party/multiparty choices exhaust the possibilities of representation.

Within this complex matrix, Zimbabweans debate issues of class privilege, democracy, and economic performance. In 1990 ZUM was both a symbol of that trend and a vehicle for aggregating and channeling political energies in a conventional way. Popular support for the upstart party was certainly not overwhelming, but its existence in an era of official unity suggests that plural and overlapping identities exist and are difficult to squeeze into one mold. It remains to be seen how long this period of debate lasts and whether Zimbabwe's rank-and-file choir, which sings both cacophonously and somewhat melodically in different keys, struggles on, in, and through the already scripted political economy in ways that challenge the plans of a state that is itself identity hyphenated.

AMBIVALENT CONCLUSIONS

These are interesting and exciting times for Zimbabwe, and for this reason there are few sharp conclusions to draw or clear lessons to reiterate. One conclusion we can draw, however, is that there has been considerable continuity with the recent colonial past in the post-1980 political economy of Zimbabwe. Yet as the country moves into its second decade of contemporary statehood, we remember all those states and many of the societies that preceded it as well as the ruptures that periodically broke and shifted the directions of seemingly unified history. We note the old stories and the new ones emerging in the narratives of women (herstories), youths, still-adjusting whites, cooperative farmers, trade unionists, industrial middle managers, and so on. Changes and

188   A LESS CONTRADICTORY FUTURE?

ongoing struggles in the world and in southern Africa will bear on
these stories, and the lively tradition of Zimbabwe watching will generate
more narratives to debate. Centrally located in the mélange, the state
will try to define true and false tales and thereby control the flow of
history and development. What is ahead for Zimbabwe is somewhat
uncertain, but none of its intersecting, diverging, and contradictory
narratives promises to be dull.

NOTES

1. For a critical discussion of Western radicals and Zimbabwe, see Ibbo
Mandaza, "Introduction: The Political Economy of Transition," in *Zimbabwe: The
Political Economy of Transition, 1980–86*, ed. Ibbo Mandaza (Dakar: Codesria,
1986), pp. 1–20.

2. Michel Foucault, "Truth and Power," in *The Foucault Reader*, ed. Paul
Rabinow (New York: Penguin, 1984), p. 64.

3. Economist Intelligence Unit, *Country Report for Zimbabwe and Malawi*,
no. 1 (London: Economist Intelligence Unit, 1990), p. 6. For further discussion
of this tendency, see Christine Sylvester, "Unities and Disunities in Zimbabwe's
1990 Election," *Journal of Modern African Studies* 28, no. 3 (1990): 375–400.

4. Interviews with trade unionists and workers in the food and clothing
industries, Harare, 1988 and 1990.

5. See discussion in Christine Sylvester, "Continuity and Discontinuity in
Zimbabwe's Development History," *African Studies Review* 28, no. 1 (1985): 19–
44.

6. "What Citizens Think of Zimbabwe's First 10 Years," *Financial Gazette*,
April 12, 1990.

7. "Zimbabwe: The Undecided Economy," Cover of *Africa South* (May–
June 1990). Quote from Patrick Bond, "Riding the Waves of Uneven Prosperity,"
p. 8. Related stories include "Work Hard, Trust ZANU and Pray for Rain," pp.
12–13; "Anxious Days for the Working Man," p. 13; "Man Who Gets Down to
Business," p. 14; "Land Reform: Art of the Impossible," pp. 15–16.

8. All quotes in this section are from Bond, "Riding the Waves of Uneven
Prosperity," p. 12.

9. Terence Ranger, *Peasant Consciousness and Guerilla War in Zimbabwe*
(Berkeley and Los Angeles: University of California Press, 1985); David Lan,
Guns and Rain: Guerrillas and Spirit Mediums in Zimbabwe (Berkeley and Los
Angeles: University of California Press, 1985); Colin Stoneman and Lionel Cliffe,
Zimbabwe: Politics, Economics and Society (London: Pinter, 1989).

10. See discussion in Christine Sylvester, "Simultaneous Revolutions: The
Zimbabwean Case," *Journal of Southern African Studies* 16, no. 3 (1990): 452–
475.

11. See Sylvester, "Unities and Disunities."

12. David Gordon, "Development Strategy in Zimbabwe: Assessments and
Prospects," in *The Political Economy of Zimbabwe*, ed. Michael Schatzberg (New
York: Praeger, 1984), p. 128.

13. In framing the situation this way, I draw on the work of several postmodernist theorists from Foucault to Jean-Francois Lyotard (*The Postmodern Condition: A Report on Knowledge* [Minneapolis: University of Minnesota Press, 1984]) to Jane Flax ("Postmodernism and Gender Relations in Feminist Theory," *Signs* 12, no. 4 [1987]: 621–643) and, with some reservations about a tendency to dichotomize state and society, the related school of thinking in African studies known as the state-society approach, described in Donald Rothchild and Naomi Chazan, eds., *The Precarious Balance: State and Society in Africa* (Boulder, Colo.: Westview Press, 1988). See Christine Sylvester, " 'Urban Women Cooperatives,' 'Progress,' and 'African Feminism' in Zimbabwe," *Differences* 3, no. 1 (1991): 29–62.

Selected Bibliography

In keeping with the term *selected*, this bibliography features mostly general works published on Zimbabwe, Southern Rhodesia, and Rhodesia or those that address topics covered in this book. Unpublished manuscripts and broader area studies appear in various chapter notes, as do references to highly specialized works.

Arnold, Millard, L. Garber, and B. Wrobel. *Zimbabwe: Report on the 1985 General Elections.* Washington, D.C.: International Human Rights Law Group, 1986.

Arrighi, Giovanni. "The Political Economy of Rhodesia." In *Essays on the Political Economy of Africa,* edited by Giovanni Arrighi and John Saul, 336–377. New York: Monthly Review Press, 1977.

Aschwanden, Herbert. *Symbols of Death: An Analysis of the Consciousness of the Karanga.* Gweru: Mambo Press, 1987.

––––––. *Symbols of Life: An Analysis of the Consciousness of the Karanga.* Gweru: Mambo Press, 1982.

Astrow, Andre. *Zimbabwe: A Revolution That Lost Its Way?* London: Zed Press, 1983.

Banana, Canaan. *Towards a Socialist Ethos.* Harare: College Press, 1987.

Banana, Canaan, ed. *Turmoil and Tenacity, Zimbabwe 1890–1990.* Harare: College Press, 1989.

Baumhogger, Goswin, with Telse Diederichsen and Ulf Engel, eds. *The Struggle for Independence: Documents on the Recent Development of Zimbabwe (1975–1980).* Hamburg: Institut fur Afrikakunde, Dokumentations—Leitstelle Afrika, 1984.

Beach, David. *The Shona and Zimbabwe, 900–1850.* Gwelo: Mambo Press, 1980.

––––––. *War and Politics in Zimbabwe, 1840–1900.* Gweru: Mambo Press, 1986.

––––––. *Zimbabwe Before 1900.* Gweru: Mambo Press, 1984.

Beinart, William. "Soil Erosion, Conservation and Ideas About Development: A Southern African Exploration, 1900 to 1960." *Journal of Southern African Studies* 11, no. 1 (1984): 52–83.

Bhebe, N. *Christianity and Traditional Religion in Western Zimbabwe, 1859–1923.* London: Longman, 1979.

Bhila, H.H.K. *Trade and Politics in a Shona Kingdom*. London: Longman, 1982.

Blake, Robert. *A History of Rhodesia*. New York: Knopf, 1978.

Bond-Stewart, Kathy. *Capitalism, Socialism and Development*. Gweru: Mambo Press, 1986.

——— . *Independence Is Not Only for One Sex*. Harare: Zimbabwe Publishing House, 1987.

——— . *Women's Problems*. Gweru: Mambo Press, 1986.

Bourdillon, Michael. *The Shona People*. Gweru: Mambo Press, 1987.

Bowman, Larry. *Politics in Rhodesia: White Politics in an African State*. Cambridge, Mass.: Harvard University Press, 1973.

Bozongwana, Wallace. *Ndebele Religion and Customs*. Gweru: Mambo Press, 1983.

Brand, C. M. "The Political Role of Unions in Rhodesia." *South African Labour Bulletin* 1 (1975).

Bratton, Michael. *Beyond Community Development: The Political Economy of Rural Administration in Zimbabwe*. Gwelo: Mambo Press, 1978.

——— . "The Comrades and the Countryside: The Politics of Agricultural Policy in Zimbabwe." *World Politics* 39, no. 2 (1987): 174–202.

——— . "The Public Service Sector in Zimbabwe." *Political Science Quarterly* 95 (1980): 441–464.

Bruwer, Andries J. *Zimbabwe: Rhodesia's Ancient Greatness*. Johannesburg: Hugh Keartland, 1965.

Bullock, Charles. *The Mashona*. Cape Town: Juta, 1928.

Bush, Ray, and Lionel Cliffe. "Agrarian Policy in Migrant Labour Societies: Reform or Transformation in Zimbabwe?" *Review of African Political Economy*, no. 29 (1984): 77–94.

Caton-Thompson, Gertrude. *The Zimbabwe Culture: Ruins and Reactions*. Oxford: Clarendon Press, 1931.

Caute, David. *Under the Skin: The Death of White Rhodesia*. Evanston, Ill.: Northwestern University Press, 1983.

Chanaiwa, David. *The Zimbabwe Controversy: A Case of Colonial Historiography*. Syracuse, N.Y.: Maxwell School of Citizenship and Public Affairs, February 1973.

Chater, Patricia. *Caught in the Crossfire*. Harare: Zimbabwe Publishing House, 1985.

Cheater, Angela. *Idioms of Accumulation: Rural Development and Class Formation Among Freeholders in Zimbabwe*. Gweru: Mambo Press, 1984.

Chidzero, Bernard. *Budget Statements*. Harare: Government Printer, 1980–present.

Chigwedere, Aeneas. *Lobola: The Pros and Cons*. Harare: Books for Africa, 1982.

Childs, H. *The History and Extent of Recognition of Tribal Law in Rhodesia*. Salisbury: Ministry of Internal Affairs, 1976.

Chitsike, L. T. *Agricultural Co-operative Development in Zimbabwe*. Harare: ZIMFEP, 1988.

Chung, Fay, and E. Ngara. *Socialism, Education and Development: A Challenge to Zimbabwe*. Harare: Zimbabwe Publishing House, 1985.

Clarke, Duncan. *Agricultural and Plantation Workers in Rhodesia: A Report on Conditions of Labour and Subsistence*. Gwelo: Mambo Press, 1977.

_____ . *The Distribution of Income and Wealth in Rhodesia*. Gwelo: Mambo Press, 1977.

_____ . *Foreign Companies and International Investment in Zimbabwe*. Gwelo: Mambo Press, 1980.

Cliffe, Lionel. "The Conservation Issue in Zimbabwe." *Review of African Political Economy* 42 (1988): 48–58.

Cliffe, Lionel, Joshua Mpofu, and Barry Munslow. "Nationalist Politics in Zimbabwe: The 1980 Elections and Beyond." *Review of African Political Economy* (May–August 1980): 44–67.

Clutton-Brock, Guy, and Molly Clutton-Brock. *Cold Comfort Confronted*. London: Mowbrays, 1972.

Cobbing, Julian. "The Absent Priesthood: Another Look at the Rhodesian Risings of 1896–97." *Journal of African History* 18, no. 1 (1977).

_____ . "Review of the Matabele Journals of Robert Moffat, 1829–1860." *Journal of African History* 20 (1979).

Cormack, I.R.N. *Towards Self-Reliance: Urban Social Development in Zimbabwe*. Gweru: Mambo Press, 1983.

Dangarembga, Tsitsi. *Nervous Conditions*. London: Women's Press, 1988.

Davidow, Jeffrey. *A Peace in Southern Africa: The Lancaster House Conference on Rhodesia, 1979*. Boulder, Colo.: Westview Press, 1984.

Davies, Rob. *The Informal Sector: A Solution to Unemployment?* Gwelo: Mambo Press, 1978.

Day, John. "Continuity and Change in the African Parties of Zimbabwe During the Struggle for Majority Rule." In *Transfer and Transformation: Political Institutions in the New Commonwealth*, edited by J. Manor and P. Lyons. Leicester: Leicester University Press, 1983.

Drinkwater, Michael. "Technical Development and Peasant Impoverishment: Land Use in Zimbabwe's Midlands Province." *Journal of Southern African Studies* 15, no. 2 (1989): 287–305.

Duggan, William. "The Native Land Husbandry Act of 1951 and the Rural African Middle Class of Southern Rhodesia." *African Affairs*, no. 79 (1980): 227–239.

Economist Intelligence Unit. *Country Report for Zimbabwe and Malawi*. London: EIU, 1980–present.

_____ . *Zimbabwe's First Five Years: Economic Prospects Following Independence*. Special Report no. 11. London: EIU, 1981.

Flower, Ken. *Serving Secretly: An Intelligence Chief on Record, Rhodesia into Zimbabwe, 1964–1981*. London: John Murray, 1987.

Gann, Lewis. *A History of Southern Rhodesia: Early Days to 1934*. New York: Humanities Press, 1969.

Gann, Lewis, and T. Henriksen. *The Struggle for Zimbabwe: The Battle in the Bush*. New York: Praeger, 1981.

Garlake, Peter. *Early Zimbabwe: From the Matopos to Inyanga*. Gweru: Mambo Press, 1982–1983.

_____ . *Great Zimbabwe: Described and Explained*. Harare: Zimbabwe Publishing House, 1982.

———. *Life at Great Zimbabwe*. Gweru: Mambo Press, 1982.

———. "Prehistory and Ideology in Zimbabwe." *Africa* 52, no. 3 (1982): 1–19.

Gasper, Des. "Rural Growth Points and Rural Industries in Zimbabwe—Ideologies and Policies." *Development and Change* 19, no. 3 (1988): 425–466.

Gelfand, Michael. *The Genuine Shona: Survival Values of an African Culture.* Gwelo: Mambo Press, 1973.

———. *Growing Up in Shona Society: From Birth to Marriage.* Gwelo: Mambo Press, 1979.

Government of Zimbabwe. *Annual Economic Review of Zimbabwe.* Harare: Government Printer, 1981.

———. *First Five Year National Development Plan, 1986–1990.* Harare: Government Printer, 1986.

———. *Growth with Equity: An Economic Policy Statement.* Harare: Government Printer, 1981.

———. *Labour and Economy: Report of the National Trade Unions Survey, Zimbabwe, 1984.* Harare: Ministry of Labour, Manpower Planning, and Social Welfare, 1984.

———. *Quarterly Digest of Statistics.* Harare: Central Statistical Office, quarterly.

———. *Report of the Commission of Inquiry into Incomes, Prices and Conditions of Service.* Harare: Government Printer, 1981.

———. *Transitional National Development Plan, 1982/83–1984/85.* Harare: Department of Finance, Economic Planning, and Development, 1982.

Hall, Richard. *Pre-historic Rhodesia.* Philadelphia: George W. Jacobs, 1909.

Hallencreutz, Carl, and Ambrose Moyo, eds. *Church and State in Zimbabwe.* Vol. 3. *Christianity South of the Zambezi.* Gweru: Mambo Press, 1988.

Handford, J. *Portrait of an Economy: Rhodesia Under Sanctions.* Salisbury: Mercury, 1986.

Herbst, Jeffrey. *State Politics in Zimbabwe.* Berkeley and Los Angeles: University of California Press, 1990.

Hodder-Williams, Richard. *White Farmers in Rhodesia, 1898–1965: A History of the Marandellas District.* London: Macmillan, 1983.

Holderness, Hardwick. *Lost Chance: Southern Rhodesia, 1945–1958.* Harare: Zimbabwe Publishing House, 1985.

Hove, Chinjerai. *Bones.* Harare: Baobob Books, 1988.

Jacobs, Susan. "State, Class, and Gendered Models of Land Resettlement." In *Women and the State in Africa*, edited by Jane Parpart and Kathleen Staudt, 161–184. Boulder, Colo.: Lynne Rienner, 1989.

Jollie, E. T. *The Real Rhodesia.* Bulawayo: Books of Rhodesia, 1971.

Kennedy, Dane. *Islands of White: Settler Society and Culture in Kenya and Southern Rhodesia, 1890–1939.* Durham, N.C.: Duke University Press, 1987.

Kriger, Norma. "The Zimbabwean War of Liberation: Struggles Within the Struggles." *Journal of Southern African Studies* 14, no. 2 (1988): 304–322.

Lan, David. *Guns and Rain: Guerrillas and Spirit Mediums in Zimbabwe.* Berkeley and Los Angeles: University of California Press, 1985.

Lessing, Doris. *Going Home.* London: Grafton Books, 1957.

Leys, Colin. *European Politics in Southern Rhodesia*. Oxford: Clarendon Press, 1959.

MacIver, David R. *Medieval Rhodesia*. London: Macmillan, 1906.

Mandaza, Ibbo, ed. *Zimbabwe: The Political Economy of Transition, 1980–86*. Dakar: Codesria, 1986.

Marechera, Dambudzo. *Mindblast*. Harare: College Press, 1984.

Martin, David, and Phyllis Johnson. *The Struggle for Zimbabwe: The Chimurenga War*. Harare: Zimbabwe Publishing House, 1981.

May, Joan. *Zimbabwean Women in Customary and Colonial Law*. Gweru: Mambo Press, 1983.

Maya, R. S. *Structural Adjustment in Zimbabwe: Its Impact on Women*. Harare: Zimbabwe Institute of Development Studies, 1989.

Moore-King, Bruce. *White Man Black War*. Harare: Baobob Books, 1988.

Mosley, Paul. *The Settler Economies: Studies in the Economic History of Kenya and Southern Rhodesia, 1900–1963*. Cambridge: Cambridge University Press, 1983.

Mudenge, S.I.G. *The Political History of Munhumutapa circa 1400–1902*. Harare: Zimbabwe Publishing House, 1988.

Mufuka, Kenneth. *Dzimbahwe: Life and Politics in the Golden Age, 1100–1500 A.D.* Harare: Zimbabwe Publishing House, 1983.

Mugabe, Robert. *Our War of Liberation: Speeches, Articles, Interviews, 1976–1979*. Gweru: Mambo Press, 1983.

Mungoshi, Charles. *Waiting for the Rain*. Harare: Zimbabwe Publishing House, 1975.

Murphree, Marshall. "The Salience of Ethnicity in African States: A Zimbabwean Case Study." *Ethnic and Racial Studies* 11, no. 2 (1988): 119–138.

Murray, D. J. *The Governmental System in Southern Rhodesia*. Oxford: Clarendon Press, 1970.

National Gallery of Zimbabwe. *Zimbabwe Heritage: Contemporary Visual Arts*. Harare: National Gallery of Zimbabwe, 1986.

Nkomo, Joshua. *Nkomo: The Story of My Life*. London: Methuen, 1984.

Nyagumbo, Maurice. *With the People: An Autobiography from the Zimbabwe Struggles*. London: Bushby, 1980.

Nyangoni, Christopher, and Gideon Nyandoro, eds. *Zimbabwe Independence Movements: Selected Documents*. New York: Barnes and Noble, 1979.

Nyathi, Andrew, with John Hoffman. *Tomorrow Is Built Today: Experiences of War, Colonialism and the Struggle for Collective Cooperatives in Zimbabwe*. Harare: Anvil Press, 1990.

Nzenza, Sekai. *Zimbabwean Woman: My Own Story*. London: Karia Press, 1988.

Palley, Claire. *The Constitutional History and Law of Southern Rhodesia, 1888–1965*. Oxford: Clarendon Press, 1966.

Palmer, Robin. *Land and Racial Domination in Rhodesia*. Berkeley and Los Angeles: University of California Press, 1977.

_____. "Land Reform in Zimbabwe, 1980–1990." *African Affairs* 89 (1990): 163–181.

Phimister, Ian. *An Economic and Social History of Zimbabwe, 1890–1948*. New York: Longman, 1988.

Randles, W.G.L. *The Empire of Monomotapa.* Gwelo: Mambo Press, 1979.

Ranger, Terence. *The African Voice in Southern Rhodesia, 1898–1930.* London: Heinemann, 1970.

——— . "The Changing of the Old Guard: Robert Mugabe and the Revival of ZANU." *Journal of Southern African Studies* 7 (1980): 71–90.

——— . *The Invention of Tribalism in Zimbabwe.* Gweru: Mambo Press, 1985.

——— . *Peasant Consciousness and Guerilla War in Zimbabwe.* Berkeley and Los Angeles: University of California Press, 1985.

——— . *Revolt in Southern Rhodesia, 1896–7.* London: Heinemann, 1978.

Rasmussen, R. K. *Mzilikazi.* Harare: Zimbabwe Educational Books, 1977.

Samkange, Stanlake. *Origins of Rhodesia.* London: Heinemann, 1968.

Samkange, Stanlake, and Tommie Marie Samkange. *Hunhuism or Ubuntuism: A Zimbabwe Indigenous Political Philosophy.* Salisbury: Graham, 1980.

Schatzberg, Michael, ed. *The Political Economy of Zimbabwe.* New York: Praeger, 1984.

Seidmann, Gay. "Women in Zimbabwe: Postindependence Struggles." *Feminist Studies* 10, no. 3 (1984): 419–440.

Shamuyarira, Nathan. *Crisis in Rhodesia.* London: Deutsch, 1965.

Shaw, W. "Towards the One-Party State in Zimbabwe: A Study in African Political Thought." *Journal of Modern African Studies* 24, no. 3 (1986): 373–394.

Shopo, T., and S. Moyo. *Vulnerable Working Households in Zimbabwe's Segmented Labour Markets.* Working Paper no. 5. Harare: Zimbabwe Institute of Development Studies, n.d.

Sithole, Masipula. *Zimbabwe Struggles Within the Struggle.* Salisbury: Rujeko, 1979.

Smith, David, and Colin Simpson, with Ian Davies. *Mugabe.* Salisbury: Pioneer Head, 1981.

Staunton, Irene, ed. *Mothers of the Revolution.* Harare: Baobob Books, 1990.

Stedman, Stephen John. *Peacemaking in Civil War: International Mediation in Zimbabwe, 1974–1980.* Boulder, Colo.: Lynne Rienner, 1991.

Stoneman, Colin, ed. *Zimbabwe's Inheritance.* London: Macmillan, 1981.

——— . *Zimbabwe's Prospects: Issues of Race, Class, State and Capital in Southern Africa.* London: Macmillan, 1988.

Stoneman, Colin, and Lionel Cliffe. *Zimbabwe: Politics, Economics and Society.* London: Pinter, 1989.

Sylvester, Christine. "Continuity and Discontinuity in Zimbabwe's Development History." *African Studies Review* 28, no. 1 (1985): 19–44.

——— . "Simultaneous Revolutions: The Zimbabwean Case." *Journal of Southern African Studies* 16, no. 3 (1990): 452–475.

——— . "Unities and Disunities in Zimbabwe's 1990 Election." *Journal of Modern African Studies* 28, no. 3 (1990): 375–400.

——— . " 'Urban Women Cooperatives,' 'Progress,' and 'African Feminism' in Zimbabwe." *Differences* 3, no. 1 (1991): 29–62.

——— . "Zimbabwe's 1985 Elections: A Search for National Mythology." *Journal of Modern African Studies* 24, no. 2 (1986): 229–256.

Thompson, Carol. *Challenge to Imperialism: The Frontline States in the Liberation of Zimbabwe.* Boulder, Colo.: Westview Press, 1985.

Todd, Judith. *An Act of Treason: Rhodesia 1965.* Harare: Longman, 1982.

―――. *The Right to Say No: Rhodesia 1972.* Harare: Longman, 1987.

Van Onselen, Charles. *Chibaro: African Mine Labour in Southern Rhodesia, 1900–1933.* Johannesburg: Raven Press, 1980.

Verrier, Anthony. *The Road to Zimbabwe, 1890–1980.* London: Jonathon Cape, 1986.

Weiner, Daniel, Sam Moyo, Barry Munslow, and Phil O'Keefe. "Land Use and Agricultural Productivity in Zimbabwe." *Journal of Modern African Studies* 23 (1985): 251–285.

Weinrich, A.K.H. *African Farmers in Rhodesia.* London: Oxford University Press, 1975.

―――. *African Marriage in Zimbabwe: And the Impact of Christianity.* Gweru: Mambo Press, 1982.

―――. *Women and Racial Discrimination in Rhodesia.* Paris: UNESCO, 1979.

Weiss, Ruth. *The Women of Zimbabwe.* London: Kesho, 1986.

Weitzer, Ronald. "In Search of Regime Security: Zimbabwe Since Independence." *Journal of Modern African Studies* 22, no. 4 (1984): 529–557.

―――. *Transforming Settler States: Communal Conflict and Internal Security in Northern Ireland and Zimbabwe.* Berkeley and Los Angeles: University of California Press, 1990.

Whitsun Foundation. *Rural Service Centres Development Study.* Salisbury: Whitsun Foundation, 1980.

Windrich, Elaine. *Britain and the Politics of Rhodesian Independence.* London: Croom Helm, 1978.

Zimbabwe Women's Bureau. *We Carry a Heavy Load: Rural Women in Zimbabwe Speak Out.* Harare: Zimbabwe Women's Bureau, 1981.

ZIMFEP. *Community Arts and the Question of Culture in the City of Harare.* Harare: ZIMFEP, 1987.

Zindi, R. *Roots Rocking in Zimbabwe.* Gweru: Mambo Press, 1985.

Acronyms

AFC	Agricultural Finance Corporation
AIDS	acquired immune deficiency syndrome
ANC	African National Congress
	South African African National Congress
ARDA	Agricultural and Rural Development Authority
BANC	Bulawayo African National Congress
BSAC	British South Africa Company
CA	communal area
CAZ	Conservative Alliance of Zimbabwe
CFU	Commercial Farmers' Union
CIDA	Canadian International Development Agency
CONSAS	Constellation of Southern African States
EEC	European Economic Community
FRELIMO	Front for the Liberation of Mozambique
FGR	Federal Republic of Germany
GAPWUZ	General Agricultural and Plantation Workers' Union
GDP	gross domestic product
GDR	German Democratic Republic
GMB	Grain Marketing Board
GNP	gross national product
IMF	International Monetary Fund
IZG	Independent Zimbabwe Group
MNR	Mozambique National Resistance
MP	member of Parliament

NAM	Non-Aligned Movement
NDP	National Democratic Party
NIBMAR	no independence before majority rule
NLHA	National Land Husbandry Act
OCCZIM	Organization of Collective Cooperatives of Zimbabwe
OPEC	Organization of Petroleum Exporting Countries
PF	Patriotic Front
PF-ZAPU	Title for ZAPU from 1980 to 1990
PRC	People's Republic of China
PTA	Preferential Trade Area
RF	Rhodesian Front Party
RMGWA	Rhodesia Mine and General Workers' Association
SADCC	Southern African Development Coordinating Conference
SAM	surface-to-air missile
SRANC	Southern Rhodesia African National Congress
TNDP	*Transitional National Development Plan*
TTL	Tribal Trust Land
UANC	United African National Council
UDI	Unilateral Declaration of Independence
UNFP	United National Federal Party
ZANLA	Zimbabwe African National Liberation Army
ZANU	Zimbabwe African National Union
ZANU(PF)	Title for ZANU from 1980 to 1990
ZANU PF	Title of the united party for ZANU and ZAPU from 1990 on
ZAPU	Zimbabwe African People's Union
	Zimbabwe Active People's Unity Movement (1989–1990)
ZCTU	Zimbabwe Congress of Trade Unions
ZIMCORD	Zimbabwe Conference on Reconstruction and Development
ZIMFEP	Zimbabwe Federation of Education with Production
ZIPRA	Zimbabwe People's Revolutionary Army
ZUM	Zimbabwe Unity Movement

About the Book and Author

More than ten years into independence, Zimbabwe is a fascinating study in contradictory history and development. Forged in the crucible of armed struggle against Rhodesian white settlers, Zimbabwe is a country in which lingering tendencies toward authoritarian rule coexist with strong liberal-nationalist currents that emerged with independence and with the form of Marxist-Leninist ideology associated with the leadership of Robert Mugabe. Here the large commercial farms of Rhodesia still stand side by side with small-scale peasant plots; crowded urban townships, created in the days when workers were discouraged from living near whites, still remain mostly segregated; remote rural villages and affluent suburban neighborhoods compete for resources; and the isolation that resulted from United Nations–imposed sanctions has been replaced by burgeoning international activity.

In this profile of one of the most distinctive countries in southern Africa, Dr. Sylvester focuses on the continuities and discontinuities in the historical patterns of Zimbabwe's political economy. She considers the politics of anticolonial struggle and of postindependence state-building; the economic policies designed to balance the needs of agriculturalists, mining interests, and industrialists; and the social pressures to define the nature of authentic culture. The book presents a portrait of a country that potentially may be the pride of the continent or may be only another example of a country whose socialist vision has not come to fruition.

Christine Sylvester is associate professor of political science at Northern Arizona University. She has traveled widely within Zimbabwe and southern Africa over the past nine years and has been a visiting research associate in the Department of Economics at the University of Zimbabwe and at the Institute of Southern African Studies at the National University of Lesotho. When she is not writing on Zimbabwe, she turns her attention to issues of feminist theory and international relations.

Index

Acquired immune deficiency
  syndrome (AIDS), 129, 135(n78)
AFC. *See* Agricultural Finance
  Corporation
Africa, southern
  and regional development, 167–169
  See also Frontline States; *specific
  countries*
African National Congress (ANC),
  52, 172
African Voice Association, 39
Age of Majority Act, 145
Agricultural Finance Corporation
  (AFC), 107
Agriculture, 97, 108(table), 183–184,
  187
  and development planning, 102–
  110, 118
  and employment, 100
  and European settlement, 19, 22–
  23
  and Rhodesia, 32, 34–35, 38–40,
  98
  See also Food; Land distribution
Agritex, 107, 108, 118
Agro-industry, 98, 117
AIDS. *See* Acquired immune
  deficiency syndrome
Alexander, Jocelyn, 75, 126–127
Amalgamated Engineering Union, 33
ANC. *See* African National Congress;
  South African National Congress
Angola, 166
Antidissidence. *See* Politics, and
  dissidence

Archaeology, 4–6, 7–8, 10, 12
Art, 137, 156–157
Askin, Steve, 171
Association of Zimbabwe Spirit
  Mediums, 155
Astrow, Andre, 142
Austin, Reg, 88
Authoritarianism, 77, 182

Banana, Canaan, 154
BANC. *See* Bulawayo African
  National Congress
Bantu Voters Association, 31, 32
Beach, David, 4, 11, 13, 83
Beinart, William, 38–39
Bindura district, 88
Bookweek Africa, 157
Botswana, 2, 166–167, 169
Brewster, Kingman, 64
British South Africa Company
  (BSAC), 17–23, 24, 32
BSAC. *See* British South Africa
  Company
Bulawayo, 2
Bulawayo African National Congress
  (BANC), 42
Bulgaria, 175

Canadian International Development
  Agency (CIDA), 177–178
Canadian University Service
  Overseas, 158
Capitalism, 97, 115, 131, 183–184
Capricorn Africa Society, 42
Carrington, Peter, 65